Getting Started with Streamlit for Data Science

Create and deploy Streamlit web applications from scratch in Python

Tyler Richards

BIRMINGHAM—MUMBAI

Getting Started with Streamlit for Data Science

Copyright © 2021 Packt Publishing

Group Product Manager: Kunal Parikh
Publishing Product Manager: Reshma Raman
Senior Editor: Mohammed Yusuf Imaratwale
Content Development Editor: Sean Lobo
Technical Editor: Devanshi Deepak Ayare
Copy Editor: Safis Editing
Project Coordinator: Aparna Ravikumar Nair
Proofreader: Safis Editing
Indexer: Rekha Nair
Production Designer: Vijay Kamble

First published: August 2021

Production reference: 1150721

Published by Packt Publishing Ltd.
Livery Place
35 Livery Street
Birmingham
B3 2PB, UK.

ISBN 978-1-80056-550-0

www.packt.com

Contributors

About the author

Tyler Richards is a data scientist at Facebook, working on community integrity. Before this gig, his focus was on helping bolster the state of US elections for the nonprofit Protect Democracy. He is a data scientist and industrial engineer by training, which he gets to make use of in fun ways such as applying machine learning to local campus elections, creating algorithms to help P&G target Tide Pod users, and finding ways to determine the best ping pong players in friend groups. He is always looking for a new project, a new adventure.

About the reviewers

Randy Zwitch is head of developer relations at Streamlit. The developer relations team at Streamlit works with community members from around the world to help develop data apps and democratize decision-making across the enterprise. Randy is also a prolific open source contributor in the Python, Julia, and R communities. In his free time, Randy is an amateur luthier, building electric guitars and other stringed instruments at `http://zwitchguitars.com/`.

Weston Willingham studied industrial and systems engineering at the University of Florida before pivoting to data science. While completing the Galvanize Data Science Immersive program, Weston built several projects including a neural network for image detection and an audio transcriber trained to his own voice to improve presentation captioning. When not reading books, Weston can be found playing jazz piano and saxophone.

Table of Contents

3
Data Visualization

4
Using Machine Learning with Streamlit

5
Deploying Streamlit with Streamlit Sharing

Section 2: Advanced Streamlit Applications

6

Beautifying Streamlit Apps

7

Exploring Streamlit Components

8

Deploying Streamlit Apps with Heroku and AWS

Section 3: Streamlit Use Cases

9

Improving Job Applications with Streamlit

10

The Data Project – Prototyping Projects in Streamlit

11

Using Streamlit for Teams

12

Streamlit Power Users

Other Books You May Enjoy

Index

Preface

Data scientists and machine learning engineers throughout the 2010s have primarily produced static analyses. We create documents to inform decisions, filled with plots and metrics about our findings, or about the models we create. Creating complete web applications that allow users to interact with analyses is cumbersome, to say the least! Enter Streamlit, a Python library for creating web applications built with data folks in mind at every step.

Streamlit shortens the development time for the creation of data-focused web applications, allowing data scientists to create web app prototypes in Python in hours instead of days.

This book takes a hands-on approach to help you learn the tips and tricks that will have you up and running with Streamlit in no time. You'll start with the fundamentals of Streamlit by creating a basic app and gradually build on this foundation by producing high-quality graphics with data visualization and testing machine learning models. As you advance through the chapters, you'll walk through practical examples of both personal and work-related data-focused web applications, and will learn about more complicated topics such as using Streamlit Components, beautifying your apps, and the quick deployment of your new apps.

Who this book is for

This book is for data scientists and machine learning engineers or enthusiasts who want to create web apps using Streamlit. Whether you're a junior data scientist looking to deploy your first machine learning project in Python to improve your resume or a senior data scientist working full time trying to convince your colleagues with a dynamic analysis, this book is for you!

What this book covers

Chapter 1, An Introduction to Streamlit, teaches the very basics of Streamlit by creating your first app.

Chapter 2, Uploading, Downloading, and Manipulating Data, looks at data; data apps need data! We'll learn how to use data efficiently and effectively in production applications.

Chapter 3, Data Visualization, teaches how to use all your favorite Python visualization libraries in Streamlit apps. There's no need to learn new visualization frameworks!

Chapter 4, Using Machine Learning with Streamlit, covers machine learning. Ever wanted to deploy your new fancy machine learning model in a user-facing app in hours? Start here for in-depth examples and tips.

Chapter 5, Deploying Streamlit with Streamlit Sharing, looks at the one-click deploy feature that Streamlit comes with. We'll learn how to remove friction in the deployment process here!

Chapter 6, Beautifying Streamlit Apps, looks at the features that Streamlit is chock-full of to make gorgeous web apps. We'll learn all the tips and tricks in this chapter.

Chapter 7, Exploring Streamlit Components, teaches how to leverage the thriving developer ecosystem around Streamlit through open source integrations called Streamlit Components. Just like LEGO, only better.

Chapter 8, Deploying Streamlit Apps with Heroku and AWS, teaches how to deploy your Streamlit applications using AWS and Heroku as an alternative to Streamlit Sharing.

Chapter 9, Improving Job Applications with Streamlit, will help you to prove your data science chops to employers using Streamlit apps through everything from apps for resume building to apps for take-home sections of interviews.

Chapter 10, The Data Project – Prototyping Projects in Streamlit, covers making apps for the Streamlit community and others, which is both fun and educational. We'll walk through some examples of projects and you'll learn how to start your own.

Chapter 11, Using Streamlit for Teams, teaches how to deploy private Streamlit repositories and enforce user authentication using the Streamlit product Streamlit for Teams.

Chapter 12, Streamlit Power Users, provides more information on Streamlit, which is already extensively used for such a young library. Learn from the best with in-depth interviews with the Streamlit founder, data scientists, analysts, and engineers.

To get the most out of this book

This book assumes that you are at least a Python novice, which means you are comfortable with basic Python syntax and have taken tutorials or classes before in Python. It is also written for users interested in data science, which includes topics such as statistics and machine learning, but does not require a data science background. If you know how to make lists and define variables and have written a `for` loop before, you have enough Python knowledge to get started!

Software/hardware covered in the book	Operating system requirements
Python 3+	Windows, macOS, or Linux
Streamlit 0.81+	
GitHub	

If you are using the digital version of this book, we advise you to type the code yourself or access the code from the book's GitHub repository (a link is available in the next section). Doing so will help you avoid any potential errors related to the copying and pasting of code.

Download the example code files

You can download the example code files for this book from GitHub at `https://github.com/tylerjrichards/Getting-Started-with-Streamlit-for-Data-Science` or through Packt's GitHub at `https://github.com/PacktPublishing/Getting-Started-with-Streamlit-for-Data-Science`. If there's an update to the code, it will be updated in these GitHub repositories.

We also have other code bundles from our rich catalog of books and videos available at `https://github.com/PacktPublishing/`. Check them out!

Download the color images

We also provide a PDF file that has color images of the screenshots and diagrams used in this book. You can download it here: `https://static.packt-cdn.com/downloads/9781800565500_ColorImages.pdf`.

Conventions used

There are a number of text conventions used throughout this book.

`Code in text`: Indicates code words in text, database table names, folder names, filenames, file extensions, pathnames, dummy URLs, user input, and Twitter handles. Here is an example: Which will be in the format `ec2-10-857-84-485.compute-1.amazonaws.com`. I made up those numbers, but yours should be close to this.

A block of code is set as follows:

```
import pandas as pd

penguin_df = pd.read_csv('penguins.csv')
print(penguin_df.head())
```

Any command-line input or output is written as follows:

```
git add .
git commit -m 'added heroku files'
git push
```

Bold: Indicates a new term, an important word, or words that you see onscreen. For instance, words in menus or dialog boxes appear in **bold**. Here is an example: We are going to be using **Amazon Elastic Compute Cloud**, or **Amazon EC2** for short.

> **Tips or important notes**
> Appear like this.

Get in touch

Feedback from our readers is always welcome.

General feedback: If you have questions about any aspect of this book, email us at `customercare@packtpub.com` and mention the book title in the subject of your message.

Errata: Although we have taken every care to ensure the accuracy of our content, mistakes do happen. If you have found a mistake in this book, we would be grateful if you would report this to us. Please visit `www.packtpub.com/support/errata` and fill in the form.

Piracy: If you come across any illegal copies of our works in any form on the internet, we would be grateful if you would provide us with the location address or website name. Please contact us at copyright@packt.com with a link to the material.

If you are interested in becoming an author: If there is a topic that you have expertise in and you are interested in either writing or contributing to a book, please visit authors.packtpub.com.

Share Your Thoughts

Once you've read *Getting Started with Streamlit for Data Science*, we'd love to hear your thoughts! Scan the QR code below to go straight to the Amazon review page for this book and share your feedback.

https://packt.link/r/1-800-56550-X

Your review is important to us and the tech community and will help us make sure we're delivering excellent quality content..

Section 1: Creating Basic Streamlit Applications

This section will introduce you to the basics of Streamlit applications, data visualization in Streamlit, how to deploy applications, and how to implement models in a Streamlit application.

The following chapters are covered in this section:

- *Chapter 1, An Introduction to Streamlit*
- *Chapter 2, Uploading, Downloading, and Manipulating Data*
- *Chapter 3, Data Visualization*
- *Chapter 4, Using Machine Learning with Streamlit*
- *Chapter 5, Deploying Streamlit with Streamlit Sharing*

1
An Introduction to Streamlit

Streamlit is a web application framework that helps you build and develop Python-based web applications that can be used to share analytics results, build complex interactive experiences, and illustrate new machine learning models. On top of that, developing and deploying Streamlit apps is incredibly fast and flexible, often turning application development time from days into hours.

In this chapter, we start out with the Streamlit basics. We will learn how to download and run demo Streamlit apps, how to edit demo apps using our own text editor, how to organize our Streamlit apps, and finally, how to make our very own. Then, we will explore the basics of data visualization in Streamlit. We will learn how to accept some initial user input, and then add some finishing touches to our own apps with text. At the end of this chapter, you should be comfortable starting to make your own Streamlit applications!

In particular, we will cover the following topics:

- Why Streamlit?
- Installing Streamlit
- Organizing Streamlit apps
- Streamlit plotting demo
- Making an app from scratch

Before we begin, we will start with the technical requirements to make sure we have everything we need to get started.

Technical requirements

Here are the installations and setup required for this chapter:

- The requirements for this book are to have Python 3.7 (or later) downloaded (`https://www.python.org/downloads/`), and have a text editor to edit Python files in. Any text editor will do. I use Sublime (`https://www.sublimetext.com/3`).

- Some sections of this book use GitHub, and a GitHub account is recommended (`https://github.com/join`). Understanding how to use Git is not necessary for this book but is always useful. If you want to get started, this link has a useful tutorial: `https://guides.github.com/activities/hello-world/`.

- A basic understanding of Python is also very useful for this book. If you are not there yet, feel free to spend some time getting to know Python better using this tutorial (`https://docs.python.org/3/tutorial/`) or any other of the freely and readily available tutorials out there, and come back here when you are ready. We also need to have the Streamlit library installed, which we will do and test in a later section called *Installing Streamlit*.

Why Streamlit?

Data scientists have become an increasingly valuable resource for companies and nonprofits over the course of the past decade. They help make data-driven decisions, make processes more efficient, and implement machine learning models to improve these decisions at a repeatable scale. One pain point for data scientists is in the process just after they have found a new insight or made a new model. What is the best way to show a dynamic result, a new model, or a complicated piece of analytics to a data scientist's colleagues? They can send a static visualization, which works in some cases but fails for complicated analyses that build on each other or on anything that requires user input. They can create a Word document (or export their Jupyter notebook as a document) that combines text and visualizations, which also doesn't work for user input and is harder to reproduce. Another option is to build out an entire web application from scratch using a framework such as Flask or Django, and then figure out how to deploy the entire app in AWS or another cloud provider. None of these options really work that well. Many are slow, don't take user input, or are suboptimal for informing the decision-making process so fundamental to data science.

Enter Streamlit. Streamlit is all about speed and interaction. It is a web application framework that helps you build and develop Python web applications. It has built-in and convenient methods for taking in user input, graphing using the most popular and powerful Python graphing libraries, and quickly deploying graphs to a web application.

I have spent the past year building Streamlit apps of all different flavors, from data projects for my personal portfolio to building quick applications for data science take-home problems, to even building mini-apps for repeatable analysis at work. I truly believe that Streamlit could be as valuable to you and your work as it has been to mine and wrote this to bring you quickly up to speed so you can accelerate your learning curve and get to building web applications in minutes and hours instead of days. If this is for you, read on! We will work in three sections, starting with an introduction to Streamlit, and ramp you up to building your own basic Streamlit applications. In part two, we'll extend this knowledge to more advanced topics such as production deployment methods and using components created by the Streamlit community for increasingly beautiful and usable Streamlit apps. And in the last part, we'll focus heavily on interviews with power users who use Streamlit at work, in academia, and for learning data science techniques. Before we begin, we need to get Streamlit set up and discuss how the rest of this book's examples will be structured.

Installing Streamlit

In order to run any Streamlit apps, you must first install Streamlit. I've used a package manager called pip to do this, but you can install it using any package manager you choose (for example, **brew**). This book uses Streamlit version 0.81, and Python 3.7, but it should work on newer versions as well.

Throughout this book, we'll be using a mix of both terminal commands and code written in Python scripts. We will signpost in which location to run the code to make this as clear as possible. To install Streamlit, run the following code in a terminal:

```
pip install streamlit
```

Now that we have Streamlit downloaded, we can call it directly from our command line using the preceding code to kick off Streamlit's demo. `streamlit hello`.

Take some time to explore Streamlit's demo and take a glance at any code that you find interesting! We're going to borrow and edit the code behind the plotting demo, which *illustrates a combination of plotting and animation with Streamlit*. Before we dive in, let's take a second and talk about how to organize Streamlit apps.

Organizing Streamlit apps

Each Streamlit app we create in this book should be contained in its own folder. It is tempting to create new files for each Streamlit app, but this promotes a bad habit that will bite us later when we talk about deploying Streamlit apps and deal with permissions and data for Streamlit.

For this book, I would recommend that you have a dedicated individual folder that will house all the apps you'll create throughout this book. I have named mine `streamlit_apps`. The following command will make a new folder called `streamlit_apps` and make it our current working directory:

```
mkdir streamlit_apps
cd streamlit_apps
```

All the code for this book is housed at `https://github.com/tylerjrichards/Getting-Started-with-Streamlit-for-Data-Science`, but I would highly recommend coding these by hand for practice.

Streamlit plotting demo

First, we're going to start to learn how to make Streamlit apps by reproducing the plotting demo we saw before in the Streamlit demo, with a Python file that we've made ourselves. In order to do that, we will do the following:

1. Make a Python file where we will house all our Streamlit code.

2. Use the plotting code given in the demo.

3. Make small edits for practice.

4. Run our file locally.

Our first step is to create a folder called `plotting_app`, which will house our first example. The following code makes this folder when run in the terminal, changes our working directory to `plotting_app`, and creates an empty Python file we'll call `plot_demo.py`:

```
mkdir plotting_app
cd plotting_app
touch plot_demo.py
```

Now that we've made a file called `plot_demo.py`, open it with any text editor (if you don't have one already, I'm partial to Sublime (`https://www.sublimetext.com/`). When you open it up, copy and paste the following code to your `plot_demo.py` file:

```python
import streamlit as st
import time
import numpy as np


progress_bar = st.sidebar.progress(0)
status_text = st.sidebar.empty()
last_rows = np.random.randn(1, 1)
chart = st.line_chart(last_rows)


for i in range(1, 101):
    new_rows = last_rows[-1, :] + np.random.randn(5,
1).cumsum(axis=0)
    status_text.text("%i%% Complete" % i)
    chart.add_rows(new_rows)
    progress_bar.progress(i)
    last_rows = new_rows
    time.sleep(0.05)


progress_bar.empty()


# Streamlit widgets automatically run the script from top to
bottom. Since
# this button is not connected to any other logic, it just
causes a plain
# rerun.
st.button("Re-run")
```

This code does a few things. First, it imports all the libraries needed and creates a line chart in Streamlit's native graphing framework that starts at a random number sampled from a normal distribution with mean 0 and variance 1. And then it runs a `for` loop that keeps sampling new random numbers in bunches of 5 and adding that to the sum we had before while waiting for a twentieth of a second so we can see the graph change, simulating an animation.

By the end of this book, you will be able to make apps like this extremely quickly. But for now, let's run this locally by typing the following code in our terminal:

```
streamlit run plot_demo.py
```

This should open a new tab with your app in your default web browser. We should see our app run as shown in the following figure:

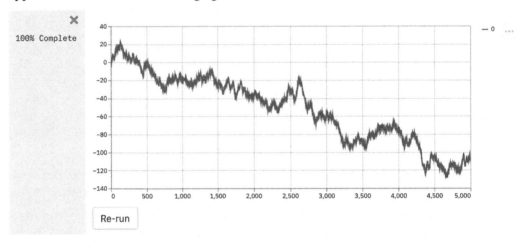

Figure 1.1 – Plotting demo output

This is how we will run every Streamlit app, by first calling `streamlit run` and then pointing Streamlit toward the Python script that houses our app's code. Now let's change something small within the app so we better understand how Streamlit works. The following code changes how many random numbers we plot on our graph, but feel free to make any changes you'd like. Make your changes using the following code, save your changes in your text editor of choice, and run the file again:

```
import streamlit as st
import time
import numpy as np

progress_bar = st.sidebar.progress(0)
status_text = st.sidebar.empty()
last_rows = np.random.randn(1, 1)
chart = st.line_chart(last_rows)

for i in range(1, 101):
    new_rows = last_rows[-1, :] + np.random.randn(50,
```

```
1).cumsum(axis=0)
    status_text.text("%i%% Complete" % i)
    chart.add_rows(new_rows)
    progress_bar.progress(i)
    last_rows = new_rows
    time.sleep(0.05)


progress_bar.empty()


# Streamlit widgets automatically run the script from top to
bottom. Since
# this button is not connected to any other logic, it just
causes a plain
# rerun.
st.button("Re-run")
```

You should notice that Streamlit detected a change to the source file and is prompting you to rerun the file if you'd like. Click **Rerun** (or **Always rerun** if you want this behavior to be the default, which I almost always do), and watch your app change.

Feel free to try making some other changes to the plotting app to get the hang of it! Once you are ready, let's move on to making our own apps.

Making an app from scratch

Now that we've tried out the apps others have made, let's make our own! This app is going to focus on using the central limit theorem, which is a fundamental theorem of statistics that says that if we randomly sample with replacement enough from any distribution, then the distribution of the mean of our samples will approximate the normal distribution.

We are not going to prove this with our app, but instead, let's try to generate a few graphs that help explain the power of the central limit theorem. First, let's make sure that we're in the correct directory (we called it streamlit_apps earlier), make a new folder called clt_app, and toss in a new file.

The following code makes a new folder called clt_app, and again creates an empty Python file, this time called clt_demo.py:

```
mkdir clt_app
cd clt_app
touch clt_demo.py
```

Whenever we start a new Streamlit app, we want to make sure to import Streamlit (often aliased in this book and elsewhere as `st`). Streamlit has unique functions for each type of content (text, graphs, pictures, and other media) that we can use as building blocks for all of our apps. The first one we'll use is `st.write()`, which is a function that takes a string (and as we'll see later, almost any Pythonic objects, such as dictionaries) and writes it directly into our web app in the order that it is called. As we are calling a Python script, Streamlit sequentially looks through the file and, every time it sees one of the functions, designates a sequential slot for that piece of content. This makes it very easy to use, as you can write all the Python you'd like, and when you want something to appear on the app you've made, you can simply use `st.write()` and you're all set.

In our `clt_demo.py` file, we can start with the basic `'Hello World'` output using `st.write()`, using the following code:

```
import streamlit as st
st.write('Hello World')
```

Now we can test this by running the following code in the terminal:

```
streamlit run clt_demo.py
```

We should see the string `'Hello World'` printed on our app, so all is good so far. The following figure is a screenshot of our app in Safari:

Figure 1.2 – Hello World app

There are three items to note in this screenshot. First, we see the string as we wrote it, which is great. Next, we see that the URL points to **localhost:8501**, which is just telling us that we're hosting this locally (that is, it's not on the internet anywhere) through port `8501`. We don't need to understand almost anything about the port system on computers, or the **Transmission Control Protocol (TCP)**. The important thing here is that this app is local to your computer. The third important item to note is the hamburger icon at the top right. The following screenshot shows us what happens when we click the icon:

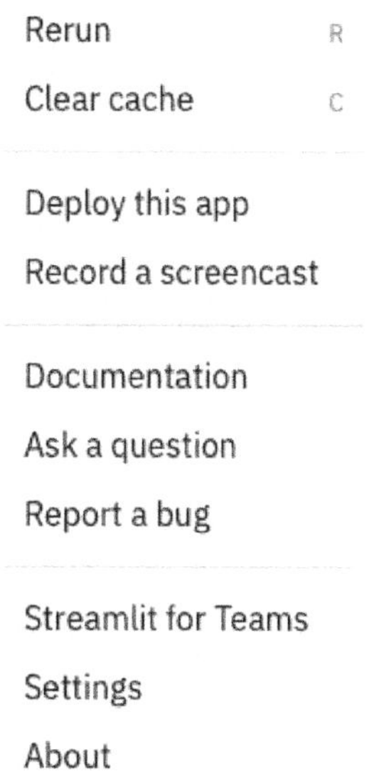

Rerun   R

Clear cache   c

Deploy this app

Record a screencast

Documentation

Ask a question

Report a bug

Streamlit for Teams

Settings

About

Figure 1.3 – Icon options

This is the default options panel for Streamlit apps. Throughout this book, we'll discuss each of these options in depth, especially the non-self-explanatory ones such as **Clear cache**. All we have to know for now is that if we want to rerun the app or find settings or the documentation, we can use this icon to find almost whatever we need.

When we host applications so that others can use them, they'll see this same icon but have some different options (for example, they will not be able to clear the cache). We'll discuss this in greater detail later as well. Now back to our central limit theorem app!

The next step is going to be generating a distribution that we want to sample from with replacement. I'm choosing the binomial here. We can read the following code as simulating 1,000 coin flips using the Python package numpy, and printing out the mean number of heads from those 1,000 coin flips:

```
import streamlit as st
import numpy as np
binom_dist = np.random.binomial(1, .5, 100)
st.write(np.mean(binom_dist))
```

Now, given what we know about the central limit theorem, we would expect that if we sampled from `binom_dist` enough times, the mean of those samples would approximate the normal distribution.

We've already discussed the `st.write()` function. Our next foray into writing content to the Streamlit app is through graphs. `st.pyplot()` is a function that lets us use all the power of the popular `matplotlib` library and push our `matplotlib` graph to Streamlit. Once we create a figure in `matplotlib`, we can explicitly tell Streamlit to write that to our app with the `st.pyplot()` function.

So, all together now! This app simulates 1,000 coin flips and stores those values in a list we call `binom_dist`. We then sample (with replacement) 100 from that list, take the mean, and store that mean in the cleverly named variable `list_of_means`. We do that 1,000 times (it's overkill – we could do this even with dozens of samples), and then plot the histogram. After we do this, the result of the following code should show a bell-shaped distribution:

```python
import streamlit as st
import numpy as np
import matplotlib.pyplot as plt
binom_dist = np.random.binomial(1, .5, 1000)

list_of_means = []
for i in range(0, 1000):
    list_of_means.append(np.random.choice(binom_dist, 100,
replace=True).mean())

fig, ax = plt.subplots()
ax = plt.hist(list_of_means)
st.pyplot(fig)
```

Each run of this app will create a new bell curve. When I ran it, my bell curve looked like the following figure. If your graph isn't exactly what you see in the next figure, that's totally fine because of the random sampling used in our code:

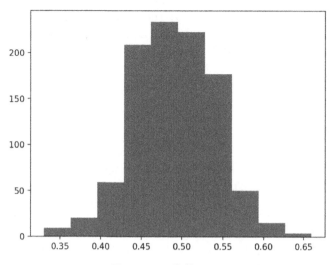

Figure 1.4 – Bell curve

As you probably noticed, we first created an empty figure and empty axes for that figure by calling `plt.subplots()`, and then assigned the histogram we created to the `ax` variable. Because of this, we were able to explicitly tell Streamlit to show the figure on our Streamlit app.

This is an important step, as in Streamlit versions, we can also skip this step, and not assign our histogram to any variable, and then call `st.pyplot()` directly afterward. The following code takes this approach:

```
import streamlit as st
import numpy as np
import matplotlib.pyplot as plt
binom_dist = np.random.binomial(1, .5, 1000)


list_of_means = []
for i in range(0, 1000):
    list_of_means.append(np.random.choice(binom_dist, 100,
replace=True).mean())


plt.hist(list_of_means)
st.pyplot()
```

I don't recommend this method, as it can give you some unexpected results. Take this example, where we want to first make our histogram of means, and then make another histogram of a new list filled only with the number 1.

Take a second and guess what the following code would do. How many graphs would we get? What would the output be?

```python
import streamlit as st
import numpy as np
import matplotlib.pyplot as plt
binom_dist = np.random.binomial(1, .5, 1000)

list_of_means = []
for i in range(0, 1000):
    list_of_means.append(np.random.choice(binom_dist, 100,
replace=True).mean())

plt.hist(list_of_means)
st.pyplot()
plt.hist([1,1,1,1])
st.pyplot()
```

I would expect this to show two histograms, the first one of list_of_means, and the second one of the lists of 1s:

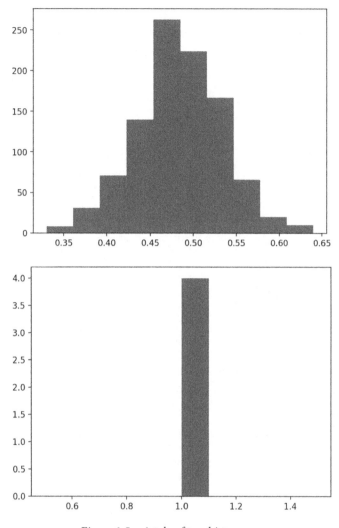

Figure 1.5 – A tale of two histograms

What we actually get is different! The second histogram has data from the first and the second list! When we call `plt.hist()` without assigning the output to anything, `matplotlib` tacks the new histogram onto the old graph that is stored globally, and Streamlit pushes that new one to our app.

Here's a solution to this issue. If we instead explicitly created two graphs, we could call the st.pyplot() function wherever we liked after the graph was generated, and have greater control over where exactly our graphs were placed. The following code separates the two graphs explicitly:

```python
import streamlit as st
import numpy as np
import matplotlib.pyplot as plt
binom_dist = np.random.binomial(1, .5, 1000)

list_of_means = []
for i in range(0, 1000):
    list_of_means.append(np.random.choice(binom_dist, 100,
replace=True).mean())

fig1, ax1 = plt.subplots()
ax1 = plt.hist(list_of_means)
st.pyplot(fig1)

fig2, ax2 = plt.subplots()
ax2 = plt.hist([1,1,1,1])
st.pyplot(fig2)
```

The preceding code plots both histograms separately by first defining separate variables for each figure and axis using plt.subplots() and then assigning the histogram to the appropriate axis. After this, we can call st.pyplot() using the created figure, which produces the following app:

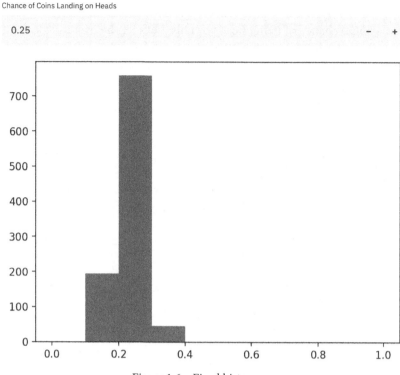

Figure 1.6 – Fixed histograms

We can clearly see in the preceding figure that the two histograms are now separated, which is the desired behavior. We will very often plot multiple visualizations in Streamlit and will use this method for the rest of the book. Now, on to accepting user input!

Using user input in Streamlit apps

As of now, our app is just a fancy way to show our visualizations. But most web apps take some user input or are dynamic, not static visualizations. Luckily for us, Streamlit has many functions to accept inputs from users, all differentiated by the object that we want to input. There are freeform text inputs with `st.text_input()`; radio buttons, `st.radio()`; numeric inputs with `st.number_input()`; and a dozen more that are extremely helpful for making Streamlit apps. We will explore most of them in detail throughout this book, but we'll start with the numeric input.

From the previous example, we assumed that the coins we were flipping were fair coins and had a 50/50 chance of being heads or tails. Let's let the user decide what the percentage chance of heads is, assign that to a variable, and use that as an input in our binomial distribution. The number input function takes a label, a minimum and maximum value, and a default value, which I have filled in the following code:

```python
import streamlit as st
import numpy as np
import matplotlib.pyplot as plt
perc_heads = st.number_input(label = 'Chance of Coins Landing
on Heads', min_value = 0.0, max_value = 1.0, value = .5)
binom_dist = np.random.binomial(1, perc_heads, 1000)

list_of_means = []
for i in range(0, 1000):
    list_of_means.append(np.random.choice(binom_dist, 100,
replace=True).mean())

fig, ax = plt.subplots()
ax = plt.hist(list_of_means, range=[0,1])
st.pyplot(fig)
```

The preceding code uses the st.number_input() function to collect our percentage, assigns the user input to a variable (perc_heads), then uses that variable to change the inputs to our binomial distribution function that we used before. It also sets our histogram's *x* axis to always be between 0 and 1, so we can better notice changes as our input changes. Try and play around with this app for a bit; change the number input and notice how the app responds whenever a user input is changed. For example, here is a result from when we set the numeric input to .25:

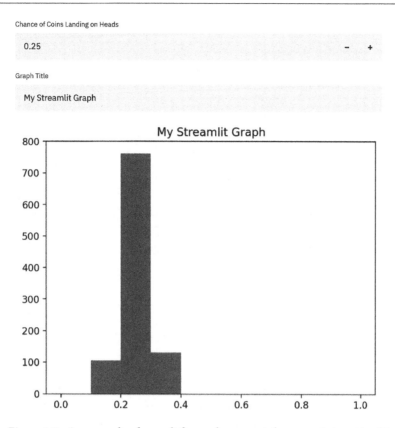

Figure 1.7 - An example of a result from when we set the numeric input to .25

As you probably noticed, every time that we changed the input of our script, Streamlit re-ran the entire application. This is the default behavior and is very important to understanding Streamlit performance; we will explore a few ways that allow us to change this default later in the book, such as adding caching or forms! We can also accept text input in Streamlit using the st.text_input() function, just as we did with the numeric input. The next bit of code takes a text input and assigns it to the title of our graph:

```
import streamlit as st
import numpy as np
import matplotlib.pyplot as plt


perc_heads = st.number_input(label='Chance of Coins Landing on
Heads', min_value=0.0,  max_value=1.0, value=.5)
graph_title = st.text_input(label='Graph Title')
binom_dist = np.random.binomial(1, perc_heads, 1000)
```

```
list_of_means = []
for i in range(0, 1000):
list_of_means.append(np.random.choice(binom_dist, 100,
replace=True).mean())

fig, ax = plt.subplots()
plt.hist(list_of_means, range=[0,1])
plt.title(graph_title)
st.pyplot(fig)
```

This creates a Streamlit app with two inputs, both a numeric input and a text input, and uses them both to change our Streamlit app. Finally, this results in a Streamlit app that looks like the next figure, with dynamic titles and probabilities:

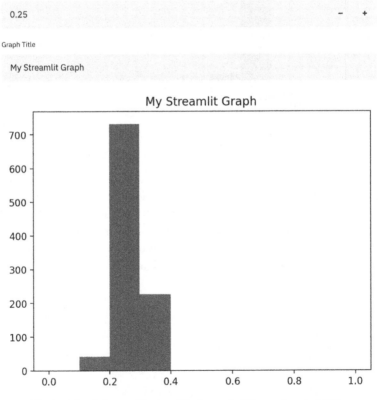

Figure 1.8 – A Streamlit app with dynamic titles and probabilities

Now that we have worked a bit with user input, let's talk about text and Streamlit apps more deeply.

Finishing touches – adding text to Streamlit

Our app is functional, but it is missing a lot of nice touches. We talked earlier about the st.write() function, which the Streamlit docs call the Swiss Army knife of Streamlit commands. Almost whatever we wrap st.write() around will work by default and it should be our go-to function if we're not sure of the best path forward.

Other than st.write(), we also can utilize other built-in functions that format our text for us, such as st.title(), st.header(), st.markdown(), and st.subheader(). Using these five functions helps to format text in our Streamlit apps easily and keeps sizing consistent for bigger apps.

More specifically, st.title() will place a large block of text in our app, st.header() uses a slightly smaller font than st.title(), and st.subheader() uses an even smaller one. Other than those three, st.markdown() will allow anyone already familiar with Markdown to use the popular markup language in our Streamlit apps. Let's try a couple of them in the following code:

```python
import streamlit as st
import numpy as np
import matplotlib.pyplot as plt

st.title('Illustrating the Central Limit Theorem with
Streamlit')
st.subheader('An App by Tyler Richards')
st.write(('This app simulates a thousand coin flips using the
chance of heads input below,'
    'and then samples with replacement from that population
and plots the histogram of the'
    ' means of the samples, in order to illustrate the Central
Limit Theorem!'))

perc_heads = st.number_input(
    label='Chance of Coins Landing on Heads', min_value=0.0,
max_value=1.0, value=.5)
binom_dist = np.random.binomial(1, perc_heads, 1000)

list_of_means = []
for i in range(0, 1000):
    list_of_means.append(np.random.choice(
```

```
        binom_dist, 100, replace=True).mean())

fig, ax = plt.subplots()
ax = plt.hist(list_of_means)
st.pyplot(fig)
```

This preceding code adds a large title (`st.title()`), adds a smaller subheader below (`st.subheader()`), and then adds some even smaller text below the subheader (`st.write()`). We also separated the long string of text in the preceding code block into three smaller strings for readability and to make it easier to edit in our text editor. It should look like the following screenshot. Note that because we are using randomly generated data for this histogram, it is OK (and expected!) if your histogram looks slightly different:

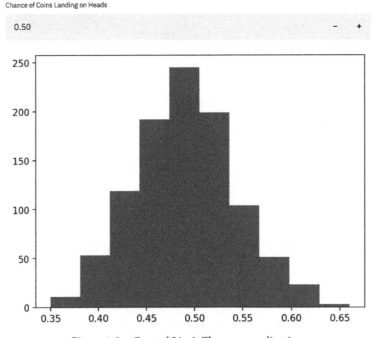

Figure 1.9 – Central Limit Theorem application

One other option Streamlit has for writing out text is `st.markdown()`, which interprets and writes Markdown-style text into your Streamlit app. If you already have familiarity with Markdown, this is a great option to test out instead of `st.write()`.

Summary

In this chapter, we started by learning how to organize our files and folders for the remainder of this book and quickly moved on to instructions for downloading Streamlit. We then built our first Streamlit application, Hello World, and learned how to run our Streamlit applications locally. Then we started building out a more complicated application to show the implications of the central limit theorem from the ground up, going from a simple histogram to accepting user input and formatting different types of text around our app for clarity and beautification.

By now, you should be comfortable with subjects such as basic data visualization, editing Streamlit apps in a text editor, and locally running Streamlit apps. We're going to dive more deeply into data manipulation in our next chapter.

2

Uploading, Downloading, and Manipulating Data

So far in this book, we have exclusively used simulated data in our Streamlit apps. This was useful for getting a good background in some of the basics of Streamlit, but most data science is not done on simulated data, but on real-world datasets that data scientists already have, or on datasets provided by users.

This chapter will focus on the world of data in Streamlit apps, covering everything you will need to know to bring datasets to life using Streamlit. We will cover data manipulation, using user imported data, flow control, debugging Streamlit apps, and speeding up our data applications using caching through an example dataset called Palmer's Penguins.

In particular, we will cover the following topics:

- The setup – Palmer's Penguins
- Debugging Streamlit apps
- Data manipulation in Streamlit

Technical requirements

For this chapter, we will need to download the Palmer's Penguins dataset, which can be found at `https://github.com/tylerjrichards/streamlit_apps/blob/main/penguin_app/penguins.csv`. The setup for this chapter, along with an explanation of the dataset, can be found in the following section.

The setup – Palmer's Penguins

For this chapter, we'll be using a delightful dataset about Arctic penguins that comes from the work of Dr. Kristen Gorman (`https://www.uaf.edu/cfos/people/faculty/detail/kristen-gorman.php`) and the Palmer Station, Antarctica LTER (`https://pal.lternet.edu/`).

> **Dataset acknowledgment**
>
> Data from the Palmer LTER data repository was supported by the Office of Polar Programs, NSF Grants OPP-9011927, OPP-9632763, and OPP-0217282.

This data is a common alternative to the famous Iris datasets and includes data on 344 individual penguins with 3 species represented. The data can be found in the GitHub repository for this book (`https://github.com/tylerjrichards/streamlit_apps`), in the `penguin_app` folder entitled `penguins.csv`.

As we've discussed before, Streamlit apps run from inside our Python script. This sets the base directory to the location of the Python file with our Streamlit app, which means we can access any other files that we put in our app directory.

First, let's create a folder for our new app in our existing `streamlit_apps` folder using the following code block:

```
mkdir penguin_app
cd penguin_app
touch penguins.py
```

After this, download the data and put the resulting CSV file (named `penguins.csv` in the example) in the `penguin_app` folder. Now, our folder should have the `penguins.py` file and our `penguins.csv` file. For our first go around, we're just going to print out the first five rows of our DataFrame using the `st.write()` function we learned earlier using the following code:

```
import streamlit as st
import pandas as pd


st.title("Palmer's Penguins")
#import our data
penguins_df = pd.read_csv('penguins.csv')
  st.write(penguins_df.head())
```

The preceding code will produce the following Streamlit app when we run `streamlit run penguins.py` in the terminal:

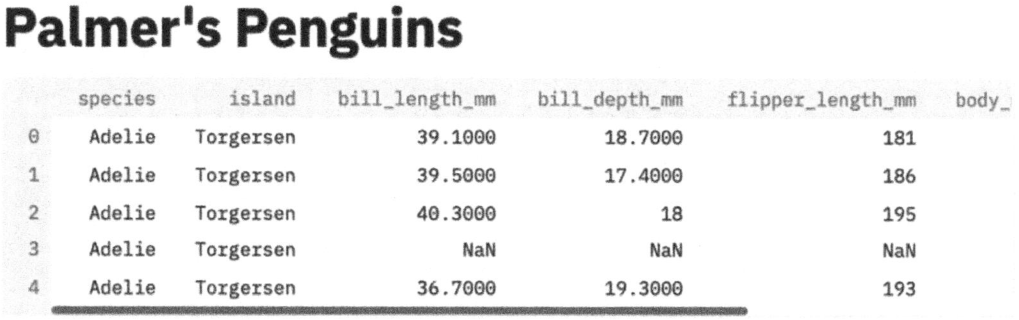

Palmer's Penguins

	species	island	bill_length_mm	bill_depth_mm	flipper_length_mm	body_
0	Adelie	Torgersen	39.1000	18.7000	181	
1	Adelie	Torgersen	39.5000	17.4000	186	
2	Adelie	Torgersen	40.3000	18	195	
3	Adelie	Torgersen	NaN	NaN	NaN	
4	Adelie	Torgersen	36.7000	19.3000	193	

Figure 2.1 – The first five penguins

Now that we have a good idea of what the data looks like, we will explore the dataset a bit more and then begin adding to our app.

Exploring Palmer's Penguins

Before we begin working with this dataset, we should make some visualizations to better understand the data. As we saw before, we have many columns in this data, from the bill length to the flipper length, to the island the penguin lives on, to even the species of penguin. For our first visualization, we can see the flipper length by body mass for the three species:

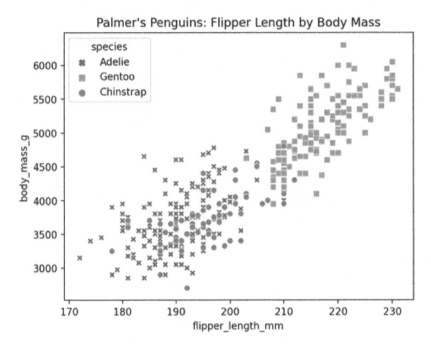

Figure 2.2 – Flippers and weight

As we can see, the Gentoo species has a high flipper length and body mass, and it appears that flipper length is correlated with body mass for all species. Next, let's look at the relationship between bill length and flipper length:

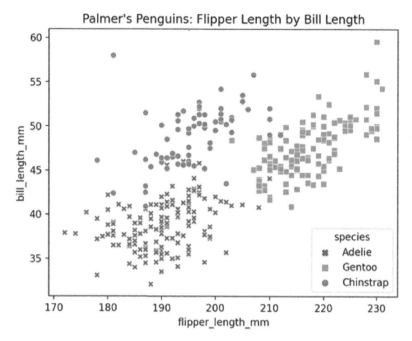

Figure 2.3 – Flippers and bills

From this graph, we can see that the Chinstrap species seem to have a longer bill than the Adelie species. There are many more combinations of variables that we could plot on a scatterplot, but could we instead make a data explorer Streamlit app do this for us?

The final goal of this mini-app is going to be to ask the user to specify one of the species of penguins and to then also choose two other variables to use for a scatterplot. We'll start by learning how to take those inputs, and then create a dynamic visualization.

The last user input that we learned about was the number input function, which won't help us here. Streamlit has a select box function (`st.selectbox()`) that allows us to ask the user to select one option from multiple options (in our case, three options), and the function returns whatever the user selects. We will use this to get the three inputs for our scatterplot:

```
import streamlit as st
import pandas as pd
import matplotlib.pyplot as plt
import seaborn as sns


st.title("Palmer's Penguins")
st.markdown('Use this Streamlit app to make your own
```

```
scatterplot about penguins!')
  selected_species = st.selectbox('What species would you like
to visualize?',
      ['Adelie', 'Gentoo', 'Chinstrap'])
  selected_x_var = st.selectbox('What do want the x variable to
be?',
      ['bill_length_mm', 'bill_depth_mm', 'flipper_length_mm',
'body_mass_g'])
  selected_y_var = st.selectbox('What about the y?',
      ['bill_length_mm', 'bill_depth_mm', 'flipper_length_mm',
'body_mass_g'])
```

This code creates three new variables from three new select boxes that the user can input in our Streamlit app. The following screenshot shows the Streamlit app from the preceding code:

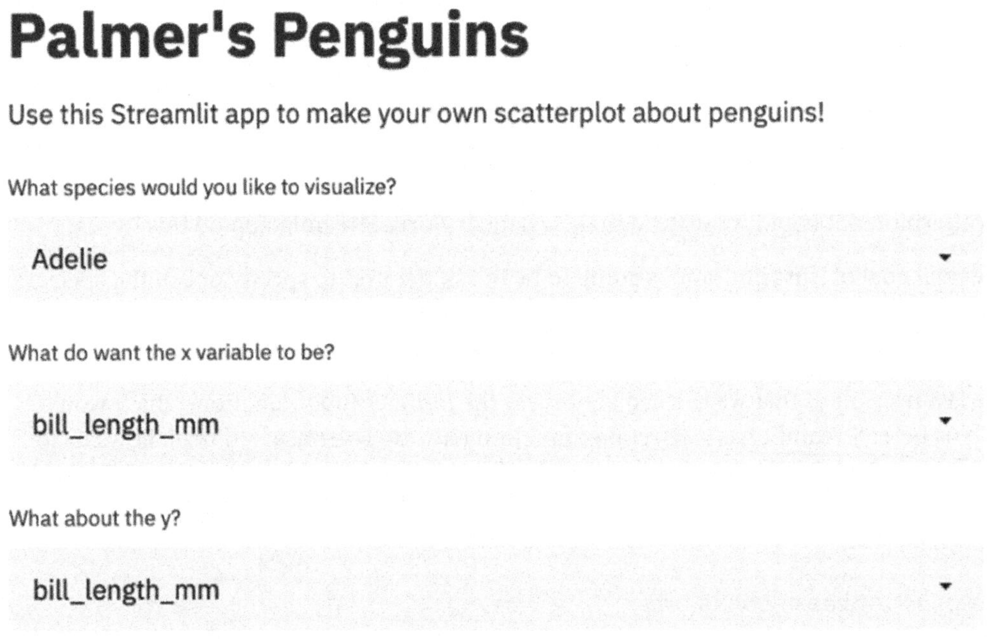

Palmer's Penguins

Use this Streamlit app to make your own scatterplot about penguins!

What species would you like to visualize?

Adelie

What do want the x variable to be?

bill_length_mm

What about the y?

bill_length_mm

Figure 2.4 – User input on penguins

Now that we have the `selected_species` variable, we can filter our DataFrame and make a quick scatterplot using the selected x and y variables, as in this next block of code:

```python
Import streamlit as st
import pandas as pd
import matplotlib.pyplot as plt
import seaborn as sns

st.title("Palmer's Penguins")
st.markdown('Use this Streamlit app to make your own
scatterplot about penguins!')
 selected_species = st.selectbox('What species would you like
to visualize?',
     ['Adelie', 'Gentoo', 'Chinstrap'])
 selected_x_var = st.selectbox('What do want the x variable to
be?',
     ['bill_length_mm', 'bill_depth_mm', 'flipper_length_mm',
'body_mass_g'])
 selected_y_var = st.selectbox('What about the y?',
     ['bill_depth_mm', 'bill_length_mm', 'flipper_length_mm',
'body_mass_g'])

penguins_df = pd.read_csv('penguins.csv')
 penguins_df = penguins_df[penguins_df['species'] == selected_
species]

fig, ax = plt.subplots()
ax = sns.scatterplot(x = penguins_df[selected_x_var],
     y = penguins_df[selected_y_var])
 plt.xlabel(selected_x_var)
 plt.ylabel(selected_y_var)
 st.pyplot(fig)
```

This bit of preceding code adds to the previous example by loading our DataFrame, filtering by species, and then plotting in the same method from the previous chapter, which will result in the same app as before but with a scatterplot attached as well, as shown in the following screenshot:

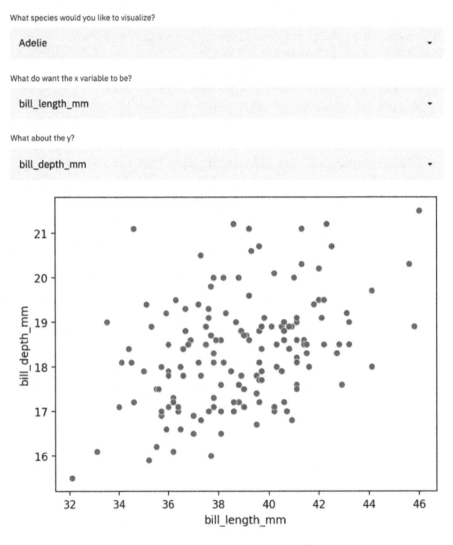

Figure 2.5 – First penguins scatterplot

Try to play around with this app and make sure that all the inputs and outputs are working correctly. Also notice that we've used the input variables to set out *x* axis and *y* axis labels, which means that those will update automatically when we make any new selections. Our graph doesn't explicitly show what species is being graphed, so let's practice making dynamic text. The following adds dynamic text to our Streamlit app's graph title with the `format()` function native to Python:

```python
import streamlit as st
import pandas as pd
import matplotlib.pyplot as plt
import seaborn as sns


st.title("Palmer's Penguins")
st.markdown('Use this Streamlit app to make your own
scatterplot about penguins!')
selected_species = st.selectbox('What species would you like
to visualize?',
     ['Adelie', 'Gentoo', 'Chinstrap'])
selected_x_var = st.selectbox('What do want the x variable to
be?',
     ['bill_length_mm', 'bill_depth_mm', 'flipper_length_mm',
'body_mass_g'])
selected_y_var = st.selectbox('What about the y?',
     ['bill_depth_mm', 'bill_length_mm', 'flipper_length_mm',
'body_mass_g'])


penguins_df = pd.read_csv('penguins.csv')
penguins_df = penguins_df[penguins_df['species'] == selected_
species]


fig, ax = plt.subplots()
ax = sns.scatterplot(x = penguins_df[selected_x_var],
     y = penguins_df[selected_y_var])
plt.xlabel(selected_x_var)
plt.ylabel(selected_y_var)
plt.title('Scatterplot of {} Penguins'.format(selected_
species))
st.pyplot(fig)
```

The preceding code adds the species to our scatterplot and results in the following Streamlit app:

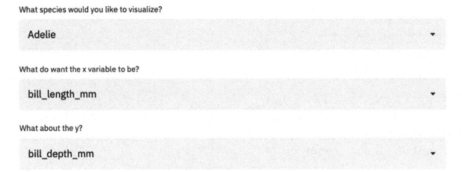

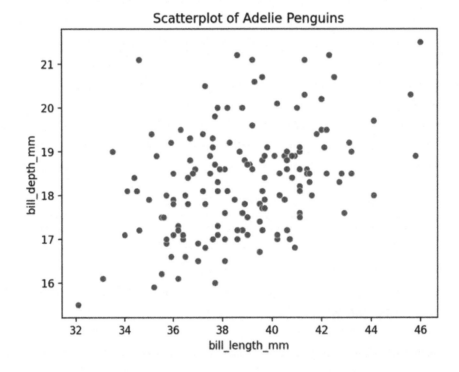

Figure 2.6 – Dynamic graph titles

This looks great! We can also graph each species by hue and shape, as we did in the introductory graphs earlier in this book. The following code does this, and also uses the Seaborn dark grid theme to stand out against Streamlit's white background a bit better:

```python
import streamlit as st
import pandas as pd
import matplotlib.pyplot as plt
import seaborn as sns


st.title("Palmer's Penguins")
st.markdown('Use this Streamlit app to make your own
scatterplot about penguins!')
selected_x_var = st.selectbox('What do want the x variable to
be?',
  ['bill_length_mm', 'bill_depth_mm', 'flipper_length_mm',
'body_mass_g'])
selected_y_var = st.selectbox('What about the y?',
  ['bill_depth_mm', 'bill_length_mm', 'flipper_length_mm',
'body_mass_g'])


penguins_df = pd.read_csv('penguins.csv')


sns.set_style('darkgrid')
markers = {"Adelie": "X", "Gentoo": "s", "Chinstrap":'o'}
fig, ax = plt.subplots()
ax = sns.scatterplot(data = penguins_df, x = selected_x_var,
  y = selected_y_var, hue = 'species', markers = markers,
  style = 'species')
plt.xlabel(selected_x_var)
plt.ylabel(selected_y_var)
plt.title("Scatterplot of Palmer's Penguins")
st.pyplot(fig)
*** Note: The code above is not in the correct format, please
fix **
```

The following screenshot shows our new and improved Palmer's Penguins app, which allows us to select *x* and *y* axes and plots a scatterplot for us with the species in a different hue and shape:

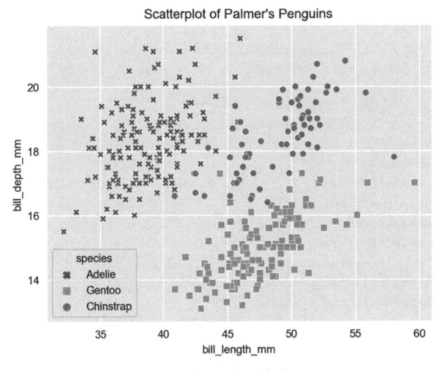

Figure 2.7 – Screenshot with shapes

> **Note**
> You are likely looking at this application through a black and white screenshot, which will only show the shape difference.

The last step for this app is to allow the user to upload their own data. What if we wanted the research team at any point to be able to upload their data to this app and see the graphed results? Or what if there were three research groups, all with their own unique data with different column names, that wanted to use a method that we created? We'll approach this problem one aspect at a time. First, how do we accept data from users?

Streamlit has a function called `file_uploader()` that allows users of the app to upload data up to 200 MB in size (as a default). It works just like the other interactive widgets we've used before, with one exception. Our default in an interactive widget-like select box is just the first value in our list, but it does not make sense to have a default uploaded file before the user actually interacts with the app! The default user uploaded file has a value of `None`.

This begins to cover a very important concept in Streamlit development, which is flow control. Flow control can be understood as thinking carefully through all the steps of your application because Streamlit will try to run the entire app at once if we're not explicit about things, such as wanting to wait until the user has uploaded a file to attempt to create a graphic or manipulate a DataFrame.

Flow control in Streamlit

As we talked about before, there are two solutions to this data upload default problem. We can provide a default file to use until the user interacts with the application, or we can stop the app until a file is uploaded. Let's start with the first option. The following code uses the `st.file_uploader()` function from within an `if` statement. If the user uploads a file, then the app uses that; if they do not, then we default to the file we have used before:

```python
import streamlit as st
import pandas as pd
import matplotlib.pyplot as plt
import seaborn as sns


st.title("Palmer's Penguins")


st.markdown('Use this Streamlit app to make your own
```

```
scatterplot about penguins!')

penguin_file = st.file_uploader('Select Your Local Penguins CSV
(default provided)')
 if penguin_file is not None:
    penguins_df = pd.read_csv(penguin_file)
 else:
    penguins_df= pd.read_csv('penguins.csv')

selected_x_var = st.selectbox('What do want the x variable to
be?',
    ['bill_length_mm', 'bill_depth_mm', 'flipper_length_mm',
'body_mass_g'])
 selected_y_var = st.selectbox('What about the y?',
    ['bill_depth_mm', 'bill_length_mm', 'flipper_length_mm',
'body_mass_g'])

fig, ax = plt.subplots()
ax = sns.scatterplot(x = penguins_df[selected_x_var],
    y = penguins_df[selected_y_var], hue = penguins_
df['species'])
 plt.xlabel(selected_x_var) plt.ylabel(selected_y_var)
 plt.title("Scatterplot of Palmer's Penguins")
st.pyplot(fig)
```

When we run the preceding code in our terminal, we see our three user inputs (the *x* axis, the *y* axis, and the dataset), and also the graph even if we have yet to upload a file. The following screenshot shows this app:

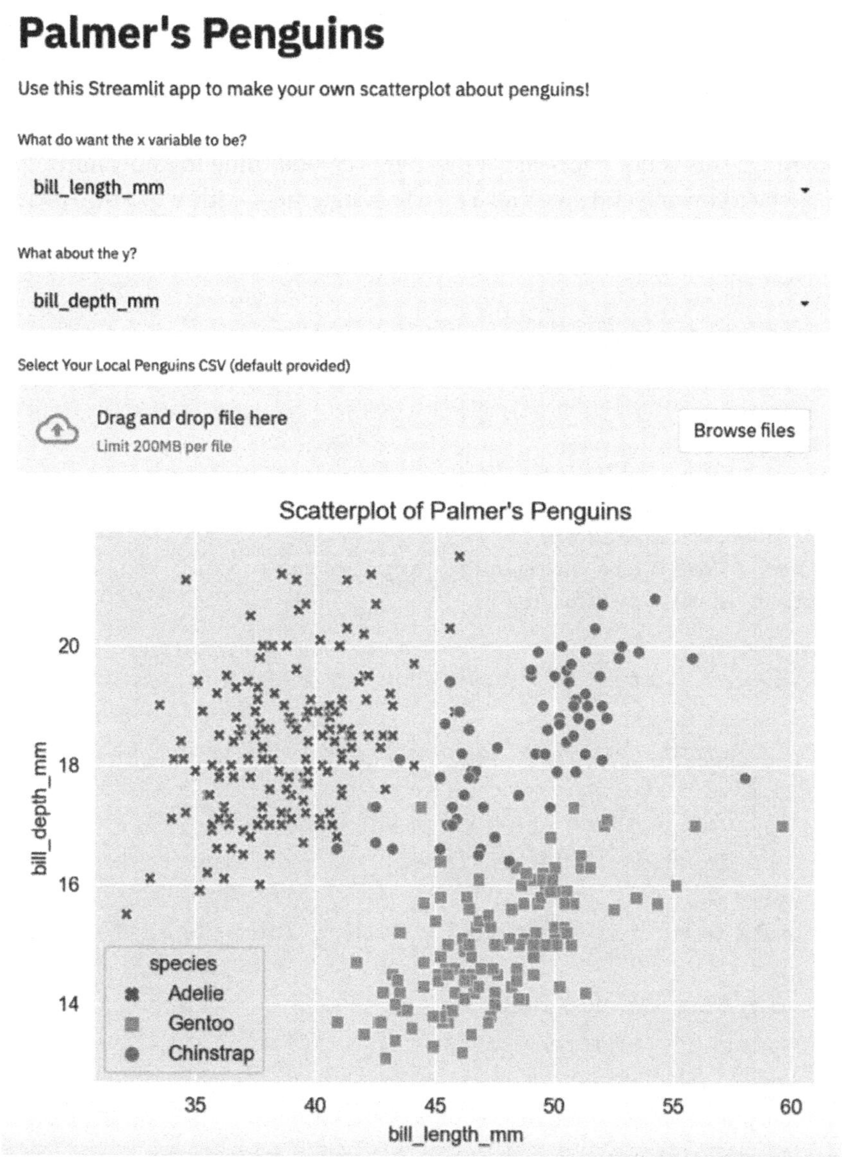
Palmer's Penguins
Use this Streamlit app to make your own scatterplot about penguins!
What do want the x variable to be?
bill_length_mm
What about the y?
bill_depth_mm
Select Your Local Penguins CSV (default provided)
Drag and drop file here
Limit 200MB per file
Browse files
Scatterplot of Palmer's Penguins
bill_depth_mm
20
18
16
14
species
Adelie
Gentoo
Chinstrap
35
40
45
50
55
60
bill_length_mm

Figure 2.8 – File input

The clear advantage of this approach is that there are always results shown in this application, but the results may not be useful to the user! For larger applications, this is a subpar solution as well because any data stored inside the app, regardless of use, is going to slow the application down. Later, in *Chapter 7, Exploring Streamlit Components*, we'll discuss all of our options for deployment, including a built-in deployment option called Streamlit Sharing.

Our second option is to stop the application entirely unless the user has uploaded a file. For that option, we're going to use a new Streamlit function called `stop()`, which (predictably) stops the flow whenever it is called. It is best practice to use this to find errors in the app and to encourage the user to make some change or describe the error that is happening. This is not necessary for us but is a good thing to know for future applications. The following code uses an `if-else` statement with `st.stop()` in the `else` statement to prevent the entire app from running when `st.file_uploader()` is unused:

```python
import streamlit as st
import pandas as pd
import matplotlib.pyplot as plt
import seaborn as sns


st.title("Palmer's Penguins")
st.markdown('Use this Streamlit app to make your own
scatterplot about penguins!')


selected_x_var = st.selectbox('What do want the x variable to
be?',
      ['bill_length_mm', 'bill_depth_mm', 'flipper_length_mm',
'body_mass_g'])
  selected_y_var = st.selectbox('What about the y?',
      ['bill_depth_mm', 'bill_length_mm', 'flipper_length_mm',
'body_mass_g'])
penguin_file = st.file_uploader('Select Your Local Penguins
CSV')
  if penguin_file is not None:
      penguins_df = pd.read_csv(penguin_file)
  else:
      st.stop()
sns.set_style('darkgrid')
markers = {"Adelie": "X", "Gentoo": "s", "Chinstrap":'o'}
fig, ax = plt.subplots()
ax = sns.scatterplot(data = penguins_df, x = selected_x_var,
   y = selected_y_var, hue = 'species', markers = markers,
   style = 'species')
plt.xlabel(selected_x_var)
```

```
plt.ylabel(selected_y_var)
plt.title("Scatterplot of Palmer's Penguins")
st.pyplot(fig)
```

As we can see with the following screenshot, until we upload our own data, we will not see a scatterplot, and the application stops. The Streamlit app simply waits to run fully until the user has uploaded their file instead of throwing an error:

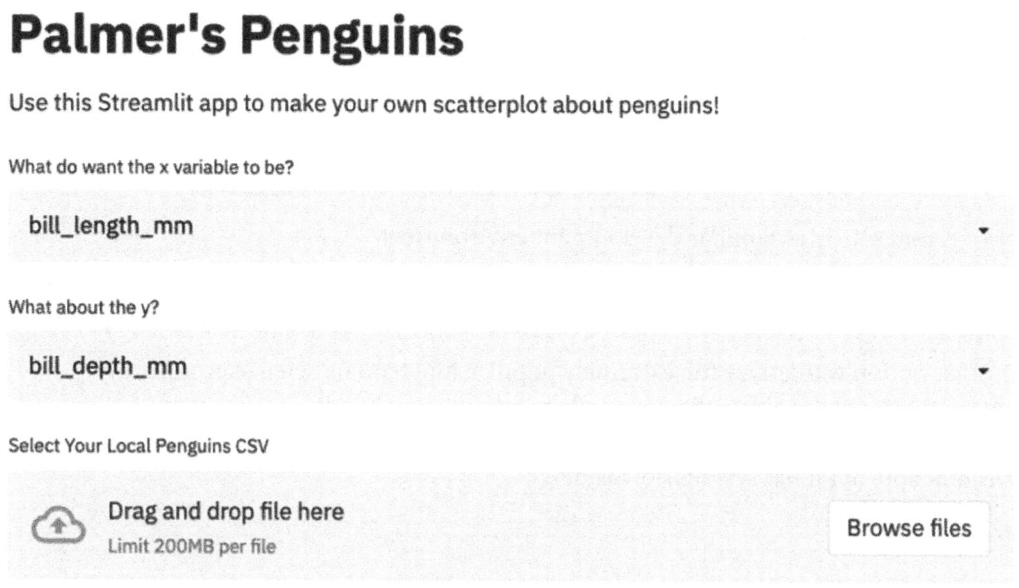

Palmer's Penguins

Use this Streamlit app to make your own scatterplot about penguins!

What do want the x variable to be?

bill_length_mm	▾

What about the y?

bill_depth_mm	▾

Select Your Local Penguins CSV

☁	**Drag and drop file here** Limit 200MB per file	**Browse files**

Figure 2.9 – Streamlit stop

Before we move on to data manipulation and create more complicated Streamlit apps, we should touch on some best practices for debugging Streamlit apps.

Debugging Streamlit apps

We broadly have two options for Streamlit development.

- Develop in Streamlit and st.write() as a debugger.
- Explore in Jupyter and then copy to Streamlit.

Developing in Streamlit

In the first option, we write our code directly in Streamlit as we're experimenting and exploring exactly what our application will do. We've basically been taking this option already, which works very well if we have less exploration work and more implementation work to do.

Pros:

- What you see is what you get
- No need to maintain both IPython and Python versions of the same app
- Better experience for learning how to write production code

Cons:

- A slower feedback loop (the entire app must run before feedback)
- A potentially unfamiliar development environment

Exploring in Jupyter and then copying to Streamlit

Another option is to utilize the extremely popular Jupyter data science product to write and test out the Streamlit app's code before placing it in the necessary script and formatting it correctly. This can be useful for exploring new methods that will live in the Streamlit app, but it has serious downsides.

Pros:

- The lightning-fast feedback loop makes it easier to experiment.
- Users may be more familiar with Jupyter.
- The full app does not have to be run to get results.

Cons:

- Jupyter may provide deceptive results if run out of order.
- 'Copying' code over from Jupyter is time-consuming.
- Python versioning may be different between Jupyter and Streamlit.

My recommendation here is to develop Streamlit apps inside the environment where they are going to be run (that is, a Python file). For debugging, heavily utilize the `st.write()` function, which can print out nearly any Python object (dictionary, DataFrame, list, string, number, graph, and so on) that you may need. Try to only use another development environment such as Jupyter as a last resort!

Data manipulation in Streamlit

Streamlit runs our Python file from the top down as a script, and so we can perform data manipulation with powerful libraries such as pandas in the same way that we might in a Jupyter notebook or a regular Python script. As we've discussed before, we can do all our regular data manipulation as normal. For our Palmer's Penguins app, what if we wanted the user to be able to filter out penguins based on their gender? The following code filters our DataFrame using pandas:

```python
import streamlit as st
import pandas as pd
import matplotlib.pyplot as plt
import seaborn as sns

st.title("Palmer's Penguins")
st.markdown('Use this Streamlit app to make your own
scatterplot about penguins!')

penguin_file = st.file_uploader(
    'Select Your Local Penguins CSV (default provided)')
if penguin_file is not None:
    penguins_df = pd.read_csv(penguin_file)
else:
    penguins_df = pd.read_csv('penguins.csv')

selected_x_var = st.selectbox('What do want the x variable to
be?',
                              ['bill_length_mm', 'bill_depth_
mm', 'flipper_length_mm', 'body_mass_g'])
selected_y_var = st.selectbox('What about the y?',
                              ['bill_depth_mm', 'bill_length_
mm', 'flipper_length_mm', 'body_mass_g'])
selected_gender = st.selectbox('What gender do you want to
filter for?',
                               ['all penguins', 'male
penguins', 'female penguins'])
if selected_gender == 'male penguins':
    penguins_df = penguins_df[penguins_df['sex'] == 'male']
elif selected_gender == 'female penguins':
```

```
    penguins_df = penguins_df[penguins_df['sex'] == 'female']
  else:
      pass

fig, ax = plt.subplots()
ax = sns.scatterplot(x=penguins_df[selected_x_var],
                      y=penguins_df[selected_y_var],
hue=penguins_df['species'])
  plt.xlabel(selected_x_var)
  plt.ylabel(selected_y_var)
  plt.title("Scatterplot of Palmer's Penguins: {}".
format(selected_gender))
  st.pyplot(fig)
```

A couple of things to note here. First, we've added another `selectbox` plugin, with male, female, and all options. We could have done this by asking for a text input, but for data manipulation, we want to restrict user action as much as possible. We also made sure to dynamically change the title, which is recommended for clarity as we want to show the user that the data has been filtered by their input directly in the graph.

An introduction to caching

As we create more computationally intensive Streamlit apps and begin to use and upload larger datasets, we should start worrying about the runtime of these apps and work to increase our efficiency whenever possible. The easiest way to make a Streamlit app more efficient is through caching, which is storing some results in memory so that the app does not repeat the same work whenever possible.

A good analogy to an app's cache is a human's short-term memory, where we keep bits of information close at hand that we think might be useful. When something is in our short-term memory, we don't have to think very hard to get access to that piece of information. In the same way, when we cache a piece of information in Streamlit, we are making a bet that we'll use that information often.

The way Streamlit caching works more specifically is by storing the results of a function in our app, and if that function is called with the same parameters by another user (or by us if we rerun the app), Streamlit does not run the same function but instead loads the result of the function from memory.

Let's prove to ourselves that this works! First, we'll create a function for our data upload part of the Penguins app, and then use the time library to artificially make the function take much longer than it would normally and see whether we can make our app faster using st.cache().

As you can see in the following code, we first made a new function called load_file(), which waits 3 seconds, and then loads the file that we need. Normally we would not intentionally slow down our app, but we want to know whether caching works:

```python
import streamlit as st
import pandas as pd
import matplotlib.pyplot as plt
import seaborn as sns
import time


st.title("Palmer's Penguins")
st.markdown('Use this Streamlit app to make your own
scatterplot about penguins!')

penguin_file = st.file_uploader(
    'Select Your Local Penguins CSV (default provided)')

def load_file(penguin_file):
    time.sleep(3)
    if penguin_file is not None:
        df = pd.read_csv(penguin_file)
    else:
        df = pd.read_csv('penguins.csv')
    return(df)
  penguins_df = load_file(penguin_file)


selected_x_var = st.selectbox('What do want the x variable to
be?',
                              ['bill_length_mm', 'bill_depth_
mm', 'flipper_length_mm', 'body_mass_g'])
  selected_y_var = st.selectbox('What about the y?',
                              ['bill_depth_mm', 'bill_length_
mm', 'flipper_length_mm', 'body_mass_g'])
  selected_gender = st.selectbox('What gender do you want to
```

```
filter for?',
                                ['all penguins', 'male
penguins', 'female penguins'])
  if selected_gender == 'male penguins':
     penguins_df = penguins_df[penguins_df['sex'] == 'male']
  elif selected_gender == 'female penguins':
     penguins_df = penguins_df[penguins_df['sex'] == 'female']
  else:
     pass
fig, ax = plt.subplots()
ax = sns.scatterplot(x=penguins_df[selected_x_var],
                     y=penguins_df[selected_y_var],
hue=penguins_df['species'])
  plt.xlabel(selected_x_var)
  plt.ylabel(selected_y_var)
  plt.title("Scatterplot of Palmer's Penguins: {}".
format(selected_gender))
  st.pyplot(fig)
```

Now, let's run this app and then select the hamburger icon in the top right and press the rerun button (we can also just press the *R* key to rerun).

We notice that each time we rerun the app, it takes at least 3 seconds. Now, let's add our cache decorator on top of the `load_file` function and run our app again:

```
import streamlit as st
import pandas as pd
import matplotlib.pyplot as plt
mport seaborn as sns
import time


st.title("Palmer's Penguins")
st.markdown('Use this Streamlit app to make your own
scatterplot about penguins!')


penguin_file = st.file_uploader(
     'Select Your Local Penguins CSV (default provided)')
  @st.cache()
def load_file(penguin_file):
```

```
    time.sleep(3)
    if penguin_file is not None:
        df = pd.read_csv(penguin_file)
    else:
        df = pd.read_csv('penguins.csv')
    return(df)
penguins_df = load_file(penguin_file)


selected_x_var = st.selectbox('What do want the x variable to
be?',
                             ['bill_length_mm', 'bill_depth_
mm', 'flipper_length_mm', 'body_mass_g'])
selected_y_var = st.selectbox('What about the y?',
                             ['bill_depth_mm', 'bill_length_
mm', 'flipper_length_mm', 'body_mass_g'])
selected_gender = st.selectbox('What gender do you want to
filter for?',
                             ['all penguins', 'male
penguins', 'female penguins'])
if selected_gender == 'male penguins':
    penguins_df = penguins_df[penguins_df['sex'] == 'male']
elif selected_gender == 'female penguins':
    penguins_df = penguins_df[penguins_df['sex'] == 'female']
else:
    pass


fig, ax = plt.subplots()
ax = sns.scatterplot(x=penguins_df[selected_x_var],
                    y=penguins_df[selected_y_var],
hue=penguins_df['species'])
plt.xlabel(selected_x_var)
plt.ylabel(selected_y_var)
plt.title("Scatterplot of Palmer's Penguins: {}".
format(selected_gender))
st.pyplot(fig)
```

As we run the app a few times, we can notice that it is much faster! When we rerun the app, two things happen. First, Streamlit checks the cache to ascertain whether that same function with the same inputs has been run before and returns the Penguins data from memory, and second, it does not run the `load_file` function at all, meaning we never run the `time.sleep(3)` command and also never spend the time required to load the data into Streamlit. We'll explore this caching function in more detail, but this method will get us the majority of the efficiency gains.

Summary

This chapter was full of fundamental building blocks that we will use vigorously throughout the remainder of this book, and that you will use to develop your own Streamlit applications.

On data, we covered how to bring our own DataFrames into Streamlit and how to accept user input in the form of a data file that brings us past only being able to simulate data. On other skillsets, we learned how to use our cache to make our data apps faster, how to control the flow of our Streamlit apps, and how to debug our Streamlit apps using `st.write()`. That's it for this chapter. Next, we'll move on to data visualization!

3
Data Visualization

Visualization is fundamental to the modern data scientist. It is often the central lens used to understand items such as statistical models (for example, via an AUC chart), the distribution of a crucial variable (via a histogram), or even important business metrics.

In the last two chapters, we used the most popular Python graphing libraries (**Matplotlib** and **Seaborn**) in our examples. This chapter will focus on extending that ability to a broad range of Python graphing libraries, along with including some graphing functions native to Streamlit.

By the end of this chapter, you should feel comfortable with using Streamlit's native graphing functions, and also using Streamlit's visualization functions to place graphs made from major Python visualization libraries in your own Streamlit app.

In this chapter, we will cover the following topics:

- San Francisco Trees – A new dataset
- Streamlit's built-in graphing functions
- Streamlit's built-in visualization options

- Importing Python visualization libraries into Streamlit. In this section, we will cover the following libraries:

  (a) **Plotly** (for interactive visualizations)

  (b) **Seaborn+Matplotlib** (for classic statistical visualizations)

  (c) **Bokeh** (for interactive visualization in web browsers)

  (d) **Altair** (for declarative, interactive visualizations)

  (e) **PyDeck** (for interactive map-based visualizations)

Technical requirements

For this chapter, we will be working with a new dataset that can be found at `https://github.com/tylerjrichards/streamlit_apps/blob/main/trees_app/trees.csv`. A further explanation of the dataset can be found in the following section.

San Francisco Trees – A new dataset

We're going to be working with all sorts of graphs in this chapter, so we're going to need a new dataset that has much more info, especially dates and locations. Enter *SF Trees*. The department of public works in San Francisco has a dataset (cleaned by the wonderful folks in the R community who run Tidy Tuesday, a weekly event where people publish interesting visualizations of new data each week) of every tree planted and maintained in the city of San Francisco. They cleverly call this dataset *EveryTreeSF – Urban Forest map*, and update this dataset every day. I have selected a random 10,000 trees with complete info and placed this data in the main GitHub repository under the `trees` folder (I'm not as clever as the data engineer in SF's DPW, I know). The GitHub repo can be found at `https://github.com/tylerjrichards/streamlit_apps`. If you would like to download the full dataset, the link is here: `https://data.sfgov.org/City-Infrastructure/Street-Tree-List/tkzw-k3nq`.

From the main `streamlit_apps` folder we've been using throughout this book, start by making a new folder, making a new Python file, and then downloading our data into the folder, the same thing as we did in *Chapter 2, Uploading, Downloading, and Manipulating Data*, but just adding some new data! You can run the following code in your terminal to set this up:

```
mkdir trees_app
cd trees_app
touch trees.py
curl https://raw.githubusercontent.com/tylerjrichards/
streamlit_apps/main/trees_app/trees.csv > trees.csv
```

I'll note here that if this does not work, or if you are on an operating system without these commands (such as Windows, for example), you can always go and download the CSV file directly by going to the GitHub repo mentioned in the preceding paragraph (`https://github.com/tylerjrichards/streamlit_apps`).

Now that we have our setup, our next step is to open our `trees.py` file in our favorite editor and get to making our Streamlit app.

> **Note**
> We will follow these exact same steps at the beginning of the rest of the chapters, so in the future, we will not cover these explicitly.

Let's start by titling our app and printing out some example rows using the following code:

```python
import streamlit as st
import pandas as pd

st.title('SF Trees')
st.write('This app analyses trees in San Francisco using'
         ' a dataset kindly provided by SF DPW')
trees_df = pd.read_csv('trees.csv')
st.write(trees_df.head())
```

We can then run the following command in our terminal and see the resulting Streamlit app in our browser:

```
streamlit run trees.py
```

Note that this is neither the easiest nor the best way to see the first few rows of a dataset, but we can do this purely because we already know that we're going to build a Streamlit app using this data. The general workflow usually begins with some data exploration outside of Streamlit (in Jupyter notebooks, through SQL queries, or whatever the preferred workflow is for you as a data scientist or analyst). That said, let's continue looking at our dataset by looking at the output of the preceding code in the new Streamlit app in our browser:

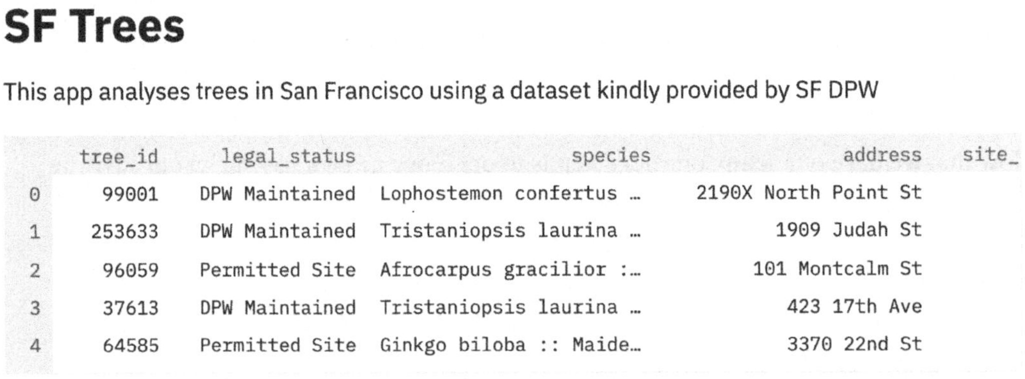

SF Trees

This app analyses trees in San Francisco using a dataset kindly provided by SF DPW

	tree_id	legal_status	species	address	site_
0	99001	DPW Maintained	Lophostemon confertus …	2190X North Point St	
1	253633	DPW Maintained	Tristaniopsis laurina …	1909 Judah St	
2	96059	Permitted Site	Afrocarpus gracilior :…	101 Montcalm St	
3	37613	DPW Maintained	Tristaniopsis laurina …	423 17th Ave	
4	64585	Permitted Site	Ginkgo biloba :: Maide…	3370 22nd St	

Figure 3.1 – The first few rows of trees

This dataset contains a huge amount of info about the trees in SF, from their width (dbh) to the longitude and latitude points, the species, their address, and even the date they were planted. Before we get started with graphing, let's talk a bit about the visualization options in front of us.

Streamlit visualization use cases

Some Streamlit users are relatively experienced Python developers with well-tested workflows in visualization libraries of their choice. For these users, the best path forward is the one we've taken so far, which is to create our graphs in our library of choice (Seaborn, Matplotlib, Bokeh, and so on) and then use the appropriate Streamlit function to write this to the app.

Other Streamlit users will have less experience in Pythonic graphing, and especially for these users, Streamlit offers a few built-in functions. We'll start with built-in libraries and move on to learning how to import the most popular and powerful libraries for our Streamlit apps.

Streamlit's built-in graphing functions

There are three built-in functions for graphing – st.line_chart(), st.bar_chart(), and st.area_chart(). They all work similarly by trying to figure out what variables you're already trying to graph, and then put them into a line, bar, or area chart, respectively. In our dataset, we have a variable called dbh, which is the width of the tree at chest height. First, we can group our DataFrame by dbh, and then push that directly to the line chart, bar chart, and area chart. The following code should group our dataset by width, count the unique trees of each width, and then make a line, bar, and area chart of each:

```
import streamlit as st
import pandas as pd

st.title('SF Trees')
st.write('This app analyses trees in San Francisco using'
        ' a dataset kindly provided by SF DPW')
trees_df = pd.read_csv('trees.csv')
df_dbh_grouped = pd.DataFrame(trees_df.groupby(['dbh']).
count()['tree_id'])
df_dbh_grouped.columns = ['tree_count']
st.line_chart(df_dbh_grouped)
st.bar_chart(df_dbh_grouped)
st.area_chart(df_dbh_grouped)
```

The preceding code should show our three graphs right after one another, as is shown in the following screenshot:

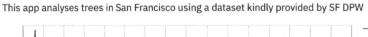

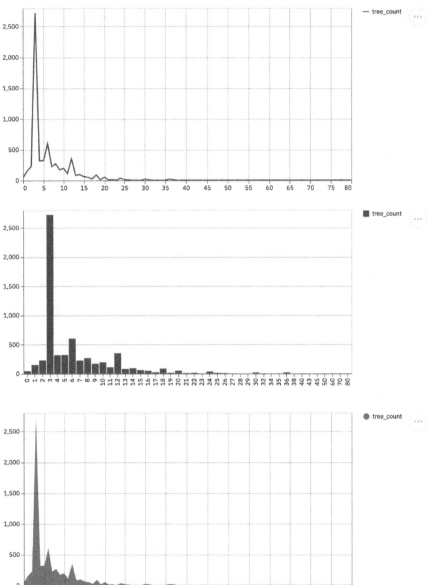

Figure 3.2 – Lines, bars, area, and tree height

We gave the function nothing except for the DataFrame, and it was able to guess correctly which items should be on the *x* and *y* axes and plot those to our Streamlit chart. Each of these charts is interactive by default! We can zoom in or out, roll out the mouse over points/bars/lines to see each data point, and even view fullscreen out of the box. These Streamlit functions are actually calling another popular graphing library called **Altair**, which we will learn how to use in more depth later in this chapter.

Now that we see the basics of the built-in (it's clear that the term *built-in* is fairly loose here, as Streamlit is built to be a great and convenient web application library, not a great visualization library) functions, let's push these functions to see how they handle more data. First, we're going to make a new column of random numbers between -500 and 500 in our df_dbh_grouped DataFrame using the numpy library and use the same plotting code that we used before. The following code plots two line charts, one before we added the new column, and one after:

```
import streamlit as st
import pandas as pd
import numpy as np


st.title('SF Trees')
st.write('This app analyses trees in San Francisco using'
         ' a dataset kindly provided by SF DPW')
trees_df = pd.read_csv('trees.csv')
df_dbh_grouped = pd.DataFrame(trees_df.groupby(['dbh']).
count()['tree_id'])
df_dbh_grouped.columns = ['tree_count']
st.line_chart(df_dbh_grouped)
df_dbh_grouped['new_col'] = np.random.randn(len(df_dbh_
grouped)) * 500
st.line_chart(df_dbh_grouped)
```

This code should produce an app that looks like the following screenshot:

SF Trees

This app analyses trees in San Francisco using a dataset kindly provided by SF DPW

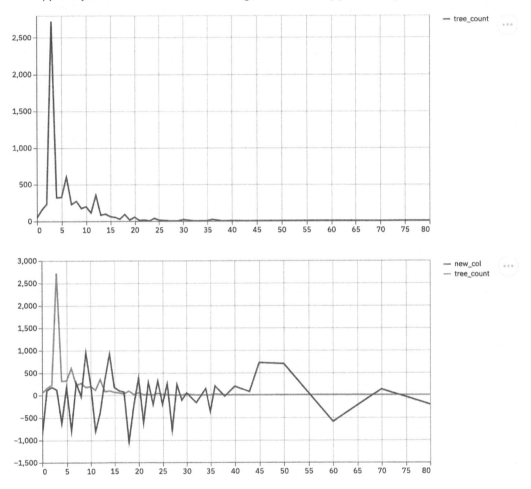

Figure 3.3 – Two sequential line charts

Again, these functions put whatever is on the index as the *x* axis and use all the columns they can as variables on the *y* axis. These built-in functions are very useful if we have an incredibly straightforward graphing problem in front of us (as in the example). However, these visualization functions are, overall, less flexible in comparison to libraries with the sole purpose of visualization and it may be difficult to debug the behavior behind these functions. The recommendation here is that if you are working with data that is easy to massage into a format where the index of the DataFrame belongs on the *x* axis, and the rest of the columns are plotted on the *y* axis, these functions will work well. For more complicated tasks, we should use other graphing libraries.

There is one more built-in Streamlit graphing function that we should discuss here, `st.map()`. Just like the preceding functions, this wraps around another Python graphing library, this time **PyDeck** instead of **Altair**, and finds columns that it thinks are longitude and latitude points by searching the DataFrame for columns with titles such as **longitude**, **long**, **latitude**, or **lat**. Then, it plots each row as its own point on a map, auto-zooms and focuses the map, and writes it to our Streamlit app. We should note that visualizing detailed maps is much more computationally intensive in comparison to the other forms of visualization that we have used so far, so we are going to sample 1,000 random rows from our DataFrame, remove null values, and try out `st.map()` using the following code:

```
import streamlit as st
import pandas as pd
import numpy as np


t.title('SF Trees')
st.write('This app analyses trees in San Francisco using'
        ' a dataset kindly provided by SF DPW')
trees_df = pd.read_csv('trees.csv')
trees_df = trees_df.dropna(subset=['longitude', 'latitude'])
trees_df = trees_df.sample(n = 1000)
st.map(trees_df)
```

This works perfectly well, right out of the box! We get a beautiful interactive map of the trees in San Francisco, as we can see in the following screenshot:

SF Trees

This app analyses trees in San Francisco using a dataset kindly provided by SF DPW

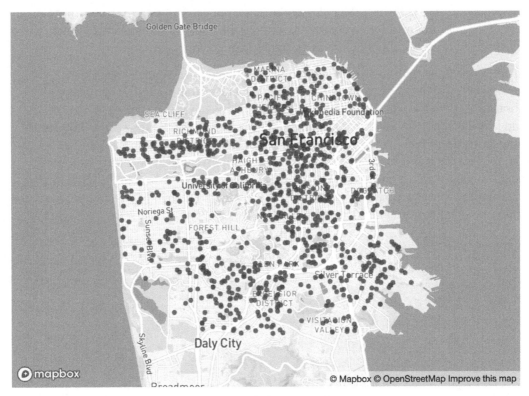

Figure 3.4 – Default SF map of trees

As with the other functions, we don't have many options for customization here other than an optional zoom parameter, but this works very well for a quick visualization.

As we've seen, these built-in functions can be useful for making Streamlit apps quickly, but we trade off speed for customizability. In practice, I rarely use these functions when I produce Streamlit apps, but often use these when doing quick visualizations of data already in Streamlit. In production, more powerful libraries, such as **Matplotlib**, **Seaborn**, and **PyDdeck**, give us the flexibility and customizability we want. The rest of this chapter will walk through six different popular Python visualization libraries.

Streamlit's built-in visualization options

For the rest of this chapter, we're going to run through the rest of the Streamlit visualization options, which are **Plotly**, **Matplotlib**, **Seaborn**, **Bokeh**, **Altair**, and **PyDeck**.

Plotly

Plotly is an interactive visualization library that many data scientists use for visualizing data in Jupyter, in the browser locally, or even hosting these graphs to be viewed on a platform for visualizations and dashboards created by the Plotly team called **Dash**. This library is very similar to Streamlit in its intent and is primarily used for internal or external dashboards (hence, the name Dash).

Streamlit allows us to call `plotly` graphs from within Streamlit apps using the `st.plotly_chart()` function, which makes it a breeze to port any Plotly or Dash dashboards. We'll test this out by making a histogram of the height of the trees in SF, essentially the same graph that we've made before. The following code makes our Plotly histogram:

```
import streamlit as st
import pandas as pd
import plotly.express as px


st.title('SF Trees')
st.write('This app analyses trees in San Francisco using'
         ' a dataset kindly provided by SF DPW')
st.subheader('Plotly Chart')
trees_df = pd.read_csv('trees.csv')


fig = px.histogram(trees_df['dbh'])
st.plotly_chart(fig)
```

As we'll notice, all the interactivity native to Plotly works by default in Streamlit. The user can scroll over the histogram bars and get the exact info about each one. There are a few other useful built-in features to Plotly that port over to Streamlit, such as the ability to zoom in and out, download the plot as a png, and select a group of data points/bars/lines. The full features can be seen in the following screenshot:

SF Trees

This app analyses trees in San Francisco using a dataset kindly provided by SF DPW

Plotly Chart

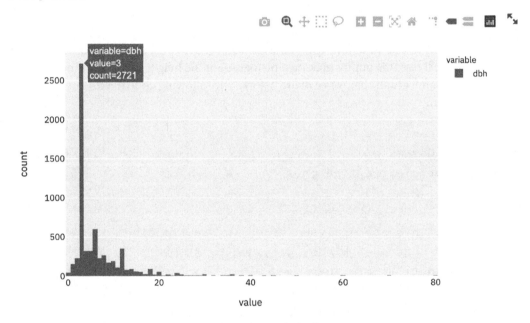

Figure 3.5 – First Plotly chart

Now that we're comfortable with Plotly, we can move on to other popular visualization libraries, **Matplotlib** and **Seaborn**.

Matplotlib and Seaborn

Earlier in this book, we learned how to use the Matplotlib and Seaborn visualization libraries inside Streamlit, so we will just go over them briefly here. There is a column called **date** in the trees dataset that corresponds to the date that the tree was planted. We can use the datetime library to figure out the age of each tree in days, and plot that histogram using Seaborn and Matplotlib, respectively. The following code creates a new column called age, which is the difference in days between the tree planting date and today, and then graphs the histogram of the age using both Seaborn and Matplotlib:

```python
import streamlit as st
import pandas as pd
import matplotlib.pyplot as plt
import seaborn as sns
import datetime as dt

st.title('SF Trees')
st.write('This app analyses trees in San Francisco using'
         ' a dataset kindly provided by SF DPW')
trees_df = pd.read_csv('trees.csv')
trees_df['age'] = (pd.to_datetime('today') -
                   pd.to_datetime(trees_df['date'])).dt.days

st.subheader('Seaborn Chart')
fig_sb, ax_sb = plt.subplots()
ax_sb = sns.histplot(trees_df['age'])
plt.xlabel('Age (Days)')
st.pyplot(fig_sb)

st.subheader('Matploblib Chart')
fig_mpl, ax_mpl = plt.subplots()
ax_mpl = plt.hist(trees_df['age'])
plt.xlabel('Age (Days)')
st.pyplot(fig_mpl)
```

In the preceding code, we defined unique subplots for each graph, created a Seaborn or Matplotlib graph for each, and then used the `st.pyplot()` function to insert each graph in order onto our Streamlit app. The preceding code should show an app similar to the following screenshot (I say similar because, depending on when you run this, the age of the trees will be different as `pd.to_datetime('today')` will return your current date:

SF Trees

This app analyses trees in San Francisco using a dataset kindly provided by SF DPW

Seaborn Chart

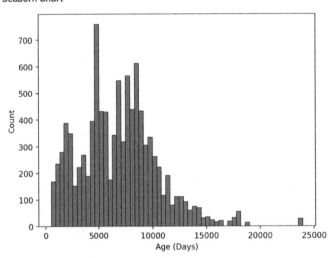

Matploblib Chart

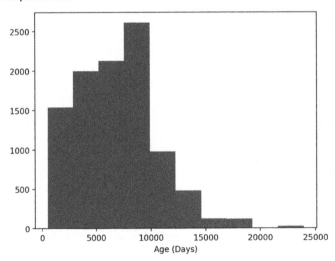

Figure 3.6 – Seaborn and Matplotlib histograms

Whether you use Seaborn or Matplotlib, you'll use the `st.pyplot()` function in the same way. Now that we're more comfortable with these libraries, we should learn about another interactive visualization library – **Bokeh**.

Bokeh

Bokeh is another web-based interactive visualization library that also has dashboarding products built on top of it. It is a direct competitor to Plotly, but is more focused on the Python ecosystem, whereas Plotly is built on top of `Plotly.js`. Either way, Bokeh is an extremely popular Python visualization package that Python users may be very comfortable using.

We can call Bokeh graphs using the same format as Plotly. First, we create the Bokeh graph, and then we use the `st.bokeh_chart()` function to write the app to Streamlit. In Bokeh, we have to first instantiate a Bokeh figure object, and then change aspects of that figure before we plot it out. The important lesson here is that if we change an aspect of the Bokeh figure object after we call the `st.bokeh_chart()` function, we will not change the graph shown on the Streamlit app. For example, when we run the following code, we will not see a new *x* axis title at all:

```
import streamlit as st
import pandas as pd
from bokeh.plotting import figure


st.title('SF Trees')
  st.write('This app analyses trees in San Francisco using'
           ' a dataset kindly provided by SF DPW')
  st.subheader('Bokeh Chart')
  trees_df = pd.read_csv('trees.csv')


scatterplot = figure(title = 'Bokeh Scatterplot')
  scatterplot.scatter(trees_df['dbh'], trees_df['site_order'])
  st.bokeh_chart(scatterplot)
  scatterplot.xaxis.axis_label = "dbh"
```

Instead, we'll have to switch the order of the last two lines, which will now show up on our app. We'll add a *y* axis for good measure as well.

```
import streamlit as st
import pandas as pd
from bokeh.plotting import figure
st.title('SF Trees')
 st.write('This app analyses trees in San Francisco using'
          ' a dataset kindly provided by SF DPW')
 st.subheader('Bokeh Chart')
 trees_df = pd.read_csv('trees.csv')


scatterplot = figure(title = 'Bokeh Scatterplot')
 scatterplot.scatter(trees_df['dbh'], trees_df['site_order'])
 scatterplot.yaxis.axis_label = "site_order"
scatterplot.xaxis.axis_label = "dbh"
 st.bokeh_chart(scatterplot)
```

The preceding code will create a Bokeh chart of dbh versus site_order, as shown in the following screenshot:

SF Trees

This app analyses trees in San Francisco using a dataset kindly provided by SF DPW

Bokeh Chart

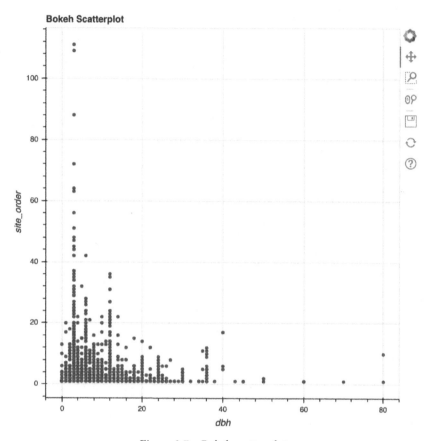

Figure 3.7 – Bokeh scatterplot

Now, onto our next visualization library – Altair!

Altair

We've already used **Altair** in this chapter through Streamlit functions such as `st.line_chart()` or `st.map()`, but now we'll explore how to use Altair directly. Altair is a declarative visualization library, which loosely means that instead of explicitly writing out each feature in a graph (such as naming *x* axes), we pass the relationships between the columns as desired, and Altair takes care of the rest.

We've made quite a few graphs with this dataset already, but why don't we explore a new column, the caretaker column? This bit of data defines who is in charge of the tree (public or private) and if public, what government organization is responsible for upkeep. Thrilling!

The following code groups our DataFrame by caretaker, and then uses that grouped DataFrame within Altair:

```
import streamlit as st
import pandas as pd
import altair as alt


st.title('SF Trees')
st.write('This app analyses trees in San Francisco using'
         ' a dataset kindly provided by SF DPW')
trees_df = pd.read_csv('trees.csv')
df_caretaker = trees_df.groupby(['caretaker']).count()['tree_
id'].reset_index()
df_caretaker.columns = ['caretaker', 'tree_count']
fig = alt.Chart(df_caretaker).mark_bar().encode(x =
'caretaker', y = 'tree_count')
st.altair_chart(fig)
```

Altair also allows us to summarize our data directly within the y value of `mark_bar()`, so we can simplify this by instead using the following code:

```
import streamlit as st
import pandas as pd
import altair as alt


st.title('SF Trees')
st.write('This app analyses trees in San Francisco using'
         ' a dataset kindly provided by SF DPW')
```

```
trees_df = pd.read_csv('trees.csv')
fig = alt.Chart(trees_df).mark_bar().encode(x = 'caretaker', y
= 'count(*):Q')
st.altair_chart(fig)
```

The preceding code will create a Streamlit app showing the count of trees by caretaker in SF, shown in the following screenshot:

SF Trees

This app analyses trees in San Francisco using a dataset kindly provided by SF DPW

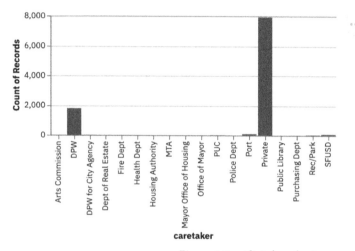

Figure 3.8 – Altair bar chart

This should be it for traditional visualization libraries, but Streamlit also allows us to use more complex visualization libraries such as **PyDeck** for geographic mapping. We have already used **PyDeck** through the native st.map() function and will explore this in more depth in the following section.

PyDeck

PyDeck is a visualization library that plots visualizations as layers on top of **Mapbox** (a mapping company with a truly exceptional free tier) maps. Both Streamlit and PyDeck have a base set of limited features available without signing up for a Mapbox account, but greatly expand their free features when we get a **Mapbox** token, which we will do in this next section.

Configuration options

In order to set up your own **Mapbox** token, which is optional, first go to www.Mapbox. com and sign up for an account. Once you have verified your account, you can find your token at https://www.Mapbox.com/install/. We will not pass our token directly to Streamlit because otherwise, we might accidentally push it to a public GitHub repository. Instead, Streamlit has a global configuration file called config.toml. To view our current settings, we can run the following command anywhere in the terminal:

```
streamlit config show
```

There are four methods that Streamlit offers for changing our default configuration settings, I'll show you my recommended option and one of the other options, which should provide you with the majority of the use cases. If you find these options insufficient, the Streamlit documentation (https://docs.streamlit.io/) goes over all four options in great detail.

The first option is to set global configuration options by directly editing the config. toml file. We can edit the file directly by opening it in our text editor. The following command will open the file in sublime. For other text editors (such as Vim and Atom), replace 'sublime' with the appropriate command or open the file directly from the text editor:

```
sublime ~/.streamlit/config.toml
```

If this fails, it likely means that we do not have the file generated already. We can either copy and paste the output of **streamlit config show** to a file at the location ~/.streamlit/config.toml, or we can run the following shortcut for Mac/Linux:

```
streamlit config show > ~/.streamlit/config.toml
```

Now that we have the file opened in sublime, we can view and edit any of the options directly. This option is great for a config option such as a **Mapbox** token, as I will never have multiple **Mapbox** accounts with multiple tokens. However, some Streamlit apps may want to use, for example, different ports than the default 8501 serverPort. It would not make sense to change a global option for a project-specific change, which leads us to the second option.

The second option is to create and edit a project-specific config.toml file. Our previous config sets our default config options, while this option is specific per Streamlit app. Here is where our individual project folders within the streamlit_apps folder come in handy!

Broadly speaking, we will do the following:

1. Check our current working directory.

2. Make a config file for our project.

3. Use the config file within PyDeck.

Our first step is to make sure our current working directory is the `trees_app` folder by running the `pwd` command in your terminal, which will show our current working directory and should end with `trees_app`' (for example, mine looks like `Users/tyler/Documents/streamlit_apps/trees_app`).

Now, we need to make a config file just for our project. First, we will make a folder called `.streamlit`, and then we will repeat the Mac/Linux shortcut we used above:

```
mkdir .streamlit
streamlit config show > .streamlit/config.toml
```

We can then edit our config options just as we did before, but this will only be applicable to our Streamlit apps when we run Streamlit from that directory.

Now, finally, we can go back to **PyDeck** graphing. Our first effort is going to be to get a base map of San Francisco, which has a city center of `37.77, -122.4`. We can do this using the following code, which first defines the initial state (where we want to start viewing the map), and then calls `st.pydeck_chart()` using that initial state:

```
import streamlit as st
import pandas as pd
import pydeck as pdk


st.title('SF Trees')
st.write('This app analyses trees in San Francisco using'
         ' a dataset kindly provided by SF DPW')
trees_df = pd.read_csv('trees.csv')


sf_initial_view = pdk.ViewState(
    latitude=37.77,
    longitude=-122.4
    )
```

```
st.pydeck_chart(pdk.Deck(
    initial_view_state=sf_initial_view
))
```

This code will produce a map of San Francisco, which we can use to layer on data points. We notice a couple of things here. First, that the black default map may be difficult to see, and second, that we need to spend time zooming in to San Francisco to get the view that we need. We can fix both these items by using the defaults suggested in the Streamlit documentation (`https://docs.streamlit.io/`), as seen in the following code:

```
import streamlit as st
import pandas as pd
import pydeck as pdk
st.title('SF Trees')
st.write('This app analyses trees in San Francisco using'
         ' a dataset kindly provided by SF DPW')
trees_df = pd.read_csv('trees.csv')

sf_initial_view = pdk.ViewState(
    latitude=37.77,
    longitude=-122.4,
    zoom=9
    )


st.pydeck_chart(pdk.Deck(
    map_style='mapbox://styles/mapbox/light-v9',
    initial_view_state=sf_initial_view,
    ))
```

The preceding code should create a map that looks like the following screenshot:

SF Trees

This app analyses trees in San Francisco using a dataset kindly provided by SF DPW

Figure 3.9 – PyDeck mapping: SF base map

This is exactly what we want! We can see the entire **SF Bay Area**, and now we need to add our layer of trees. The **PyDeck** library has tooltips for interactivity, which do not deal well with null values in our dataset, so we will remove null values before we map these points in the following code. We'll also increase the zoom value to 11 so we can see each point better:

```
import streamlit as st
import pandas as pd
import pydeck as pdk


st.title('SF Trees')
 st.write('This app analyses trees in San Francisco using'
          ' a dataset kindly provided by SF DPW')
```

```
trees_df = pd.read_csv('trees.csv')
trees_df.dropna(how='any', inplace=True)

sf_initial_view = pdk.ViewState(
    latitude=37.77,
    longitude=-122.4,
    zoom=11
    )

sp_layer = pdk.Layer(
    'ScatterplotLayer',
    data = trees_df,
    get_position = ['longitude', 'latitude'],
    get_radius=30)
st.pydeck_chart(pdk.Deck(
    map_style='mapbox://styles/mapbox/light-v9',
    initial_view_state=sf_initial_view,
    layers = [sp_layer]
    ))
```

The best values for both the zoom and radius parameters are dependent on your visualization preferences. Try a few options out to see what looks the best. The preceding code will make the following map:

SF Trees

This app analyses trees in San Francisco using a dataset kindly provided by SF DPW

Figure 3.10 – Mapping SF trees

As with previous maps, this is interactive by default, so we can zoom into different parts of San Francisco to see where the places with the highest tree density are. For our next change to this map, we are going to add another layer, this time of hexagons, which will be colored based on the density of the trees in SF. We can use the same code as above, but change the scatterplot layer to a hexagon layer. We also will include the option to have the hexagon extrude vertically, which isn't necessary, but it is certainly a fun visualization style.

Our last change is to change the pitch or the angle at which we are viewing the map. The default pitch, as we can see, is nearly directly down at the city, which will not work if we are trying to view vertical hexagons on our map. The following code implements each one of these changes:

```python
import streamlit as st
import pandas as pd
import pydeck as pdk

st.title('SF Trees')
 st.write('This app analyses trees in San Francisco using'
          ' a dataset kindly provided by SF DPW')
 trees_df = pd.read_csv('trees.csv')
 trees_df.dropna(how='any', inplace=True)

sf_initial_view = pdk.ViewState(
     latitude=37.77,
     longitude=-122.4,
     zoom=11,
     pitch=30
     )

hx_layer = pdk.Layer(
     'HexagonLayer',
     data = trees_df,
     get_position = ['longitude', 'latitude'],
     radius=100,
     extruded=True)

st.pydeck_chart(pdk.Deck(
     map_style='mapbox://styles/mapbox/light-v9',
     initial_view_state=sf_initial_view,
     layers = [hx_layer]
     ))
```

As with the previous map, the optimal radius and pitch parameters will change based on your visualizations. Try changing each one of these around a few times to see whether you can get the hang of it! The preceding code will produce the following app:

SF Trees

This app analyses trees in San Francisco using a dataset kindly provided by SF DPW

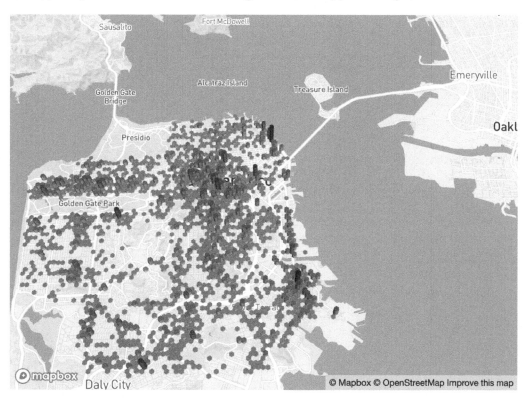

Figure 3.11 – Final San Francisco Trees map

From this screenshot, we can see that **PyDeck** creates darker circles where there exists a higher density of trees in SF. We can observe from this many interesting details, such as the fact that the dataset seems to be missing trees from the famous Golden Gate Park on the west side of the city, and that the area around the Golden Gate Bridge also seems to have very few trees in the dataset.

Summary

After this chapter, you hopefully have a solid understanding of how to leverage the incredible open source Python visualization libraries to make web apps in Streamlit.

First, we learned how to use the default visualization options, such as `st.line_chart()` and `st.map()`, and then we dove into interactive libraries such as Plotly, mapping libraries such as PyDeck, and everything in between.

In our next chapter, we will cover how to use machine learning in Streamlit.

4
Using Machine Learning with Streamlit

A very common situation data scientists find themselves in is at the end of the model creation process, not knowing exactly how to convince non-data scientists that their model is worthwhile. They might have performance metrics from their model or some static visualizations but have no easy way to allow others to interact with their model.

Before Streamlit, there were a couple of other options, the most popular being creating a full-fledged app in Flask or Django or turning their model into an **Application Programming Interface (API)** and pointing developers toward it. These are great options but tend to be time-consuming and suboptimal for valuable use cases such as prototyping an app.

The incentives on teams are a little misaligned here. A data scientist wants to create the best models for their teams, but if they need to take a day or two (or, if they have experience, a few hours) of work to turn their model into a Flask or Django app, it doesn't make much sense to build this out until they think they are nearly complete with the modeling process. The benefit of Streamlit is that it helps us turn this arduous process into a frictionless app creation experience. In this chapter, we'll go over how to create **Machine Learning (ML)** prototypes in Streamlit, how to add user interaction to your ML apps, and also how to understand the ML results.

Specifically, the following topics are covered in this chapter:

- The standard ML workflow
- Predicting penguin species
- Utilizing a pre-trained ML model in Streamlit
- Training models inside Streamlit apps
- Understanding ML results

The standard ML workflow

The first step to creating an app that uses ML is the ML model itself. There are dozens of popular workflows for creating your own ML models. It's likely you might have your own already! There are two parts of this process to consider:

- The generation of the ML model
- The use of the ML model in production

If the plan is to train a model once and then use this model in our Streamlit app, the best method is to create this model outside of Streamlit (for example, in a Jupyter notebook or in a standard Python file) first, and then use this model within the app.

If the plan is to use the user input to train the model inside our app, then we can no longer create the model outside of Streamlit and instead will need to run the model training within the Streamlit app.

We will start by building our ML models outside of Streamlit and move on to training our models inside of Streamlit apps after.

Predicting penguin species

The dataset that we will primarily use in this chapter is the same Palmer's Penguins dataset that we used in *Chapter 1*, *An Introduction to Streamlit*. As is typical, we will create a new folder that will house our new Streamlit app and accompanying code. The following code creates this new folder within our streamlit_apps folder and copies the data from our penguin_app folder. If you haven't downloaded the Palmer's Penguins data yet, please follow the instructions in the *The Setup: Palmer's Penguins* section in *Chapter 2*, *Uploading, Downloading, and Manipulating Data*:

```
mkdir penguin_ml
cp penguin_app/penguins.csv penguin_ml
```

```
cd penguin_ml
touch penguins_ml.py
touch penguins_streamlit.py
```

As you may have noticed in the preceding code, there are two Python files here, one to create the ML model (`penguins_ml.py`) and the second to create the Streamlit app (`penguins_streamlit.py`). We will start with the `penguins_ml.py` file, and once we have a model we are happy with, we will move on to the `penguins_streamlit.py` file.

> **Note**
>
> You can also opt to create the model in a Jupyter notebook, which is less reproducible by design (as cells can be run out of order) but is still incredibly popular.

Let's get re-familiarized with the `penguins.csv` dataset. The following code will read the dataset and print out the first five rows:

```
import pandas as pd


penguin_df = pd.read_csv('penguins.csv')
print(penguin_df.head())
```

The output of the preceding code, when we run our Python file `penguins_ml.py` in the terminal, will look something like the following screenshot:

```
↳  penguin_ml git:(main) × python3 penguins_ml.py
    species     island  bill_length_mm  bill_depth_mm  flipper_length_mm  body_mass_g     sex  year
0   Adelie  Torgersen            39.1           18.7              181.0       3750.0    male  2007
1   Adelie  Torgersen            39.5           17.4              186.0       3800.0  female  2007
2   Adelie  Torgersen            40.3           18.0              195.0       3250.0  female  2007
3   Adelie  Torgersen             NaN            NaN                NaN          NaN     NaN  2007
4   Adelie  Torgersen            36.7           19.3              193.0       3450.0  female  2007
```

Figure 4.1 – First five penguins

For this app, we are going to attempt to create an app that will help researchers in the wild know what species of penguin they are looking at. It will predict the species of the penguin given some measurements of the bill, flippers, and body mass, and knowledge about the sex and location of the penguin.

This next section is not an attempt to make the best ML model possible, but just to create something as a quick prototype for our Streamlit app that we can iterate off of. So in that light, we are going to drop our few rows with null values, and not use the `year` variable in our features as it does not fit with our use case. We will need to define our features and output variables, and do one-hot-encoding (or as pandas calls it, creating dummy variables for our text columns) on our features, and factorize our output variable (turn it from a string into a number). The following code should get our dataset in a better spot to run through a classification algorithm:

```python
import pandas as pd
penguin_df = pd.read_csv('penguins.csv')
penguin_df.dropna(inplace=True)
output = penguin_df['species']
features = penguin_df[['island', 'bill_length_mm', 'bill_depth_mm',
       'flipper_length_mm', 'body_mass_g', 'sex']]
features = pd.get_dummies(features)
print('Here are our output variables')
print(output.head())
print('Here are our feature variables')
print(features.head())
```

Now when we run our Python file `penguins_ml.py` again, we see the output and feature variables separated, as shown in the following screenshot:

```
⊢  penguin_ml git:(main) × python3 penguins_ml.py
Here is what our unique output variables represent
Index(['Adelie', 'Gentoo', 'Chinstrap'], dtype='object')
Here are our feature variables
   bill_length_mm  bill_depth_mm  flipper_length_mm  ...  island_Torgersen  sex_female  sex_male
0            39.1           18.7              181.0  ...                 1           0         1
1            39.5           17.4              186.0  ...                 1           1         0
2            40.3           18.0              195.0  ...                 1           1         0
4            36.7           19.3              193.0  ...                 1           1         0
5            39.3           20.6              190.0  ...                 1           0         1
```

Figure 4.2 – Output variables

Now, we want to create a classification model using a subset (in this case, 80%) of our data, and get the accuracy of said model. The following code runs through those steps using a random forest model, but you can use other classification algorithms if you would like. Again, the point here is to get a quick prototype to show to the penguin researchers for feedback!

```python
import pandas as pd
from sklearn.metrics import accuracy_score
from sklearn.ensemble import RandomForestClassifier
from sklearn.model_selection import train_test_split


penguin_df = pd.read_csv('penguins.csv')
penguin_df.dropna(inplace=True)
output = penguin_df['species']
features = penguin_df[['island', 'bill_length_mm', 'bill_depth_
mm',
                        'flipper_length_mm', 'body_mass_g',
'sex']]
features = pd.get_dummies(features)
output, uniques = pd.factorize(output)

x_train, x_test, y_train, y_test = train_test_split(
    features, output, test_size=.8)
rfc = RandomForestClassifier(random_state=15)
rfc.fit(x_train, y_train)
y_pred = rfc.predict(x_test)
score = accuracy_score(y_pred, y_test)
print('Our accuracy score for this model is {}'.format(score))
```

We now have a pretty good model for predicting the species of penguins! Our last step in the model generating process is to save the two parts of this model that we need the most – the model itself and the `uniques` variable, which maps the factorized output variable to the species name that we recognize. To the previous code, we will add a few lines that will save these objects as pickle files (files that turn a Python object into something we can save directly and import easily from another Python file such as our Streamlit app). More specifically, the `open()` function creates two pickle files, the `pickle.dump()` function writes our Python files to said files, and the `close()` function closes the files. The wb in the `open()` function stands for *write bytes*, which tells Python that we want to write, not read, to this file:

```python
import pandas as pd
from sklearn.metrics import accuracy_score
from sklearn.ensemble import RandomForestClassifier
from sklearn.model_selection import train_test_split
import pickle


penguin_df = pd.read_csv('penguins.csv')
penguin_df.dropna(inplace=True)
output = penguin_df['species']
features = penguin_df[['island', 'bill_length_mm', 'bill_depth_
mm',
                        'flipper_length_mm', 'body_mass_g',
'sex']]
features = pd.get_dummies(features)
output, uniques = pd.factorize(output)


x_train, x_test, y_train, y_test = train_test_split(
    features, output, test_size=.8)
rfc = RandomForestClassifier(random_state=15)
rfc.fit(x_train, y_train)
y_pred = rfc.predict(x_test)
score = accuracy_score(y_pred, y_test)
print('Our accuracy score for this model is {}'.format(score))
```

```
rf_pickle = open('random_forest_penguin.pickle', 'wb')
pickle.dump(rfc, rf_pickle)
rf_pickle.close()
output_pickle = open('output_penguin.pickle', 'wb')
pickle.dump(uniques, output_pickle)
output_pickle.close()
```

We now have two more files in our penguin_ml folder, a file called random_forest_ penguin.pickle, which contains our model, and output_penguin_.pickle, which has the mapping between penguin species and the output of our model. This is it for the penguins_ml.py function! We can move on to our Streamlit app.

Utilizing a pre-trained ML model in Streamlit

Now that we have our model, we want to load it (along with our mapping function as well) into Streamlit. In our file, penguins_streamlit.py, that we created before, we will again use the pickle library to load our files using the following code. We use the same functions as before, but instead of wb, we use the rb parameter, which stands for *read bytes*. To make sure these are the same Python objects that we used before, we will use the st.write() function that we are so familiar with already to check:

```
import streamlit as st
import pickle


rf_pickle = open('random_forest_penguin.pickle', 'rb')
map_pickle = open('output_penguin.pickle', 'rb')
rfc = pickle.load(rf_pickle)
unique_penguin_mapping = pickle.load(map_pickle)
st.write(rfc)
st.write(unique_penguin_mapping)
```

As with our previous Streamlit apps, we run the following code in the terminal to run our app:

```
streamlit run penguins_streamlit.py
```

We now have our random forest classifier, along with the penguin mapping! Our next step is to add Streamlit functions to get the user input. In our app, we used island, bill length, bill depth, flipper length, body mass, and sex to predict the penguin species, so we will need to get each of these from our user. For island and sex, we know which options were in our dataset already and want to avoid having to parse through user text, so we will use `selectbox`. For the other data, we just need to make sure that the user has input a positive number, so we will use the `st.number_input()` function and make the minimum value `0`. The following code takes these inputs in and prints them out on our Streamlit app:

```python
import streamlit as st
import pickle

rf_pickle = open('random_forest_penguin.pickle', 'rb')
map_pickle = open('output_penguin.pickle', 'rb')
rfc = pickle.load(rf_pickle)
unique_penguin_mapping = pickle.load(map_pickle)
rf_pickle.close()
map_pickle.close()

island = st.selectbox('Penguin Island', options=[
                      'Biscoe', 'Dream', 'Torgerson'])
sex = st.selectbox('Sex', options=['Female', 'Male'])
bill_length = st.number_input('Bill Length (mm)', min_value=0)
bill_depth = st.number_input('Bill Depth (mm)', min_value=0)
flipper_length = st.number_input('Flipper Length (mm)', min_
value=0)
body_mass = st.number_input('Body Mass (g)', min_value=0)

st.write('the user inputs are {}'.format(
    [island, sex, bill_length,
        bill_depth, flipper_length, body_mass]))
```

The preceding code should make the following app. Try it out and see if it works by changing the values and seeing if the output changes as well. Streamlit is designed so that, by default, each time a value is changed, the entire app reruns. The following screenshot shows the app live, with some values that I've changed. We can either change numeric values with the (+ and -) buttons on the right-hand side, or we can just enter the values manually:

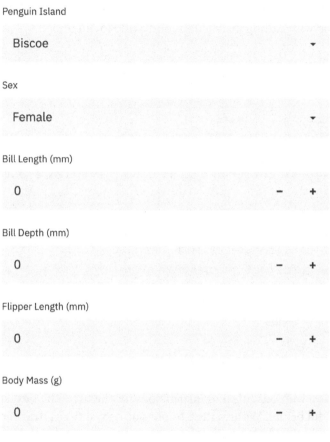

the user inputs are ['Biscoe', 'Female', 0, 0, 0, 0]

Figure 4.3 – Model inputs

Now we have all our inputs, and we also have our model. The next step is to format the data into the same format as our preprocessed data, for example, our model does not have one variable called sex but instead has two variables called sex_female and sex_male. Once our data is in the right shape, we can call the predict function and map the prediction to our original species list to see how our model functions. The following code does exactly this, and also adds some basic titles and instructions to the app to make it more usable. This app is rather long, so I will break it up into multiple sections for readability, starting with adding instructions and a title to our app:

```python
import streamlit as st
import pickle

st.title('Penguin Classifier')
st.write("This app uses 6 inputs to predict the species of penguin using"
         "a model built on the Palmer's Penguin's dataset. Use the form below"
         " to get started!")

rf_pickle = open('random_forest_penguin.pickle', 'rb')
map_pickle = open('output_penguin.pickle', 'rb')
rfc = pickle.load(rf_pickle)
unique_penguin_mapping = pickle.load(map_pickle)
rf_pickle.close()
map_pickle.close()
```

We now have an app with our title and instructions for the user. The next step is to get the user inputs as we did before. We also need to put our sex and island variables into the correct format, as discussed before:

```python
island = st.selectbox('Penguin Island', options=[
                      'Biscoe', 'Dream', 'Torgerson'])
sex = st.selectbox('Sex', options=['Female', 'Male'])
bill_length = st.number_input('Bill Length (mm)', min_value=0)
bill_depth = st.number_input('Bill Depth (mm)', min_value=0)
flipper_length = st.number_input('Flipper Length (mm)', min_value=0)
```

```
body_mass = st.number_input('Body Mass (g)', min_value=0)


island_biscoe, island_dream, island_torgerson = 0, 0, 0
if island == 'Biscoe':
    island_biscoe = 1
elif island == 'Dream':
    island_dream = 1
elif island == 'Torgerson':
    island_torgerson = 1


sex_female, sex_male = 0, 0
if sex == 'Female':
    sex_female = 1
elif sex == 'Male':
    sex_male = 1
```

All of our data is in the correct format! The last step here is using the `predict()` function on our model with our new data, which this final section takes care of:

```
new_prediction = rfc.predict([[bill_length, bill_depth,
flipper_length,
                               body_mass, island_biscoe,
island_dream,
                               island_torgerson, sex_female,
sex_male]])
prediction_species = unique_penguin_mapping[new_prediction][0]
st.write('We predict your penguin is of the {} species'.
format(prediction_species))
```

Now our app should look like the following screenshot. I have added some example values to the inputs, but you should play around with changing the data to see if you can make the species change!

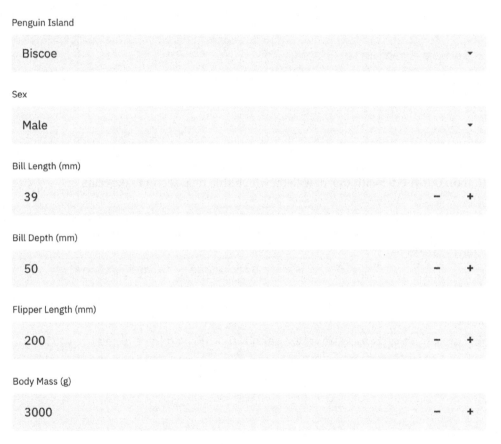

Penguin Classifier

This app uses 6 inputs to predict the species of penguin usinga model built on the Palmer's Penguin's dataset. Use the form below to get started!

Penguin Island

Biscoe

Sex

Male

Bill Length (mm)

39

Bill Depth (mm)

50

Flipper Length (mm)

200

Body Mass (g)

3000

We predict your penguin is of the Adelie species

Figure 4.4 – Full Streamlit prediction

We now have a full Streamlit app that utilizes our pre-trained ML model, takes user input, and outputs the prediction. Next, we will discuss how to train models directly within Streamlit apps!

Training models inside Streamlit apps

Often, we may want to have the user input change how our model is trained. We may want to accept data from the user or ask the user what features they would like to use, or even allow the user to pick the type of machine learning algorithm they would like to use. All of these options are feasible in Streamlit, and in this section, we will cover the basics around using user input to affect the training process. As we discussed in the section above, if a model is going to be trained only once, it is probably best to train the model outside of Streamlit and import the model into Streamlit. But what if, in our example, the penguin researchers have the data stored locally, or do not know how to retrain the model but have the data in the correct format already? In cases like these, we can add the `st.file_uploader()` option and include a method for these users to input their own data, and get a custom model deployed for them without having to write any code. The following code will add a user option to accept data and will use the preprocessing/training code that we originally had in `penguins_ml.py` to make a unique model for this user. It is important to note here that this will only work if the user has data in the exact same format and style that we used, which may be unlikely. One other potential add-on here is to show the user what format the data needs to be in for this app to correctly train a model as expected!

```python
import streamlit as st
import seaborn as sns
import matplotlib.pyplot as plt
import pandas as pd
import pickle
from sklearn.metrics import accuracy_score
from sklearn.ensemble import RandomForestClassifier
from sklearn.model_selection import train_test_split


st.title('Penguin Classifier')
st.write("This app uses 6 inputs to predict the species of penguin using "
         "a model built on the Palmer's Penguin's dataset. Use the form below"
         " to get started!")


penguin_file = st.file_uploader('Upload your own penguin data')
```

This first section imports the libraries that we need, adds the title – as we have used before, and adds the `file_uploader()` function. What happens, however, when the user has yet to upload a file? We can set the default to load our random forest model if there is no penguin file, as shown in the next section of code:

```
if penguin_file is None:
    rf_pickle = open('random_forest_penguin.pickle', 'rb')
    map_pickle = open('output_penguin.pickle', 'rb')
    rfc = pickle.load(rf_pickle)
    unique_penguin_mapping = pickle.load(map_pickle)
    rf_pickle.close()
    map_pickle.close()
```

The next problem we need to solve is how to take in the user's data, clean it, and train a model based on it. Luckily, we can reuse the model training code that we have already created and put it within our `else` statement in the next code block:

```
else:
    penguin_df = pd.read_csv(penguin_file)
    penguin_df = penguin_df.dropna()
    output = penguin_df['species']
    features = penguin_df[['island', 'bill_length_mm', 'bill_
depth_mm',
                           'flipper_length_mm', 'body_mass_g',
'sex']]
    features = pd.get_dummies(features)
    output, unique_penguin_mapping = pd.factorize(output)

    x_train, x_test, y_train, y_test = train_test_split(
        features, output, test_size=.8)
    rfc = RandomForestClassifier(random_state=15)
    rfc.fit(x_train, y_train)
    y_pred = rfc.predict(x_test)
    score = round(accuracy_score(y_pred, y_test), 2)
    st.write('We trained a Random Forest model on these data,'
             ' it has a score of {}! Use the '
             'inputs below to try out the
model.'.format(score))
```

We have now created our model within the app and need to get the inputs from the user for our prediction. This time, however, we can make an improvement on what we have done before. As of now, each time a user changes an input in our app, the entire Streamlit app will rerun. We can use the st.form() and st.submit_form_button() functions to wrap the rest of our user inputs in and allow the user to change all of the inputs and submit the entire form at once instead of multiple times:

```python
with st.form('user_inputs'):
island = st.selectbox('Penguin Island', options=[
                        'Biscoe', 'Dream', 'Torgerson'])
sex = st.selectbox('Sex', options=['Female', 'Male'])
bill_length = st.number_input('Bill Length (mm)', min_value=0)
bill_depth = st.number_input('Bill Depth (mm)', min_value=0)
flipper_length = st.number_input('Flipper Length (mm)', min_
value=0)
body_mass = st.number_input('Body Mass (g)', min_value=0)
st.form_submit_button()

island_biscoe, island_dream, island_torgerson = 0, 0, 0
if island == 'Biscoe':
    island_biscoe = 1
elif island == 'Dream':
    island_dream = 1
elif island == 'Torgerson':
    island_torgerson = 1

sex_female, sex_male = 0, 0
if sex == 'Female':
    sex_female = 1
elif sex == 'Male':
    sex_male = 1
```

Now that we have the inputs with our new form, we need to create our prediction and write the prediction to the user, as shown in the next block:

```python
new_prediction = rfc.predict([[bill_length, bill_depth,
flipper_length,
                                body_mass, island_biscoe,
```

```
island_dream,
                                island_torgerson, sex_female,
sex_male]])
prediction_species = unique_penguin_mapping[new_prediction][0]
st.write('We predict your penguin is of the {} species'.
format(prediction_species))
```

And there we go! We now have a Streamlit app that allows the user to input their own data and trains a model based on their data and outputs the results, as shown in the next screenshot:

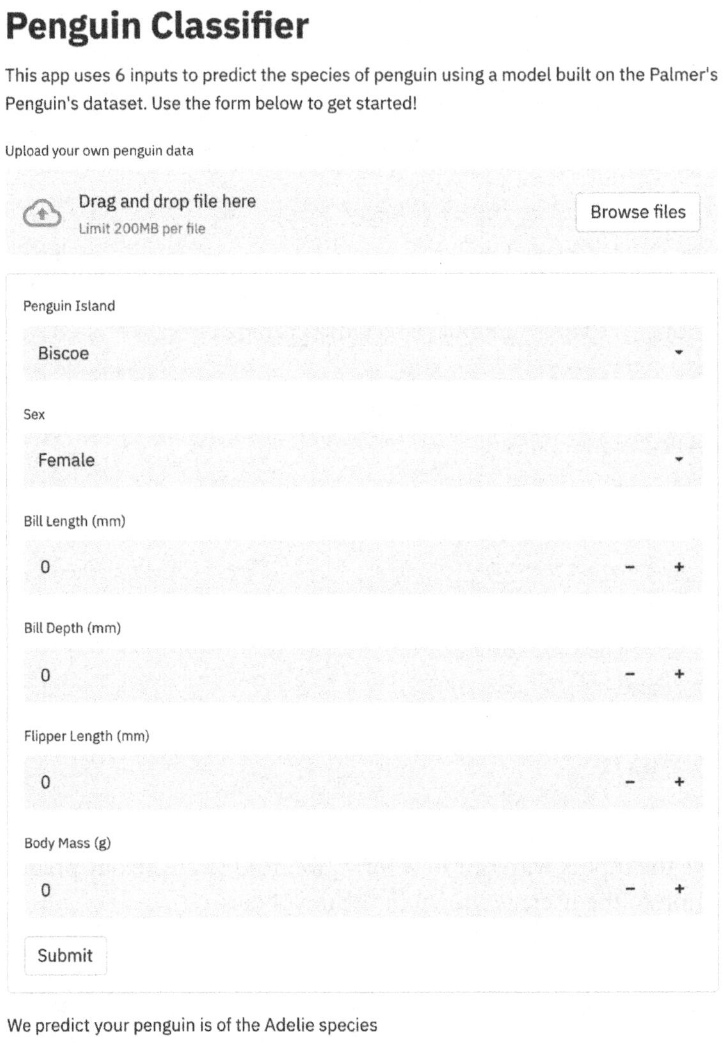

Figure 4.5 – Penguin classifier predictions

There are potential improvements here, such as through using caching functions (explored in *Chapter 2, Uploading, Downloading, and Manipulating Data*), as one example. Apps like these where users bring their own data are significantly harder to build, especially without a universal data format. It is more common as of this writing to see Streamlit apps that show off impressive ML models and use cases rather than apps that build them directly in-app (especially with more computationally expensive model training). As we mentioned before, Streamlit developers often will provide references to the required data format before asking for user input in the form of a dataset. However, this option of allowing users to bring their own data is available and practical, especially to allow for quick iterations on model building.

Understanding ML results

So far, our app might be useful, but often just showing a result is not good enough for a data app. We also should show some explanation as to why they got the result that they did! In order to do this, we can include in the output of the app that we have already made a section that helps users understand the model better.

To start, random forest models already have a built-in feature importance method derived from the set of individual decision trees that make up the random forest. We can edit our `penguins_ml.py` file to graph this importance, and then call that image from within our Streamlit app. We could also graph this directly from within our Streamlit app, but it is more efficient to make this graph once in `penguins_ml.py` instead of every time our Streamlit app reloads (which is every time a user changes a user input!). The following code edits our `penguins_ml.py` file and adds the feature importance graph, saving it to our folder. We also call the `tight_layout()` feature, which helps format our graph better and makes sure we avoid any labels getting cut off. This set of code is long, and the top half of the file remains unchanged, so only the section on library importing and data cleaning has been omitted:

```
x_train, x_test, y_train, y_test = train_test_split(
    features, output, test_size=.8)
rfc = RandomForestClassifier(random_state=15)
rfc.fit(x_train, y_train)
y_pred = rfc.predict(x_test)
score = accuracy_score(y_pred, y_test)
print('Our accuracy score for this model is {}'.format(score))


rf_pickle = open('random_forest_penguin.pickle', 'wb')
```

```
pickle.dump(rfc, rf_pickle)
rf_pickle.close()
output_pickle = open('output_penguin.pickle', 'wb')
pickle.dump(uniques, output_pickle)
output_pickle.close()


fig, ax = plt.subplots()
ax = sns.barplot(rfc.feature_importances_, features.columns)
plt.title('Which features are the most important for species
prediction?')
plt.xlabel('Importance')
plt.ylabel('Feature')
plt.tight_layout()
fig.savefig('feature_importance.png')
```

Now when we rerun pengiuns_ml.py, we should see a file called feature_
importance.png, which we can call from our Streamlit app. Let's do that now! We can
use the st.image() function to load an image from our png and print it to our penguin
app. The following code adds our image to the Streamlit app and also improves our
explanations around the prediction we made. Because of the length of this code block,
we will just show the new code from the point where we start to predict using the
user's data:

```
new_prediction = rfc.predict([[bill_length, bill_depth,
flipper_length,
                              body_mass, island_biscoe,
island_dream,
                              island_torgerson, sex_female,
sex_male]])
prediction_species = unique_penguin_mapping[new_prediction][0]


st.subheader("Predicting Your Penguin's Species:")
st.write('We predict your penguin is of the {} species'
        .format(prediction_species))
st.write('We used a machine learning (Random Forest) model to '
        'predict the species, the features used in this
prediction '
        ' are ranked by relative importance below.')
st.image('feature_importance.png')
```

Now, the bottom of your Streamlit app should look like the following screenshot (note: your string might be slightly different based on your inputs).

Predicting Your Penguin's Species:

We predict your penguin is of the Adelie species

We used a machine learning (Random Forest) model to predict the species, the features used in this prediction are ranked by relative importance below.

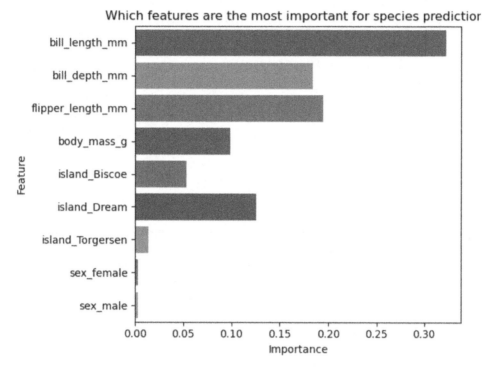

Figure 4.6 – Feature importance screenshot

As we can see, bill length, bill depth, and flipper length are the most important variables according to our random forest model. A final option for explaining how our model works is to plot the distributions of each of these variables by species, and also plot some vertical lines representing the user input. Ideally, the user can begin to understand the underlying data holistically, and therefore will understand the predictions that come from the model as well. To do this, we will need to actually import the data into our Streamlit app, which we have not done previously. The following code imports the penguin data we used to build the model, and plots three histograms (for *bill length*, *bill depth*, and *flipper length*) along with the user input as a vertical line, starting from the model explanation section:

```
st.subheader("Predicting Your Penguin's Species:")
st.write('We predict your penguin is of the {} species'
        .format(prediction_species))
st.write('We used a machine learning (Random Forest) model to '
        'predict the species, the features used in this
prediction '
        ' are ranked by relative importance below.')
st.image('feature_importance.png')


st.write('Below are the histograms for each continuous variable
'
        'separated by penguin species. The vertical line '
        'represents your the inputted value.')

```

Now that we have set up our app for the histograms, we can use the `displot()` function in the Seaborn visualization library to create our three histograms for our most important variables:

```
fig, ax = plt.subplots()
ax = sns.displot(x=penguin_df['bill_length_mm'],
                hue=penguin_df['species'])
plt.axvline(bill_length)
plt.title('Bill Length by Species')
st.pyplot(ax)


fig, ax = plt.subplots()
ax = sns.displot(x=penguin_df['bill_depth_mm'],
```

```
                    hue=penguin_df['species'])
plt.axvline(bill_depth)
plt.title('Bill Depth by Species')
st.pyplot(ax)


fig, ax = plt.subplots()
ax = sns.displot(x=penguin_df['flipper_length_mm'],
                    hue=penguin_df['species'])
plt.axvline(flipper_length)
plt.title('Flipper Length by Species')
st.pyplot(ax)
```

The preceding code should create the app shown in the following figure, which is our app in its final form. For viewing ease, we will just show the first histogram:

Below are the histograms for each continuous variable separated by penguin species. The vertical line represents your the inputted value.

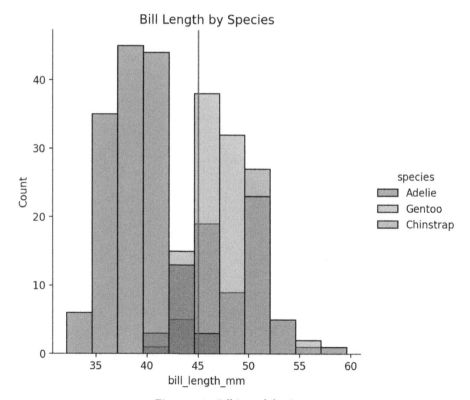

Figure 4.6 – Bill Length by Species

As always, the completed and final code can be found at `https://github.com/tylerjrichards/Getting-Started-with-Streamlit-for-Data-Science`. That completes this section. We have now created a fully formed Streamlit app that takes a pre-built model and user input and outputs both the result of the prediction and an explanation of the output as well.

Summary

In this chapter, we learned some ML basics: how to take a pre-built ML model and use it within Streamlit, how to create our own models from within Streamlit, and also how to use user input to understand and iterate on ML models. Hopefully, at the end of this chapter, you feel comfortable with each of these. We will dive into the world of deploying Streamlit using Streamlit sharing next!

5
Deploying Streamlit with Streamlit Sharing

So far in this book, we have focused on Streamlit app development, from creating complex visualizations to deploying and creating **machine learning** (**ML**) models. In this chapter, we will learn how to deploy these applications so they can be shared with anyone with internet access. This is a crucial part of Streamlit apps, as, without the ability to deploy a Streamlit app, the friction still exists for users or consumers of your work. If we believe that Streamlit removes the friction between creating data science analysis/products/ models and sharing them with others, then we must also believe that the ability to widely share apps is just as crucial as the ease of development.

There are three main ways to deploy Streamlit apps: through a product created by Streamlit called *Streamlit Sharing*, through a cloud provider such as *Amazon Web Services* or *Heroku*, or through another product created by Streamlit called *Streamlit for Teams*. All three of these options are paid, but Streamlit Sharing has a free tier and Amazon Web Services regularly gives away free credit to students, first-time users, and start-ups, and Heroku has a free tier as well. The easiest and preferred method for most Streamlit users is Streamlit Sharing, so we will cover that directly here, and will cover Amazon Web Services, Heroku, and Streamlit for Teams later in this book, in *Chapter 8, Deploying Streamlit Apps with Heroku and AWS*, and *Chapter 10, The Data Project – Prototyping Projects in Streamlit*.

In this chapter, we will cover the following topics:

- Getting started with Streamlit Sharing

- A quick primer on GitHub

- Deploying with Streamlit Sharing

- Debugging Streamlit Sharing

Technical requirements

This chapter requires access to Streamlit Sharing, which as of this writing is in beta. You can request Streamlit Sharing access at `https://streamlit.io/sharing-sign-up`. They send out new admissions each week! If you are still waiting for Streamlit Sharing access and want to deploy an app immediately, feel free to move on to *Chapter 8, Deploying Streamlit Apps with Heroku and AWS*, where we deploy on AWS and Heroku.

This chapter also requires a free GitHub account, which can be attained at `https://www.github.com`. A full Primer on GitHub, along with detailed setup instructions, can be found in the section *A quick primer on GitHub* later in this chapter.

The code for this chapter can be found in the following GitHub repository:

`https://github.com/PacktPublishing/Getting-started-with-Streamlit-for-Data-Science`

Getting started with Streamlit Sharing

Streamlit Sharing is Streamlit's answer to a fast deployment process and is certainly my first recommendation for deploying your Streamlit applications. I remember the first time I deployed an app on Streamlit Sharing, I thought that there was no way that it was all that simple. We only need to push our code to a Github repository, point Streamlit to said repository, and it takes care of the rest. There are times when we care about "the rest," such as when we want to configure the amount of storage space or memory available, but often, letting Streamlit Sharing handle deployment, resourcing, and link creation makes our development significantly easier.

The goal here will be to take the Palmer's penguins ML app we have already created and deploy it using Streamlit Sharing. Before we get started, Streamlit Sharing runs using GitHub. If you are already familiar with Git and GitHub, feel free to skip over this section and make a GitHub repository with our `penguins_ml` folder.

A quick primer on GitHub

GitHub, and the language Git, are collaboration tools for software engineers and data scientists that provide a framework for version control. We do not need to know everything about how they work to use Streamlit Sharing, but we do need to be able to create our own repositories (which act like shared folders) and update them as we update our applications. There are two options for dealing with Git and GitHub, via the command line and via a product called GitHub Desktop. Primarily in this book, so far, we have stayed on the command line, and this tutorial will stick there. However, if you would like to use GitHub Desktop instead, head over to `https://desktop.github.com` and follow along with the instructions provided there.

Now, use the following steps to get started with Git and GitHub on the command line:

1. First, go to `https://www.github.com` and make a free account there.

2. Then, we need to download the language Git onto our own computer and connect to our GitHub account with Git. We can do this on a Mac using `brew` in our terminal:

    ```
    brew install git
    ```

3. We are also going to want to set a global username and email in Git (if we haven't already), which is recommended by GitHub. The following code sets these globally:

    ```
    git config --global user.name "My Name"
    git config --global user.email myemail@email.com
    ```

Now that we have our GitHub account, and we also have Git installed locally, we need to create our first repository! We already have our folder with the files that we need inside it, called `penguin_ml`, so we should make sure that is the working directory we are working in (if you aren't sure, the command `pwd` will return our working directory). We are going to work with the final version of the `penguins_streamlit.py` app, which is shown with brief explanations for some context in the following code:

```
import streamlit as st
import seaborn as sns
import matplotlib.pyplot as plt
import pandas as pd
import pickle


st.title('Penguin Classifier')
st.write("This app uses 6 inputs to predict the species of
```

```
penguin using "
        "a model built on the Palmer's Penguin's dataset. Use
the form below"
        " to get started!")

penguin_df = pd.read_csv('penguins.csv')
rf_pickle = open('random_forest_penguin.pickle', 'rb')
map_pickle = open('output_penguin.pickle', 'rb')
rfc = pickle.load(rf_pickle)
unique_penguin_mapping = pickle.load(map_pickle)
rf_pickle.close()
map_pickle.close()
```

This first section imports our libraries, sets up the titles for our app, and loads the model that we created using the penguins_ml.py file. This section will fail if we do not have the random_forest_penguin.pickle and output_penguin.pickle files. You can either go to *Chapter 4, Using Machine Learning with Streamlit*, to create these files or head over to https://github.com/tylerjrichards/Getting-Started-with-Streamlit-for-Data-Science/tree/main/penguin_ml to find them directly:

```
with st.form('user_input'):
island = st.selectbox('Penguin Island', options=[
                    'Biscoe', 'Dream', 'Torgerson'])
sex = st.selectbox('Sex', options=['Female', 'Male'])
bill_length = st.number_input('Bill Length (mm)', min_value=0)
bill_depth = st.number_input('Bill Depth (mm)', min_value=0)
flipper_length = st.number_input('Flipper Length (mm)', min_
value=0)
body_mass = st.number_input('Body Mass (g)', min_value=0)
st.form_submit_button()

island_biscoe, island_dream, island_torgerson = 0, 0, 0
if island == 'Biscoe':
    island_biscoe = 1
elif island == 'Dream':
    island_dream = 1
```

```
elif island == 'Torgerson':
    island_torgerson = 1

sex_female, sex_male = 0, 0
if sex == 'Female':
    sex_female = 1
elif sex == 'Male':
    sex_male = 1


new_prediction = rfc.predict([[bill_length, bill_depth,
flipper_length,
                              body_mass, island_biscoe,
island_dream,
                              island_torgerson, sex_female,
sex_male]])
prediction_species = unique_penguin_mapping[new_prediction][0]
```

This next section grabs all the user input we need for our prediction, from the island the researcher is on to the sex of the penguin, to the penguin's bill and flipper measurements, which prepares us for the predicting of the penguin species in the following code:

```
st.subheader("Predicting Your Penguin's Species:")
st.write('We predict your penguin is of the {} species'
        .format(prediction_species))
st.write('We used a machine learning (Random Forest) model to '
        'predict the species, the features used in this
prediction '
        ' are ranked by relative importance below.')
st.image('feature_importance.png')
```

And now this final section creates multiple histograms to explain the prediction by the model, showing the bill length/bill depth/flipper length separated by the species in hue. We use those three variables because our feature importance graph told us those were the best predictors of species in *Chapter 4, Using Machine Learning with Streamlit*:

```python
st.write('Below are the histograms for each continuous variable '
         'separated by penguin species. The vertical line '
         'represents your the inputted value.')

fig, ax = plt.subplots()
ax = sns.displot(x=penguin_df['bill_length_mm'],
                 hue=penguin_df['species'])
plt.axvline(bill_length)
plt.title('Bill Length by Species')
st.pyplot(ax)


fig, ax = plt.subplots()
ax = sns.displot(x=penguin_df['bill_depth_mm'],
                 hue=penguin_df['species'])
plt.axvline(bill_depth)
plt.title('Bill Depth by Species')
st.pyplot(ax)


fig, ax = plt.subplots()
ax = sns.displot(x=penguin_df['flipper_length_mm'],
                 hue=penguin_df['species'])
plt.axvline(flipper_length)
plt.title('Flipper Length by Species')
st.pyplot(ax)
```

Now that we are in the correct folder with the right files, we will use the following code to initialize our first repository, and to add and then commit all our files to the repository:

```
git init
git add .
git commit -m 'our first repo commit'
```

Our next step is to connect the Git repository on our local device to our GitHub account:

1. First, we need to set up a new repository by going back to the GitHub website and clicking the **New repository** button as shown in the following screenshot:

Figure 5.1 – Setting up a new repository

2. We can then fill out our repository name (penguin_ml), and click **Create repository**:

Owner *   **Repository name** *

    🐧 tylerjrichards ▾   /   penguin_ml   ⚠

Great repository names are s   The repository **penguin_ml** already exists on this account.   okish-tribble?

Description (optional)

◉ 📖 **Public**
         Anyone on the internet can see this repository. You choose who can commit.

○ 🔒 **Private**
         You choose who can see and commit to this repository.

Initialize this repository with:
Skip this step if you're importing an existing repository.

☐ **Add a README file**
     This is where you can write a long description for your project. Learn more.

☐ **Add .gitignore**
     Choose which files not to track from a list of templates. Learn more.

☐ **Choose a license**
     A license tells others what they can and can't do with your code. Learn more.

    Create repository

Figure 5.2 – Repo creation

3. Now that we have a new repository on GitHub, and also a repository locally, we need to connect the two. The following code connects the two repositories and pushes our code to the GitHub repo, GitHub also suggests how to connect two repositories after you click **Create repository**:

```
git branch -M main
git remote add origin https://github.com/{insert_
username}/penguin_ml.git
git push -u origin main
```

We should now see our `penguin_ml` files in our GitHub! If and when we have new code to push to our repository, we can follow the general format of using `git add .` to add the file changes, `git commit -m "commit message"`, and then finally `git push` to push the changes to our repository.

We can now move on to the deployment process on the Streamlit side.

Deploying with Streamlit Sharing

Now that all our necessary files are in the GitHub repository, we have almost all that we need to deploy our application. You can use the following list of steps to deploy our application:

1. When we deploy to Streamlit Sharing, Streamlit uses its own servers to host the app. Because of this, we need to explicitly tell Streamlit which Python libraries are required for our app to run. The following code installs a very helpful library called `pipreqs` and creates a `requirements.txt` file in the format we need for Streamlit:

```
pip install pipreqs
pipreqs .
```

2. When we look at our `requirements.txt` file, we can see that `pipreqs` looked through all of our Python files and checked what we imported and used, and created a file that Streamlit can use to install the exact same versions of our libraries to prevent errors:

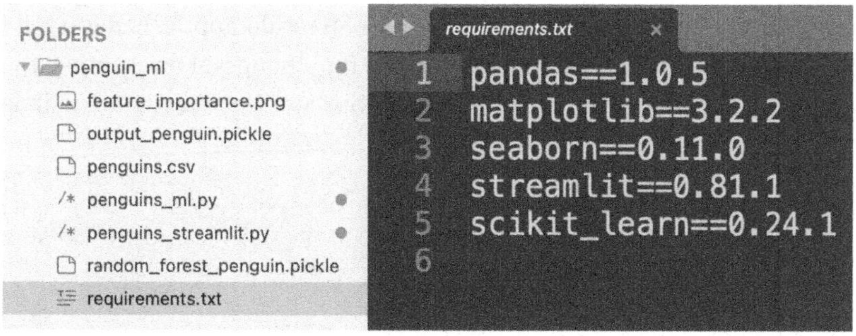

Figure 5.3 – Requirements.txt

3. We have a new file, so we need to also add it to our GitHub repository. The following code adds `requirements.txt` to our repository:

```
git add requirements.txt
git commit -m 'add requirements file'
git push
```

4. Now, our last step is to sign up for Streamlit Sharing (`share.streamlit.io`) and click the **New App** button. After that, we can point Streamlit Sharing directly to our Python file that hosts our app's code, which in our case is called `penguins_streamlit.py`. You should also change the username from my personal GitHub username (`tylerjrichards`) to your own:

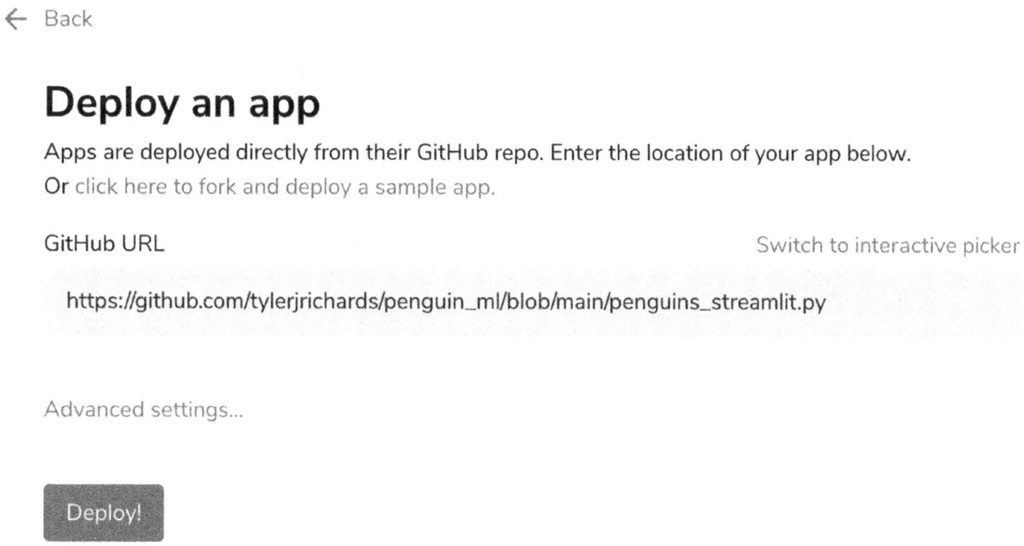

← Back

Deploy an app

Apps are deployed directly from their GitHub repo. Enter the location of your app below.
Or click here to fork and deploy a sample app.

GitHub URL   Switch to interactive picker

https://github.com/tylerjrichards/penguin_ml/blob/main/penguins_streamlit.py

Advanced settings...

Deploy!

Figure 5.4 – Adding URLs

After the app builds, we have a fully deployed Streamlit app. Whenever we make changes to the GitHub repository, we will see our changes. For example, the following code makes a change to the title of our app (for brevity, we will only show enough code to illustrate the change):

```
import streamlit as st
import seaborn as sns
import matplotlib.pyplot as plt
import pandas as pd
import pickle

st.title('Penguin Classifier: A Machine Learning App')
st.write("This app uses 6 inputs to predict the species
of penguin using "
        "a model built on the Palmer's Penguin's
dataset. Use the form below"
        " to get started!")

penguin_df = pd.read_csv('penguins.csv')
rf_pickle = open('random_forest_penguin.pickle', 'rb')
map_pickle = open('output_penguin.pickle', 'rb')
rfc = pickle.load(rf_pickle)
unique_penguin_mapping = pickle.load(map_pickle)
rf_pickle.close()
map_pickle.close()
```

5. Now, to push the change, we need to update our GitHub repository. We will do that using the following code:

```
git add .
git commit -m 'changed our title'
git push
```

When we go back to our app, your app will have its own unique URL. If you ever cannot find your Streamlit apps, you can always find them at `share.streamlit.io`. Now the top of our app should look like the following screenshot:

Penguin Classifier: A Machine Learning App

This app uses 6 inputs to predict the species of penguin using a model built on the Palmer's Penguin's dataset. Use the form below to get started!

Penguin Island

Biscoe ▾

Sex

Female ▾

Figure 5.5 – Our deployed Streamlit app

> **Note**
> It may take a couple of minutes for the app to reload!

Now we have a fully deployed Streamlit app! We can share this link with friends, with colleagues, or on social media sites such as Twitter (if you make an interesting Streamlit app with the help of this book, please tweet it at me *@tylerjrichards*, I would love to see it!). Now, to learn how to debug our Streamlit apps.

Debugging Streamlit Sharing

Streamlit Sharing also gives us access to the logs of our apps themselves, which will show up on our terminal if we are deploying our apps locally. At the bottom right, whenever we are viewing our own applications, there is a **Manage Application** button, which allows us to access our logs. From this menu of options, we can reboot, delete, or download logs from our app, along with viewing our other available apps and logging out from Streamlit.

Streamlit Secrets

When creating and deploying Streamlit apps, you may want to use some information that is not viewable by the user of your app. The default in Streamlit Sharing is for public GitHub repositories with entirely public code, data, and models. But if, say, you want to use a private API key as many APIs (for example, Twitter's scraping API, or the Google Maps API) require, or want to programmatically access data stored in a password protected database, or even if you would like to password protect your Streamlit app, you need a way to expose a bit of data to Streamlit that is private. Streamlit's answer to this is Streamlit Secrets, which lets us set hidden and private "secrets" in each app. Let's start with password protecting our Streamlit applications, specifically our existing penguin app.

To start out, we can edit the top of our app to require the user to enter a password before the rest of the application loads. We can use the st.stop() function to stop the app from running if the password is incorrect using the following code:

```python
import streamlit as st
import seaborn as sns
import matplotlib.pyplot as plt
import pandas as pd
import pickle
from sklearn.metrics import accuracy_score
from sklearn.ensemble import RandomForestClassifier
from sklearn.model_selection import train_test_split


st.title('Penguin Classifier')
st.write("This app uses 6 inputs to predict the species of penguin using "
         "a model built on the Palmer's Penguin's dataset. Use the form below"
         " to get started!")

password_guess = st.text_input('What is the Password?')
if password_guess != 'streamlit_password':
    st.stop()
penguin_file = st.file_uploader('Upload your own penguin data')
```

This code will result in the next screenshot, and the rest will only load if the user inputs the string `streamlit_password` in the text input box:

Penguin Classifier

This app uses 6 inputs to predict the species of penguin using a model built on the Palmer's Penguin's dataset. Use the form below to get started!

What is the Password?

Figure 5.6 – Password checker

To create a Streamlit Secret, we just need to head over to our Streamlit Sharing main page at `https://share.streamlit.io/`, and click the **Edit secrets** option, as shown in the next screenshot:

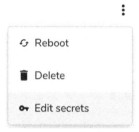

⟳ Reboot

🗑 Delete

⚬┐ Edit secrets

Figure 5.7 – Secrets

Once we click the **Edit secrets** button, we can add new Streamlit Secrets to our app:

Edit Secrets   ✕

Provide environment variables and other secrets to your app using TOML format. This information is encrypted and served securely to your app at runtime. Learn more about Secrets in our docs. Changes take around a minute to propagate.

```
password = 'streamlit_is_great'
```

Save

Figure 5.8 – Our first Streamlit Secret

Our last step is to read Streamlit Secrets from our deployed app within our code, which we can do by calling `st.secrets` and calling the variable we created in Secrets. The following code replaces our hardcoded password with the Streamlit Secret:

```
st.title('Penguin Classifier')
st.write("This app uses 6 inputs to predict the species of
penguin using "
        "a model built on the Palmer's Penguin's dataset. Use
the form below"
        " to get started!")

password_guess = st.text_input('What is the Password?')
if password_guess != st.secrets["password"]:
   st.stop()

penguin_file = st.file_uploader('Upload your own penguin data')
```

This code will create the following Streamlit app, password protected with the Streamlit Secret that we set:

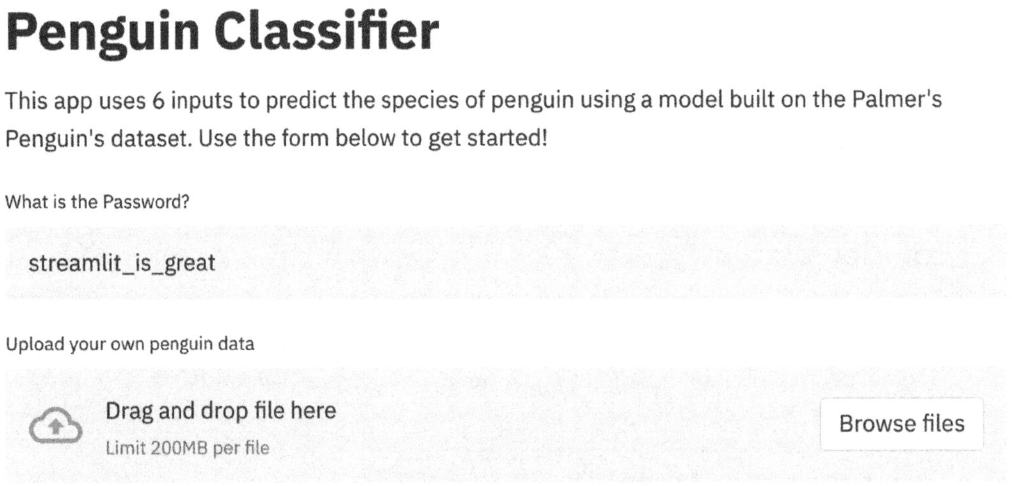

Penguin Classifier

This app uses 6 inputs to predict the species of penguin using a model built on the Palmer's Penguin's dataset. Use the form below to get started!

What is the Password?

> streamlit_is_great

Upload your own penguin data

> ☁ **Drag and drop file here**   Browse files
> Limit 200MB per file

Figure 5.9 – Deployed password

When we push this code to our GitHub repository and reboot our Streamlit app, we will then have a password-protected Streamlit app deployed on Streamlit Sharing! We can use this same method for private API keys, or any other use case where we need to hide data from the user of the app.

Summary

In this chapter, we've learned how to get started with Git and GitHub on the command line, how to debug apps on Streamlit Sharing, how to use Streamlit Secrets to use private data on public apps, and how to deploy our apps quickly using Streamlit Sharing. This completes part one of this book! Congratulations for making it to this point. The next section will use all of part one as a building block for more advanced topics such as more complicated formatting and beautification of our Streamlit apps and using valuable open source community-built add-ons called Streamlit components.

In the next chapter, we will cover beautifying Streamlit apps through themes, columns, and many more features.

Section 2: Advanced Streamlit Applications

This section covers the basics of Streamlit and will show you how to create your first app. *Section 2* explores Streamlit through complex applications and use cases and intends to make you an expert Streamlit user.

The following chapters are covered in this section:

- *Chapter 6, Beautifying Streamlit Apps*
- *Chapter 7, Streamlit Components*
- *Chapter 8, Deploying Streamlit Apps with Heroku and AWS*

6
Beautifying Streamlit Apps

Welcome to Section 2 of the book! In *Section 1, Creating Basic Streamlit Applications*, we focused on the basics – visualization, deployment, and data munging, all the topics that are crucial to getting started with Streamlit. In this part of the book, the purpose is to explore Streamlit through more complex applications and use cases, with the intent of turning you into an expert Streamlit user.

Throughout this chapter, we'll work with elements including sidebars, columns, colors, and themes to extend our ability to make beautiful Streamlit applications. By the end of this chapter, you should feel much more comfortable creating applications that are better than the average **Minimum Viable Product** (**MVP**). We'll start by learning about columns and move on to the rest of the elements discussed, weaving each into the main Streamlit app for the chapter.

Specifically, in this chapter, we will cover the following topics:

- Setting up the SF (San Francisco) Trees dataset

- Working with columns in Streamlit

- Exploring page configuration

- Using the Streamlit sidebar

- Picking colors with Color Picker
- Utilizing Streamlit themes

Technical requirements

This chapter requires a free GitHub account, which can be obtained at `https://www.github.com`. A full primer on GitHub, along with detailed setup instructions, can be found in the *A quick primer on GitHub* section in the previous chapter, *Chapter 5, Deploying Streamlit with Streamlit Sharing*.

Setting up the SF Trees dataset

For this chapter, we will be working with the SF Trees dataset again, the same dataset that we used in *Chapter 3, Data Visualization*. As we did in the previous chapters, we need to follow this list of steps for the setup:

1. Create a new folder for the chapter.
2. Add our data to the folder.
3. Create a Python file for our app.

Let's see each of these steps in detail.

In our main `streamlit_apps` folder, run the following code in your terminal to make a new folder cleverly called `pretty_trees`. You can also create a new folder manually outside the terminal:

```
mkdir pretty_trees
```

Now, we need to move our data from *Chapter 3, Data Visualization*, into our folder for this chapter. The following code copies the data into the correct folder:

```
cp trees_app/trees.csv pretty_trees
```

If you do not have the `trees_app` folder and have not yet completed *Chapter 3, Data Visualization*, you can also download the necessary data from `https://github.com/tylerjrichards/Getting-Started-with-Streamlit-for-Data-Science` within the folder entitled `trees_app`.

Now that we have our data ready, we need to create a Python file to host our Streamlit app's code; the following code does precisely this:

```
touch pretty_trees.py
```

The `pretty_trees` file will hold our Python code, so go ahead and open it up in the text editor of your choice and the chapter can officially begin with us learning how to work with columns in Streamlit!

Working with columns in Streamlit

In all of our apps prior to this point, we have viewed each Streamlit task as a top-down experience. We output text as our title, collect some user input below, and then put our visualizations below that. However, Streamlit allows us to format our app into dynamic columns using the `st.beta_columns()` feature. As of now, the columns feature is in beta (hence the `beta_` in the function name), but the feature should be out of beta at some point in 2021, where it will be called `st.columns()`.

We can divide our Streamlit app into multiple columns of variable lengths, and then treat each column as its own unique space in our app to include text, graphs, images, or anything else we would like.

The syntax for columns in Streamlit uses `with` notation, which you may already be familiar with for use cases such as resource management and dealing with opening and writing to files in Python. The easiest way to think about `with` notation in Streamlit columns is that they are self-contained blocks of code that tell Streamlit exactly where to place items in our apps. Let's check out an example to see how it works. The following code imports our SF Trees dataset and creates three columns of equal length within it, writing text into each one:

```python
import streamlit as st
import pandas as pd

st.title('SF Trees')
st.write('This app analyses trees in San Francisco using'
         ' a dataset kindly provided by SF DPW')
trees_df = pd.read_csv('trees.csv')

col1, col2, col3 = st.beta_columns((1,1,1))

with col1:
    st.write('First column')

with col2:
```

```
        st.write('Second column')

with col3:
        st.write('Third column')
```

The preceding code will create the app shown in the following screenshot:

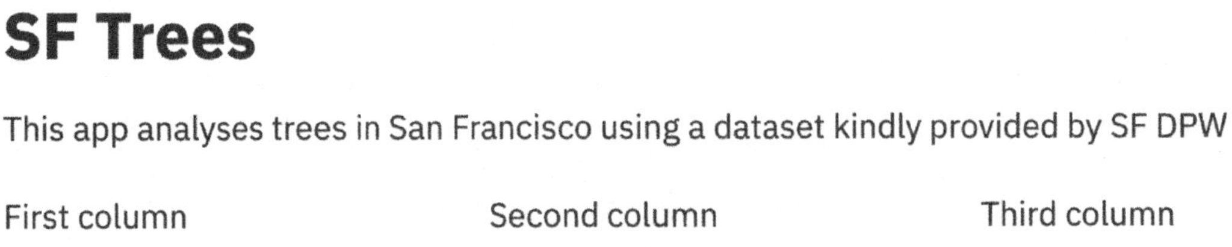

SF Trees

This app analyses trees in San Francisco using a dataset kindly provided by SF DPW

First column   Second column   Third column

Figure 6.1 – First three columns

As we can see, `st.beta_columns()` defines three columns of equal length, and we use the `with` notation to print some text in each. We can also call the `st.write()` function (or any other Streamlit function that writes content to our Streamlit app) directly on our predefined columns for the same outcome, as shown in the following code. The following code will have the exact same output as the preceding code block:

```
import streamlit as st
import pandas as pd

st.title('SF Trees')
st.write('This app analyses trees in San Francisco using'
         ' a dataset kindly provided by SF DPW')
trees_df = pd.read_csv('trees.csv')

col1, col2, col3 = st.beta_columns((1,1,1))

col1.write('First column')
col2.write('Second column')
col3.write('Third column')
```

As we write more complex Streamlit apps with more content in each column, `with` statements tend to make for cleaner apps that are easier to understand and debug. The majority of this book will use `with` statements whenever possible.

In Streamlit, the column width is relative to the size of the other defined columns. Because of this, if we scale up the width of each column to 10 instead of 1, our app will not change at all. Additionally, we can also pass a single number into st.beta_columns(), and st.beta_columns() will return that number of columns of equal width. The following code block shows three options for column width that all result in the same column widths:

```
#option 1
col1, col2, col3 = st.beta_columns((1,1,1))
#option 2
col1, col2, col3 = st.beta_columns((10,10,10))
#option 3
col1, col2, col3 = st.beta_columns(3)
```

As a final example, the following code block allows the user input to determine the width of each column. Go ahead and play around with the resulting app to better understand how we can use columns to change the format behind our Streamlit apps:

```
import streamlit as st
import pandas as pd

st.title('SF Trees')
st.write('This app analyses trees in San Francisco using'
         ' a dataset kindly provided by SF DPW')
trees_df = pd.read_csv('trees.csv')

first_width = st.number_input('First Width', min_value=1,
value=1)
second_width = st.number_input('Second Width', min_value=1,
value=1)
third_width = st.number_input('Third Width', min_value=1,
value=1)

col1, col2, col3 = st.beta_columns(
        (first_width,second_width,third_width))

with col1:
        st.write('First column')
```

```
with col2:
    st.write('Second column')


with col3:
    st.write('Third column')
```

In *Chapter 3*, *Data Visualization*, we used the following code to show the difference between the built-in Streamlit functions st.line_chart(), st.bar_chart(), and st.area_chart():

```
import streamlit as st
import pandas as pd


st.title('SF Trees')
st.write('This app analyses trees in San Francisco using'
         ' a dataset kindly provided by SF DPW')
trees_df = pd.read_csv('trees.csv')
df_dbh_grouped = pd.DataFrame(trees_df.groupby(['dbh']).count()
['tree_id'])
df_dbh_grouped.columns = ['tree_count']
st.line_chart(df_dbh_grouped)
st.bar_chart(df_dbh_grouped)
st.area_chart(df_dbh_grouped)
```

The preceding code block creates the following Streamlit app, with three graphs of San Francisco trees grouped by their width placed one right after the other (only the two graphs are shown for brevity):

SF Trees

This app analyses trees in San Francisco using a dataset kindly provided by SF DPW

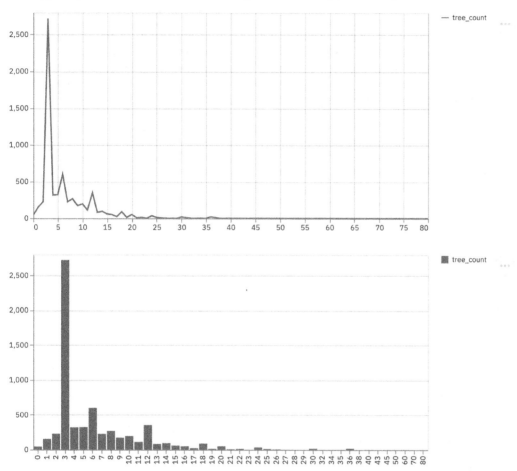

Figure 6.2 – SF line and bar charts

The point of this exercise was to better understand the three Streamlit functions, but how can we do that if we need to scroll to see them all? Let's improve on this by putting our three graphs side by side using three columns. The following code predefines three equally wide columns and places one graph in each:

```
import streamlit as st
import pandas as pd
st.title('SF Trees')
st.write('This app analyses trees in San Francisco using'
```

```
            ' a dataset kindly provided by SF DPW')
trees_df = pd.read_csv('trees.csv')
df_dbh_grouped = pd.DataFrame(trees_df.groupby(['dbh']).count()
['tree_id'])
df_dbh_grouped.columns = ['tree_count']
col1, col2, col3 = st.beta_columns(3)


with col1:
        st.line_chart(df_dbh_grouped)
with col2:
        st.bar_chart(df_dbh_grouped)
with col3:
        st.area_chart(df_dbh_grouped)
```

When we run the preceding code, we get a strange result shown in the following screenshot:

SF Trees

This app analyses trees in San Francisco using a dataset kindly provided by SF DPW

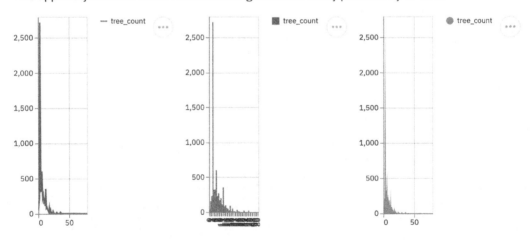

Figure 6.3 – Skinny graphs

This is most certainly not what we wanted! Each graph is far too narrow. Luckily for us, this brings us to our next mini-topic, page configuration in Streamlit.

Exploring page configuration

Streamlit allows us to configure a few essential page-specific features at the top of each Streamlit app. So far, we have been using the Streamlit defaults, but at the top of our Streamlit app, we can manually configure everything, from the page title shown on the web browser used to open our Streamlit apps, to the page layout, to the sidebar default state (we will cover the sidebar in the *Using the Streamlit sidebar* section!).

The default for Streamlit apps is to have a centered page layout, which is why there is copious white space on the edges of our apps. The following code sets up our Streamlit app in a wide format instead of our default centered one:

```
import streamlit as st
import pandas as pd
st.set_page_config(layout='wide')
st.title('SF Trees')
st.write('This app analyses trees in San Francisco using'
        ' a dataset kindly provided by SF DPW')
trees_df = pd.read_csv('trees.csv')
df_dbh_grouped = pd.DataFrame(trees_df.groupby(['dbh']).count()
['tree_id'])
df_dbh_grouped.columns = ['tree_count']
col1, col2, col3 = st.beta_columns(3)


with col1:
    st.line_chart(df_dbh_grouped)
with col2:
    st.bar_chart(df_dbh_grouped)
with col3:
    st.area_chart(df_dbh_grouped)
```

When we run the preceding code, we now see that our three graphs are well spaced and we can easily compare between the three. The following screenshot shows the Streamlit app in a wide format:

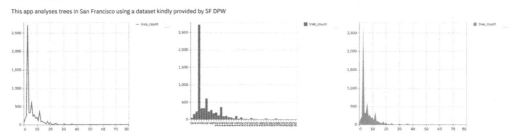

Figure 6.4 – Wide-format graphs

This concludes our exploration of using columns in Streamlit, and also concludes our first look at page configuration defaults. We will increasingly use both of these skills in the remainder of the book. Our next topic is to introduce the Streamlit sidebar.

Using the Streamlit sidebar

As we have already seen in Streamlit, when we start to both accept large amounts of user input and also start to develop longer Streamlit apps, we often lose the ability for the user to see both their input and the output on the same screen. In other cases, we may want to put all the user input into its own section to clearly separate input and output in our Streamlit app. For both of these use cases, we can use the Streamlit sidebar, which allows us to place a minimizable sidebar on the left side of the Streamlit app and add any Streamlit component to it.

To begin with, we can make a basic example that takes one of the graphs from our preceding app and filter the data behind it based on the user's input. In this case, we can ask the user to specify the type of tree owner (for example, a private owner, or the Department of Public Works), and filter on those conditions using the st.multiselect() function, which allows the user to select multiple options from a list:

```
import streamlit as st
import pandas as pd


st.title('SF Trees')
st.write('This app analyses trees in San Francisco using'
         ' a dataset kindly provided by SF DPW. The '
         'histogram below is filtered by tree owner.')
```

```
trees_df = pd.read_csv('trees.csv')
owners = st.sidebar.multiselect(
    'Tree Owner Filter', trees_df['caretaker'].unique())

if owners:
    trees_df = trees_df[trees_df['caretaker'].isin(owners)]
df_dbh_grouped = pd.DataFrame(trees_df.groupby(['dbh']).count()
['tree_id'])
df_dbh_grouped.columns = ['tree_count']

st.line_chart(df_dbh_grouped)
```

The preceding code will create the following Streamlit app. As we have done before, we hide the owners variable within an if statement, as we would like the app to run with the entire dataset if the user has yet to select from the options. The sidebar allows the user to easily see both the options they selected and the output to our app:

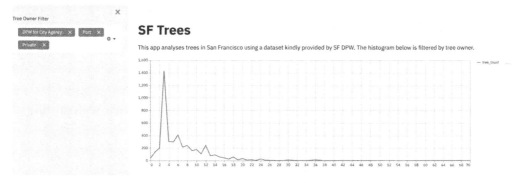

Figure 6.5 – First sidebar

Our next step for this app is going to be to add a few more visualizations, starting with the tree map we created in *Chapter 3*, *Data Visualization*, and then combine the sidebar with what we have already learned about columns in this chapter.

The following code places the map of trees throughout San Francisco, filtered by our multi-select box, below the histogram:

```
import streamlit as st
import pandas as pd

trees_df = pd.read_csv('trees.csv')
owners = st.sidebar.multiselect(
```

```
        'Tree Owner Filter', trees_df['caretaker'].unique())
```

```
st.title('SF Trees')
st.write('This app analyses trees in San Francisco using'
         ' a dataset kindly provided by SF DPW. The '
         'histogram below is filtered by tree owner.')
st.write('The current analysis is of trees owned by {}'.
format(owners))
```

```
if owners:
    trees_df = trees_df[trees_df['caretaker'].isin(owners)]
df_dbh_grouped = pd.DataFrame(trees_df.groupby(['dbh']).count()
['tree_id'])
df_dbh_grouped.columns = ['tree_count']
```

```
st.line_chart(df_dbh_grouped)
```

```
trees_df = trees_df.dropna(subset=['longitude', 'latitude'])
trees_df = trees_df.sample(n = 1000, replace=True)
st.map(trees_df)
```

The following screenshot shows the Streamlit app from the preceding code, with the line chart just above the new map of the trees in SF, filtered by tree owner:

Figure 6.6 – Filtered map with sidebar

Our next step for this application is going to be to combine what we learned about columns with the sidebar by adding another graph on top of the geographic map. In *Chapter 3, Data Visualization*, we created a histogram of the age of the trees. We can use that as our third graph in this Streamlit app. The following code block does this, and also switches the line graph into the same library (`seaborn`) as our tree age graph:

```python
import streamlit as st
import pandas as pd
import seaborn as sns
import datetime as dt
import matplotlib.pyplot as plt

st.title('SF Trees')
st.write('This app analyses trees in San Francisco using'
         ' a dataset kindly provided by SF DPW. The '
         'histogram below is filtered by tree owner.')

trees_df = pd.read_csv('trees.csv')
trees_df['age'] = (pd.to_datetime('today') -
                   pd.to_datetime(trees_df['date'])).dt.days

owners = st.sidebar.multiselect(
    'Tree Owner Filter', trees_df['caretaker'].unique())
if owners:
    trees_df = trees_df[trees_df['caretaker'].isin(owners)]

df_dbh_grouped = pd.DataFrame(trees_df.groupby(['dbh']).count()
['tree_id'])
df_dbh_grouped.columns = ['tree_count']
```

This first section does the following:

1. It loads the trees dataset.
2. It adds an age column based on the date column in our dataset.
3. It creates a multi-select widget on the sidebar.
4. It filters based on the sidebar.

Our next step is to create our three graphs:

```
#define multiple columns, add two graphs
col1, col2 = st.beta_columns(2)
with col1:
      st.write('Trees by Width')
      fig_1, ax_1 = plt.subplots()
      ax_1 = sns.histplot(trees_df['dbh'])
      plt.xlabel('Tree Width')
      st.pyplot(fig_1)
with col2:
      st.write('Trees by Age')
      fig_2, ax_2 = plt.subplots()
      ax_2 = sns.histplot(trees_df['age'])
      plt.xlabel('Age (Days)')
      st.pyplot(fig_2)

st.write('Trees by Location')
trees_df = trees_df.dropna(subset=['longitude', 'latitude'])
trees_df = trees_df.sample(n = 1000, replace=True)
st.map(trees_df)
```

As we have already discussed in *Chapter 3*, *Data Visualization*, built-in Streamlit functions such as st.map() and st.line_chart() are useful for quick visualizations but lack some configurability options, such as proper titles or axis renaming. The following screenshot shows our Streamlit application with a few tree owner filters pre-set:

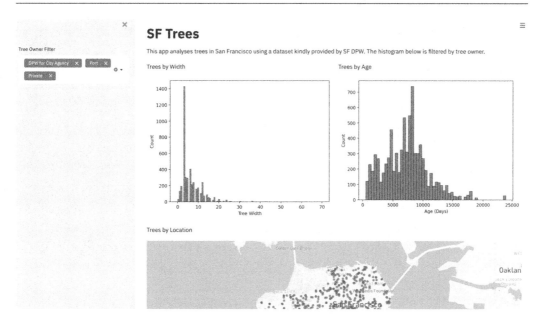

Figure 6.7 – Three filtered graphs

Our next feature to discuss in this chapter is how to get and use user input on color, which will be covered in the next section.

Picking colors with Color Picker

Colors are very difficult to take in as user input in applications. If a user wants red, do they want light red or dark red? Maroon or a pinkish red? Streamlit's approach to this problem is st.color_picker(), which lets the user pick a color, and returns that color in a hex string (which is a unique string that defines very specific color shades used by most graphing libraries as input). The following code adds this color picker to our previous app and changes the color of the Seaborn graphs to be based on the color that the user selects:

```
import streamlit as st
import pandas as pd
import seaborn as sns
import datetime as dt
import matplotlib.pyplot as plt

st.title('SF Trees')
st.write('This app analyses trees in San Francisco using'
        ' a dataset kindly provided by SF DPW. The '
```

```
                'histogram below is filtered by tree owner.')


#load trees dataset, add age column in days
trees_df = pd.read_csv('trees.csv')
trees_df['age'] = (pd.to_datetime('today') -
                pd.to_datetime(trees_df['date'])).dt.days
#add tree owner filter to sidebar, then filter, get color
owners = st.sidebar.multiselect(
    'Tree Owner Filter', trees_df['caretaker'].unique())
graph_color = st.sidebar.color_picker('Graph Colors')
if owners:
    trees_df = trees_df[trees_df['caretaker'].isin(owners)]


#group by dbh for leftmost graph
df_dbh_grouped = pd.DataFrame(trees_df.groupby(['dbh']).count()
['tree_id'])
df_dbh_grouped.columns = ['tree_count']
```

The change here from our previous app is to add the graph_color variable, which is a result of the st.color_picker() function. We added a name to this color picker and placed the color picker in the sidebar right under the owner's multi-select widget. Now that we have the color input from the user, we can use this to change the colors in our graphs, as shown in the following code:

```
#define multiple columns, add two graphs
col1, col2 = st.beta_columns(2)
with col1:
    st.write('Trees by Width')
    fig_1, ax_1 = plt.subplots()
    ax_1 = sns.histplot(trees_df['dbh'],
        color=graph_color)
    plt.xlabel('Tree Width')
    st.pyplot(fig_1)
with col2:
    st.write('Trees by Age')
    fig_2, ax_2 = plt.subplots()
    ax_2 = sns.histplot(trees_df['age'],
```

```
                color=graph_color)
        plt.xlabel('Age (Days)')
        st.pyplot(fig_2)


st.write('Trees by Location')
trees_df = trees_df.dropna(subset=['longitude', 'latitude'])
trees_df = trees_df.sample(n = 1000, replace=True)
st.map(trees_df)
```

When you run this Streamlit app, you can see exactly how the color picker works (this book is published in grayscale, so is not visible in the hard copy). It has a default color (in our case, black) that you can change by selecting the component and then clicking on your color of choice. The following screenshot shows both the component when clicked on and the result in our SF Trees app:

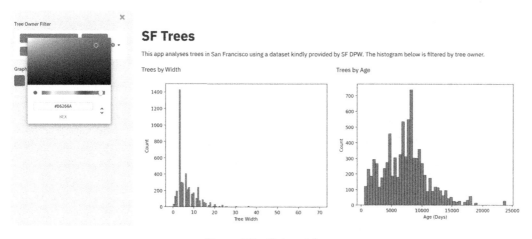

Figure 6.8 – Color picker

Now that we know how to change the colors of visualizations in Streamlit, how can we change the entire format and color scheme of Streamlit apps themselves? The next chapter explores Streamlit themes, and how to set up different themes to beautify Streamlit apps.

Utilizing Streamlit themes

So far, our applications have all had the exact same background and color scheme, apart from the previous section on the color picker. Streamlit allows us to update our applications and change the color of the background and the various components in our app as a customization feature. Using this, we can create Streamlit apps that default to dark mode, or that have the perfect colors for our app, or even create themes that ensure that people affected by color-blindness can see all of our visualizations.

There are two ways to edit the *theme* of an app – through the UI or through the same `config.toml` setup we used in *Chapter 3*, *Data Visualization*. When we run our Streamlit apps, in the top-right corner, there is a little hamburger icon. When we click that icon and then click **Settings**, we will see the following options pop up in the middle of our screen:

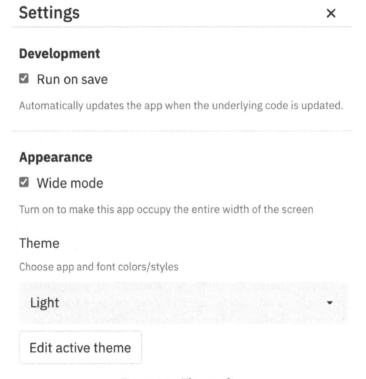

Figure 6.9 – Theme edits

Using the preceding menu, we can switch between **Light** and **Dark** themes, and when we click on **Edit active theme**, we can see all of our theme editing options as demonstrated in the following screenshot:

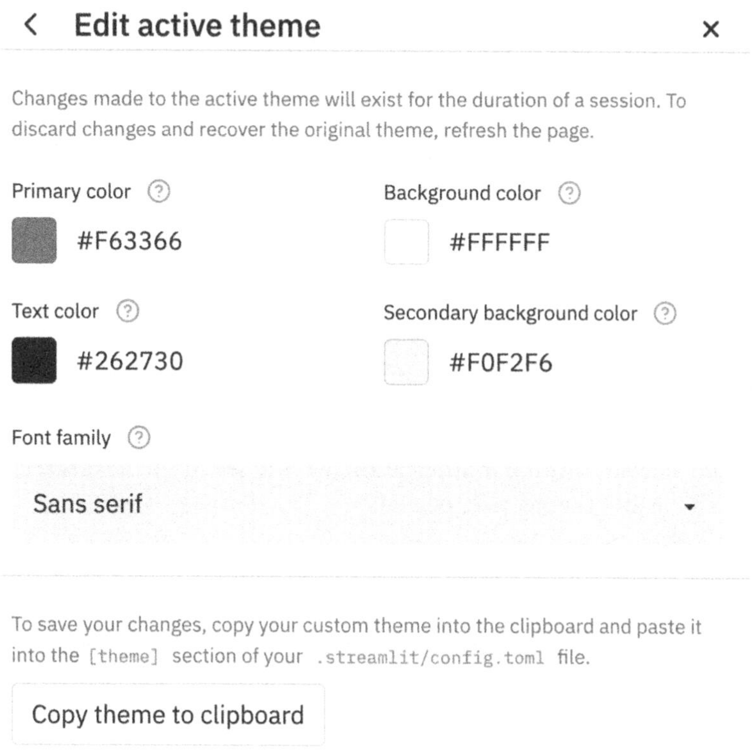

← **Edit active theme**   ✕

Changes made to the active theme will exist for the duration of a session. To discard changes and recover the original theme, refresh the page.

Primary color ⑦   Background color ⑦

⬜ #F63366   ⬜ #FFFFFF

Text color ⑦   Secondary background color ⑦

⬛ #262730   ⬜ #F0F2F6

Font family ⑦

Sans serif   ▾

To save your changes, copy your custom theme into the clipboard and paste it into the [theme] section of your .streamlit/config.toml file.

Copy theme to clipboard

Figure 6.10 – Editing active themes

From the preceding screenshot, we can observe that the following can be switched:

- **Primary color**: For interactive colors
- **Background color**: Background of the app
- **Secondary background color**: Background within components
- **Text color/font**: The color and font of the app text

Feel free to click on them and change the colors and see how this affects your Streamlit app. Once you have found a few colors that you like for our SF Trees app, you can add them to the theme section of your .streamlit/config.toml file as the instructions in **Settings** tell you to, and this will change the theme whenever you open the app. The following code block is added to the config.toml file and shows the colors I have selected for my theme:

```
[theme]


# Primary accent color for interactive elements.
```

```
primaryColor = "#de8ba1"


# Background color for the main content area.
backgroundColor = "#f4f1ea"


# Background color used for the sidebar and most interactive
widgets.
secondaryBackgroundColor = "#9fe4cc"


# Color used for almost all text.
textColor = "#262730"
```

When we save this file and rerun our application, we will see in the next screenshot that our app now has a custom theme, as expected:

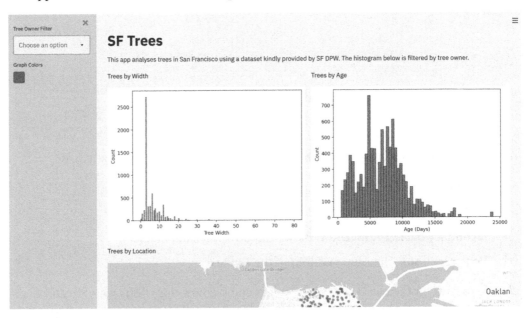

Figure 6.11 – Custom theme output

The easiest way I have found to make your Streamlit themes look great is to edit in the in-browser editor live, and then copy and paste your results to the Streamlit configuration file, as we just did in this example. But, as with all things, have fun with it! Try new combinations and make your Streamlit apps as beautiful as they can be.

Summary

This concludes our adventures with the SF Trees dataset, and with learning about the various ways to make our Streamlit apps more aesthetically pleasing. We covered separating our apps into columns and page configuration, along with gathering user input in the sidebar, getting specific colors in user input through the `st.color_picker()` feature, and finally learning how to use Streamlit themes.

In the next chapter, we will learn about the open source community around Streamlit, by understanding how to download and use Streamlit components built by users.

7
Exploring Streamlit Components

Streamlit has a full-time team of developers working on new features but also thrives because it is open to community-driven development. Undoubtedly, there will be community members who want a specific feature that did not make it onto the roadmap of priorities. Streamlit Components allow them the flexibility to go out and make it themselves, and immediately use their idea in their own Streamlit apps.

Our priority in this chapter is to learn how to find and use community-made Streamlit Components. For that, we will run through three excellent Streamlit apps, one to learn how to embed code into our Streamlit apps, another for adding beautiful animations to them, and a third to embed easy automated **exploratory data analysis (EDA)** to Streamlit apps.

In this chapter, we will cover the following topics:

- Using Streamlit Components: `streamlit-embedcode`
- Using Streamlit Components: `streamlit-lottie`
- Using Streamlit Components: `streamlit-pandas-profiling`
- Finding more components

Let's look at the technical requirements in the next section.

Technical requirements

Before we can work with new Streamlit Components, we need to download them first. We can download each using `pip` (or any other package manager), just as we did with Streamlit in *Chapter 1, An Introduction to Streamlit*. These are the components to be downloaded:

- `streamlit-embedcode`: To download this library, run the following code in your terminal:

```
pip install streamlit-embedcode
```

`streamlit-embedcode` makes it easy to import code blocks from other locations (such as a GitHub gist) and show them directly in your apps, and was created by Randy Zwitch, a Streamlit employee.

- `streamlit-lottie`: To download this library, run the following code in your terminal:

```
pip install streamlit-lottie
```

`streamlit-lottie` uses the `lottie` open source library to allow us to add web-native animations (such as a **Graphics Interchange Format** (**GIF**) file) into our Streamlit apps. It is frankly a wonderful library for beautifying Streamlit apps and was created by Andy Fanilo, a prolific Streamlit app creator.

- `streamlit-pandas-profiling`: To download this library, run the following code in your terminal:

```
pip install streamlit-pandas-profiling
```

The popular `pandas` Python library is the standard Python data analysis library and often tops the list of the most popular and useful Python libraries for data scientists. `pandas-profiling` creates an automatically generated EDA on top of any DataFrame we create and shows us everything, from descriptive statistics to how many duplicate rows we have. It was created by a Streamlit user who goes by the name of *Okld* on GitHub (`https://github.com/okld`).

Now that we have the three libraries installed, we can move on to learning about the first one: `streamlit-embedcode`.

Using Streamlit Components – streamlit-embedcode

If we want to display code on Streamlit, we can easily just treat the code as text and use the familiar st.write(), which takes text as input, or st.markdown(), which takes markdown as input. This might work well for small snippets but will be a struggle to format easily, and may not look good for the average user or longer bits of code. As a result, streamlit-embedcode was created to help solve this problem.

Showing snippets of code to others is a commonly solved problem; a few solutions that are out there include sharing snippets with GitHub gists (which are like mini GitHub repositories with only one text file) with GitLab snippets (which are the same as gists but for GitLab) and using Pastebin, which is a shared text/code snippets freeway outside of GitHub/GitLab. Now, we can make a Python file with some example Streamlit code, put it in a GitHub gist, and call it from a new Streamlit app. To do so, we'll follow these steps:

1. For each of these options, we will start by making a quick Streamlit app that just exists to show users the code behind the Palmer's Penguins Streamlit app. We can house this app in its own component_example folder using the following code from our streamlit_apps folder:

    ```
    mkdir component_example
    cd component_example
    touch gist_example.py
    ```

2. Next, we need to navigate to https://gist.github.com/ to create our very own gist. After we sign in to GitHub, we need to title the gist and then paste our code from Palmer's Penguins to copy it to the following code block (which includes a brief explanation in the middle of it):

    ```
    import streamlit as st
    import pandas as pd
    import matplotlib.pyplot as plt
    import seaborn as sns

    st.title("Palmer's Penguins")
    st.markdown('Use this Streamlit app to make your own
    scatterplot about penguins!')

    selected_x_var = st.selectbox('What do want the x
    variable to be?',
    ```

```
    ['bill_length_mm', 'bill_depth_mm', 'flipper_length_
mm', 'body_mass_g'])
selected_y_var = st.selectbox('What about the y?',
    ['bill_depth_mm', 'bill_length_mm', 'flipper_length_
mm', 'body_mass_g'])
```

```
penguin_file = st.file_uploader('Select Your Local
Penguins CSV')
if penguin_file is not None:
    penguins_df = pd.read_csv(penguin_file)
else:
    st.stop()
```

This first section imports our libraries, adds some text for a title, gathers some inputs from the user, and downloads the right dataset. Now, we would just like to make a scatterplot graph, and then that will conclude the code that goes into our gist. Again, the exact code here does not actually matter because it does not execute within a gist—it is instead a prettier way to send code to others. The following code snippet illustrates the process:

```
sns.set_style('darkgrid')
markers = {"Adelie": "X", "Gentoo": "s", "Chinstrap":'o'}
fig, ax = plt.subplots()
ax = sns.scatterplot(data = penguins_df, x = selected_x_
var,
   y = selected_y_var, hue = 'species', markers = markers,
  style = 'species')
plt.xlabel(selected_x_var)
plt.ylabel(selected_y_var)
plt.title("Scatterplot of Palmer's Penguins")
st.pyplot(fig)
```

Now, we should have a GitHub gist that looks like this:

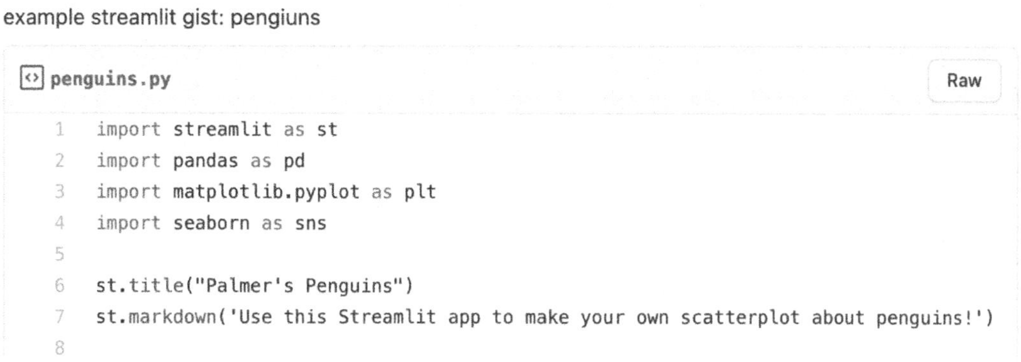

example streamlit gist: pengiuns

```
<>  penguins.py                                                              Raw

1    import streamlit as st
2    import pandas as pd
3    import matplotlib.pyplot as plt
4    import seaborn as sns
5
6    st.title("Palmer's Penguins")
7    st.markdown('Use this Streamlit app to make your own scatterplot about penguins!')
8
```

Figure 7.1 – GitHub gist example

3. When we save our GitHub gist, we can link directly to it from within our Streamlit apps. In the gist_example.py Python file, we need to import the github_gist() function from our new library and use it on the GitHub gist we just created. The following code does this for my own gist, but you should replace the gist link with your own:

```
import streamlit as st
from streamlit_embedcode import github_gist

st.title("Github Gist Example")
st.write("Code from Palmer's Penguin Streamlit app.")
github_gist('https://gist.github.com/
tylerjrichards/9dcf6df0c17ccb7b91baafbe3cdf7654')
```

Now, if we ever need to edit the code in the gist, we can instead edit the underlying gist and the Streamlit apps will update automatically. When we start up our Streamlit apps held in `gist_example.py`, we will get the following Streamlit app:

Github Gist Example

Code from Palmer's Penguin Streamlit app.

```python
 1   import streamlit as st
 2   import pandas as pd
 3   import matplotlib.pyplot as plt
 4   import seaborn as sns
 5
 6   st.title("Palmer's Penguins")
 7   st.markdown('Use this Streamlit app to make your own scatterplot about penguins!')
 8
 9   selected_x_var = st.selectbox('What do want the x variable to be?',
10     ['bill_length_mm', 'bill_depth_mm', 'flipper_length_mm', 'body_mass_g'])
11   selected_y_var = st.selectbox('What about the y?',
12     ['bill_depth_mm', 'bill_length_mm', 'flipper_length_mm', 'body_mass_g'])
13
14   penguin_file = st.file_uploader('Select Your Local Penguins CSV')
15   if penguin_file is not None:
16           penguins_df = pd.read_csv(penguin_file)
17   else:
18           st.stop()
19
20   sns.set_style('darkgrid')
21   markers = {"Adelie": "X", "Gentoo": "s", "Chinstrap":'o'}
22   fig, ax = plt.subplots()
23   ax = sns.scatterplot(data = penguins_df, x = selected_x_var,
24     y = selected_y_var, hue = 'species', markers = markers,
25     style = 'species')
26   plt.xlabel(selected_x_var)
27   plt.ylabel(selected_y_var)
```

Figure 7.2 – Streamlit apps with GitHub gist

> **Note**
>
> For any public Streamlit apps, we can always simply access the source code for the app in the **Settings** tab. So, this method is not very useful for showing the code behind the Streamlit apps as this is already built-in, but is more useful for showing often-used code blocks such as a generic bit of code to make a **machine learning** (**ML**) model or a more generic **Structured Query Language** (**SQL**) query that users may learn from.

Now, let's switch over to learning about how to add beautiful animations to our app using `streamlit-lottie`!

Using Streamlit Components – streamlit-lottie

As we talked about at the beginning of this chapter, `lottie` is a web-native, open source library created by *Airbnb* to make putting animations on your website just as easy as putting static images on it. It is very common for large, profitable tech companies to put out open source software as a way of giving back to the developer community (or, more likely, to recruit developers who think their software is cool), and this is no exception. In this case, `streamlit-lottie` wraps around `lottie` files and places them directly into our Streamlit apps.

To do this, we first need to import the `streamlit-lottie` library, and then point the `st_lottie()` function to our `lottie` file. We can either import a local `lottie` file or, more likely, we can find a useful animation file on the free site (`https://lottiefiles.com/`) and load it from there into our app.

To test this out, we can add a cute penguin animation (`https://lottiefiles.com/39646-cute-penguin`) to the top of the Penguins app we created earlier in *Chapter 4, Using Machine Learning with Streamlit*. In our new `components_example` folder, we can add a new `penguin_animated.py` file using the following code:

```
touch penguin_animated.py
```

Then, in this new file, we can make this new app. The following code block makes a function, as shown in the example from the `streamlit-lottie` library (`https://github.com/andfanilo/streamlit-lottie`), that allows us to load `lottie` files from the URL and then loads this animation at the top of the application:

```
import streamlit as st
from streamlit_lottie import st_lottie
import requests
import pandas as pd
```

```
import matplotlib.pyplot as plt
import seaborn as sns


def load_lottieurl(url: str):
    r = requests.get(url)
    if r.status_code != 200:
        return None
    return r.json()


lottie_penguin = load_lottieurl('https://assets9.lottiefiles.
com/private_files/1f30_1ntyk83o.json')
st_lottie(lottie_penguin, height=200)
```

The previous section of code uses the requests library to define a function that we can use to load lottie files from a link. In this case, I have pre-filled a link that takes us to a cute penguin animation. We can then load our file using our new function, and call that file using the st_lottie() function we imported from our streamlit-lottie library. Next, we can finish out the app with our previously defined user inputs and scatterplot. The code is illustrated in the following snippet:

```
st.title("Palmer's Penguins")
st.markdown('Use this Streamlit app to make your own
scatterplot about penguins!')

selected_x_var = st.selectbox('What do want the x variable to
be?',
  ['bill_length_mm', 'bill_depth_mm', 'flipper_length_mm',
'body_mass_g'])
selected_y_var = st.selectbox('What about the y?',
  ['bill_depth_mm', 'bill_length_mm', 'flipper_length_mm',
'body_mass_g'])

penguin_file = st.file_uploader('Select Your Local Penguins
CSV')
if penguin_file is not None:
    penguins_df = pd.read_csv(penguin_file)
else:
```

```
        penguins_df = pd.read_csv('penguins.csv')

sns.set_style('darkgrid')
markers = {"Adelie": "X", "Gentoo": "s", "Chinstrap":'o'}
fig, ax = plt.subplots()
ax = sns.scatterplot(data = penguins_df, x = selected_x_var,
    y = selected_y_var, hue = 'species', markers = markers,
    style = 'species')
plt.xlabel(selected_x_var)
plt.ylabel(selected_y_var)
plt.title("Scatterplot of Palmer's Penguins")
st.pyplot(fig)
```

This code block will create the following app, which is simply our *Palmer's Penguins* app with the cute penguin animation on top (the app has been cropped for brevity):

Palmer's Penguins

Use this Streamlit app to make your own scatterplot about penguins!

What do want the x variable to be?

bill_length_mm	▾

What about the y?

bill_depth_mm	▾

Select Your Local Penguins CSV

☁	**Drag and drop file here** Limit 200MB per file	Browse files

Figure 7.3 – Adorable penguin animation

streamlit-lottie also allows us to change the animation speed, width, and height through the speed, width, and height parameters respectively. If the animation goes too slowly for your taste, increase the speed to a number such as 1.5 or 2, which will increase the speed by 50% or 100%. The height and width parameters, however, are the pixel height/width of the animation and default to the native size of the animation (the penguin animation is ~700 pixels by ~400 pixels, for example). In the following code block, we change the speed, width, and height of our animation:

```python
import streamlit as st
from streamlit_lottie import st_lottie
import requests
import pandas as pd
import matplotlib.pyplot as plt
import seaborn as sns


def load_lottieurl(url: str):
    r = requests.get(url)
    if r.status_code != 200:
        return None
    return r.json()


lottie_penguin = load_lottieurl('https://assets9.lottiefiles.
com/private_files/lf30_lntyk83o.json')
st_lottie(lottie_penguin, speed=1.5, width=800, height=400)
```

The following code block is the same as for the other app but instead, we have changed the speed, width, and height of our animation to 1.5, 800, and 400. It takes a while to get used to how these inputs interact, as animations can have different sizes and speeds! You can see the different settings being applied here:

```python
st.title("Palmer's Penguins")
st.markdown('Use this Streamlit app to make your own
scatterplot about penguins!')

selected_x_var = st.selectbox('What do want the x variable to
be?',
  ['bill_length_mm', 'bill_depth_mm', 'flipper_length_mm',
'body_mass_g'])
```

```python
selected_y_var = st.selectbox('What about the y?',
  ['bill_depth_mm', 'bill_length_mm', 'flipper_length_mm',
'body_mass_g'])
```

```python
penguin_file = st.file_uploader('Select Your Local Penguins
CSV')
if penguin_file is not None:
    penguins_df = pd.read_csv(penguin_file)
else:
    penguins_df = pd.read_csv('penguins.csv')
```

```python
sns.set_style('darkgrid')
markers = {"Adelie": "X", "Gentoo": "s", "Chinstrap":'o'}
fig, ax = plt.subplots()
ax = sns.scatterplot(data = penguins_df, x = selected_x_var,
  y = selected_y_var, hue = 'species', markers = markers,
  style = 'species')
plt.xlabel(selected_x_var)
plt.ylabel(selected_y_var)
plt.title("Scatterplot of Palmer's Penguins")
st.pyplot(fig)
```

When we make the penguin animation much larger by increasing the width and height in comparison to the previous version, we see the impact on the animation size, as illustrated in the following screenshot. When you run this yourself, you will also notice the animation speed increase as well. I would strongly encourage running this app, as the penguin animation is really quite adorable:

Palmer's Penguins

Use this Streamlit app to make your own scatterplot about penguins!

What do want the x variable to be?

bill_length_mm   ▾

What about the y?

bill_depth_mm   ▾

Select Your Local Penguins CSV

☁ **Drag and drop file here**
    Limit 200MB per file   Browse files

Figure 7.4 – Final penguin animation app

And that completes our tour of `streamlit-lottie`! I have started getting into the habit of putting a nice animation at the top of each and every Streamlit apps I create—it creates a sense of design that makes Streamlit apps feel more purposeful, and immediately alerts the user to the fact that this is not a static document but instead a dynamic and interactive application. Now, let's move on to `pandas-profiling`!

Using Streamlit Components – streamlit-pandas-profiling

`pandas-profiling` is a very powerful Python library that automates some of the EDA that is often the first step in any data analysis, modeling, or even data engineering task. Before a data scientist begins almost any data work, they want to start with a good understanding of the distributions of their underlying data, the number of missing rows, correlations between variables, and many other basic pieces of information. As we mentioned before, this library automates the process and then places this interactive analytics document into a Streamlit app for the user.

Behind the Streamlit component called `pandas-profiling`, there is a full Python library with the same name that the component imports its functions from. The Streamlit component here actually renders the output from the `pandas-profiling` Python library in a way that becomes very easy to integrate. For this segment, we will first learn how to implement the library, and then explore the generated output.

For our example, we will actually continue with our code from the previous section on Palmer's Penguins and add our automatically generated profile to the bottom of the app. The code for this is only a few lines—we need to generate a report for our dataset and then use the Streamlit component to add it to our app. The next code block imports the necessary libraries, and then creates and adds to our app a profile based on the `penguins_df` variable we have defined:

```
import streamlit as st
from streamlit_lottie import st_lottie
import requests
import pandas as pd
import matplotlib.pyplot as plt
import seaborn as sns
from pandas_profiling import ProfileReport
from streamlit_pandas_profiling import st_profile_report

def load_lottieurl(url: str):
```

```
    r = requests.get(url)
    if r.status_code != 200:
        return None
    return r.json()


lottie_penguin = load_lottieurl('https://assets9.lottiefiles.
com/private_files/lf30_lntyk83o.json')
st_lottie(lottie_penguin, speed=1.5, width = 800, height = 400)


st.title("Palmer's Penguins")
st.markdown('Use this Streamlit app to make your own
scatterplot about penguins!')


selected_x_var = st.selectbox('What do want the x variable to
be?',
  ['bill_length_mm', 'bill_depth_mm', 'flipper_length_mm',
'body_mass_g'])
selected_y_var = st.selectbox('What about the y?',
  ['bill_depth_mm', 'bill_length_mm', 'flipper_length_mm',
'body_mass_g'])
```

This section uses the same `streamlit-lottie` library but also loads the `pandas_profiling` and `streamlit-pandas-profiling` library for our use. This is a good lesson—we can treat Streamlit Components as unique Lego blocks, combining them at will to create new and interesting Streamlit applications. The following section reads in our DataFrame and adds a pandas profile to our dataset! Here's the code:

```
penguin_file = st.file_uploader('Select Your Local Penguins
CSV')
if penguin_file is not None:
    penguins_df = pd.read_csv(penguin_file)
else:
    penguins_df = pd.read_csv('penguins.csv')


sns.set_style('darkgrid')
markers = {"Adelie": "X", "Gentoo": "s", "Chinstrap":'o'}
fig, ax = plt.subplots()
ax = sns.scatterplot(data = penguins_df, x = selected_x_var,
```

```
    y = selected_y_var, hue = 'species', markers = markers,
    style = 'species')
plt.xlabel(selected_x_var)
plt.ylabel(selected_y_var)
plt.title("Scatterplot of Palmer's Penguins")
st.pyplot(fig)


st.title('Pandas Profiling of Penguin Dataset')
penguin_profile = ProfileReport(penguins_df, explorative=True)
st_profile_report(penguin_profile)
```

The resulting app contains this profile, which starts with an overview that contains information on the number of variables, any warnings about the dataset (for example, we are warned that some rows are missing gender information for our penguin dataset), and other base information. The following screenshot shows the top section of the profile:

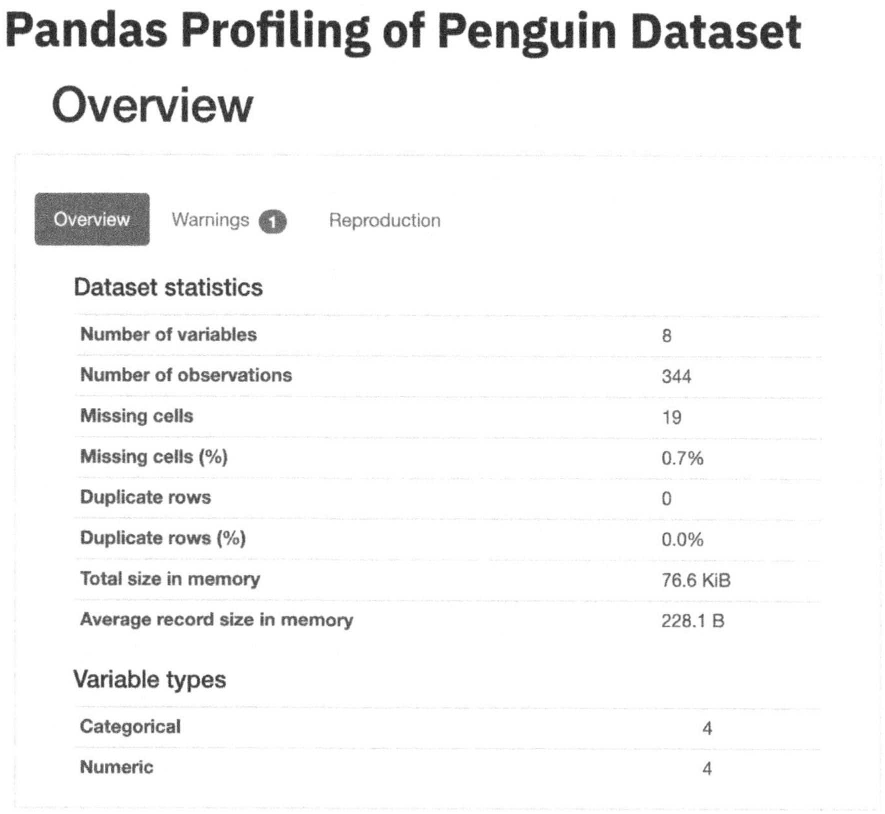

Pandas Profiling of Penguin Dataset

Overview

Overview	Warnings **1**	Reproduction

Dataset statistics

Number of variables	8
Number of observations	344
Missing cells	19
Missing cells (%)	0.7%
Duplicate rows	0
Duplicate rows (%)	0.0%
Total size in memory	76.6 KiB
Average record size in memory	228.1 B

Variable types

Categorical	4
Numeric	4

Figure 7.5 – pandas profile

I would strongly encourage you to try out this component yourself and see the massive amount of information generated from these couple of lines of code. It includes histograms and basic statistics about each variable, sample rows from the beginning and end of the dataset, and even a correlation matrix with an explanation of a few different correlation variables. The following screenshot shows the correlation section output for our penguin dataset—we can immediately see that body mass is positively correlated with the flipper length of our penguins:

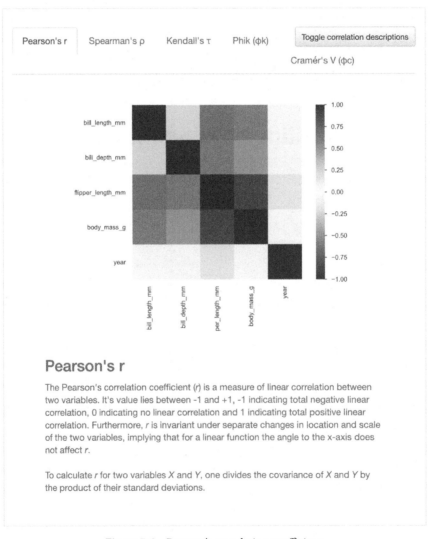

Figure 7.6 – Pearson's correlation coefficient

> **Note**
>
> Try this out yourself to see the full spectrum of colors.

Hopefully, you now have a solid understanding of how to use this component to add EDA, which should help if you are inviting users to bring their own dataset, as in the penguin example.

Finding more components

These three components are a tiny percentage of all the components the community has created, and by the time you may be reading this, I am sure the number of components out there will be dramatically higher. The best place to find new and interesting components is on either the Streamlit website at `https://streamlit.io/gallery?type=components&category=featured` or the discussion forums at `https://discuss.streamlit.io/tag/custom-components`. When you find a component that you think is interesting, try it out by downloading it with `pip` as we did earlier, and read enough documentation to get started!

Summary

At this point, I hope you feel very comfortable downloading and using Streamlit Components, which you have learned about here, as well as comfortable with finding new Streamlit components created by the community. You should also understand how to add GitHub gist examples, Lottie animations, and automatic `pandas-profiling` features to the apps you build.

In the next chapter, we will dive more deeply into deploying your own Streamlit apps with a cloud provider such as **Amazon Web Services (AWS)**.

8
Deploying Streamlit Apps with Heroku and AWS

In *Chapter 5, Deploying Streamlit with Streamlit Sharing*, we learned how to deploy our Streamlit applications with Streamlit Sharing. Streamlit Sharing is quick, easy, and very effective for most applications but has a few downsides, mainly that we are limited by only being able to host three free applications at once and that we also are limited in the computational power at hand. The following excerpt is from the Streamlit Sharing page:

Apps get up to 1 CPU, 800 MB of RAM, and 800 MB of dedicated storage in a shared execution environment.

If you are in a situation where you want to deploy more than three applications at a time, or you want more compute as you run, for example, more complex ML models that would benefit from a GPU or more RAM, then this chapter is for you! We will cover how to set up accounts with AWS and Heroku and how to fully deploy your Streamlit applications there.

In this chapter, we will cover the following topics:

- Choosing between AWS, Streamlit Sharing, and Heroku
- Deploying Streamlit with Heroku
- Deploying Streamlit with AWS

Technical requirements

Here is a list of installments required for this chapter:

- **Heroku account**: Heroku is a popular platform that data scientists and software engineers use to host their applications, models, and APIs (application programming interfaces), and is owned by Salesforce. To get a Heroku account, please head over to `https://signup.heroku.com` to make your free account.

- **Heroku Command-Line Interface (CLI)**: To use Heroku effectively, we will need to download the Heroku CLI, which will allow us to run Heroku commands. To download this, please follow the instructions listed here: `https://devcenter.heroku.com/articles/heroku-cli`.

- **Amazon Web Services (AWS) account**: Before we can use AWS, we first need to sign up for our own Amazon account, which you can do at `https://aws.amazon.com/free`. Thankfully, there is a generous free tier available for students with .edu accounts, for start-up founders and entrepreneurs, and also for non-profits. Once you do this, I would strongly recommend setting billing alerts on your account (see `https://console.aws.amazon.com/billing/home?#preferences` for more details) to make sure that you do not overshoot your free tier, and when you have deployed your own app, to make sure you are not spending more than desired.

- **PuTTy** (Windows only): If you are using Windows, you will need to download and install the PuTTY program, which allows Windows OSes to use a protocol called **Secure Shell (SSH)**. To download PuTTY, head over to `https://www.putty.org/` and follow the installation instructions. Then, wherever we are using SSH in this chapter, open PuTTY and follow the directions as normal!

Now that we have the requirements, let's begin!

Choosing between AWS, Streamlit Sharing, and Heroku

At a high level, whenever we are trying to deploy our Streamlit application such that users on the internet can see our applications, what we are really doing is renting a computer owned by someone else (such as Amazon) and giving that computer a set of instructions to start up our application. Choosing which platform to use is difficult to know how to do without either having a background in deploying systems or without trying each option out first, but there are a few heuristics that should help you out. The two most important factors for this decision are the flexibility of the system and the time it takes to get up and running. Note that these two factors directly trade off with one another. If you are using Streamlit Sharing, you cannot say "I want this to run on a macOS, and I want to add two GPUs to this app," and so on, but in return, you get a wildly simple process where you can simply point Streamlit Sharing to your GitHub repository, and it will take care of all the other little decisions that need to be made.

On the other hand, AWS and Heroku give you much more flexibility but take time to set up (as you will find out!). The biggest difference between the two is that Heroku is a *Platform as a Service product*, while Amazon is an *Infrastructure as a Service product*, which means, in practical terms, that Heroku gives you more flexibility than Streamlit Sharing by allowing you to do things such as provide more computational resources, and is faster to deploy than AWS, as you can see in the following graphic:

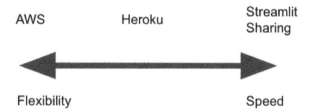

Figure 8.1 – Heroku versus AWS versus Sharing

The AWS advantage, however, is in its extreme flexibility. AWS will let you choose between Ubuntu, macOS, Windows, and Red Hat Linux, between dozens of different database types, and is seemingly infinitely customizable. When you are making your Streamlit applications, if you want to get out a quick prototype to test out an idea, Streamlit Sharing is perfect for you. For full-fledged public applications that need more compute, Heroku might be the best call. And if you require ultimate flexibility for a complex ML application, or if you are running a business entirely on Streamlit, then AWS might be the best call. Throughout the rest of this chapter, we will dive into how to deploy your own app on both AWS and Heroku, as we have covered Streamlit Sharing directly in *Chapter 5*, *Deploying Streamlit with Streamlit Sharing*. Let's get started with Heroku!

Deploying Streamlit with Heroku

Heroku is slightly faster and simpler than AWS, and more cumbersome than Streamlit Sharing. But if you have run out of your Streamlit Sharing repositories, or need some more compute than Sharing has to offer but require fewer configuration options than the infinite ones provided by AWS, then Heroku is the place for you. One other win is that you can get custom URLs for your apps with Heroku, which Streamlit Sharing does not support (yet!). To deploy our Streamlit apps on Heroku, we need to do the following:

1. Set up and log in to Heroku.
2. Clone and configure our local repository.
3. Deploy to Heroku.

Let's look at each of these steps in detail!

Setting up and logging in to Heroku

In the *Technical requirements* section of this chapter, we covered how to download Heroku and create an account. Now, we need to log in to our Heroku from our command line by running the following command and logging in when prompted:

```
heroku login
```

This will take us to the Heroku page, and once we log in, we will be good to go. This command will keep you logged in on your machine indefinitely unless your password changes or you purposely log out of Heroku.

Cloning and configuring our local repository

Next, we need to change our directory to where the penguin machine learning app is located. My app folder is inside my `Documents` folder, so the following command takes me there, but your folder might be different:

```
cd ~/Documents/penguin_ml
```

If you do not already have the repository downloaded locally with a corresponding repository on GitHub, go ahead and stop by *Chapter 5, Deploying Streamlit with Streamlit Sharing*, to see how to get started with GitHub. Instead, you can also run the following command to download the repository locally from my personal GitHub, just as we did with deploying from AWS:

```
git clone https://github.com/tylerjrichards/penguin_ml.git
```

It is highly encouraged that you practice with your own GitHub repository, as this is much better practice than cloning an app from me to use to deploy to Heroku.

Now we need to create a Heroku app with a unique name for our app with the next command (the app will be deployed as this name with `.heroku.com` appended to the end of it). Mine will be `penguin-machine-learning`, but go ahead and pick your own!

```
heroku create penguin-machine-learning
```

Once we have this, we need to explicitly make the connection between our Git repository and the Heroku app we have just created, which can be done with the following command:

```
heroku git:remote -a penguin-machine-learning
```

And finally, we are going to add two files to our repository that are needed to start up with Heroku, the `Procfile` file and the `streamlit_setup.sh` file. Heroku uses something called a **Procfile** as a way to declare which commands the app should perform when starting up, and also to tell Heroku what type of application this is. For our Heroku apps, we also need this Procfile to configure some setup for our app specific to Streamlit apps (such as the port configuration), and then also to run the `streamlit run` command to launch our app. Let's start by creating the `streamlit_setup.sh` file using the following command:

```
touch streamlit_setup.sh
```

We can open this file with our text editor and put the following lines inside it, which creates our familiar `config.toml` file in the base directory:

```
mkdir -p ~/.streamlit


echo "[server]
headless = true
port = $PORT
enableCORS = false
" > ~/.streamlit/config.toml
```

Once we save this file, we need to create a Procfile that runs this `streamlit_setup.sh` file and then also runs our Streamlit app:

```
touch Procfile
```

Within the `Procfile` file we just created, we will next add the following line:

```
web: sh streamlit_setup.sh && streamlit run penguins_streamlit.
py
```

Now that we have our Streamlit app all set up, our final step is to deploy to Heroku!

Deploying to Heroku

Before we deploy, we have a couple of new files on our app, so we need to add those to our Git repository using the following commands:

```
git add .
git commit -m 'added heroku files'
git push
```

And now, our final step in this chapter is to push to Heroku, which we can do with this next command:

```
git push heroku main
```

This will kick off the Heroku build, and soon enough we will see our Penguin app deployed to Heroku for anyone to go and view. The app we have been working on and just deployed can be found at the following link (with a screenshot attached!), `https://penguin-machine-learning.herokuapp.com/`, and the GitHub repository for this app can be found at `https://github.com/tylerjrichards/penguin_ml`. It is the same as the app we deployed on AWS earlier in the chapter, shown in the following screenshot:

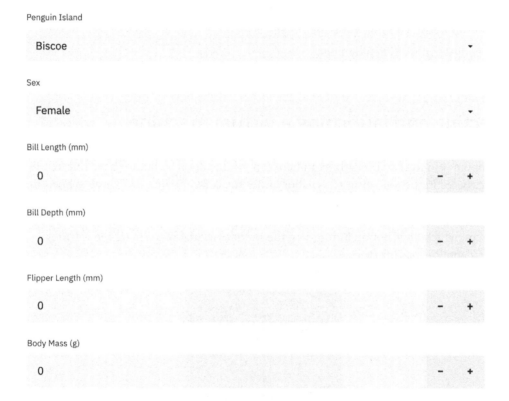

Penguin Classifier: A Machine Learning App

This app uses 6 inputs to predict the species of penguin using a model built on the Palmer's Penguin's dataset. Use the form below to get started!

Penguin Island

Biscoe

Sex

Female

Bill Length (mm)

0

Bill Depth (mm)

0

Flipper Length (mm)

0

Body Mass (g)

0

Predicting Your Penguin's Species:

We predict your penguin is of the Adelie species

We used a machine learning (Random Forest) model to predict the species, the features used in this prediction are ranked by relative importance below.

Figure 8.2 – Heroku App deployment

We have now successfully deployed one of our Streamlit apps on the Heroku platform, but if we need more control over the types of servers behind our app, we need to build directly on AWS, as demonstrated in the next section!

Deploying Streamlit with AWS

In comparison to deploying with Heroku, deploying apps on AWS is significantly more cumbersome but has seemingly infinite options. There are a few steps to deploying your own apps with AWS, and these include the following:

1. Selecting and launching a virtual machine
2. Installing the necessary software
3. Cloning and running your app
4. Long-term AWS deployment

We will run through these sequentially!

Selecting and launching a virtual machine

AWS has literally hundreds of service options for everything from deploying ML models to compute resources to everything in between. In this book so far, we have referred to the services listed in the following screenshot under the central name *AWS*, but to be more precise, we are going to be using **Amazon Elastic Compute Cloud**, or **Amazon EC2** for short. This next screenshot shows the breadth of services available just for compute resources, which does not include any of the services available for machine learning, business applications, or storage:

Figure 8.3 – AWS Compute

Amazon EC2 is a dynamic, pay-as-you-go service that will scale automatically based on use. If there are 10, 100, or 10,000 concurrent users of your Streamlit app, EC2 will change the compute resources given to your application to accommodate the users. You pay for what you use!

To get started, head over to `https://console.aws.amazon.com/ec2/v2/home` and click the button that says **Launch instance**, as shown in the following screenshot. Your default region may be different than mine, which is totally fine! AWS regions allow you to select where you want the compute to be physically located, in case your app needs low latency, or there are regulatory reasons for where your data is hosted (for example, because of **General Data Privacy Regulation** (**GDPR**), in the European Union). The overwhelming majority of the time, the default region AWS puts you in is perfectly fine:

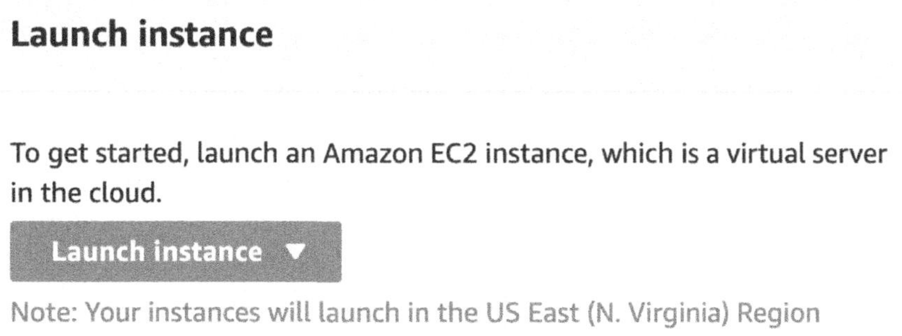

Launch instance

To get started, launch an Amazon EC2 instance, which is a virtual server in the cloud.

Launch instance ▼

Note: Your instances will launch in the US East (N. Virginia) Region

Figure 8.4 – EC2 launch

Once you launch your instance, there are seven tabs:

- **Choose AMI** (Amazon Machine Image) or the OS used by your virtual machine
- **Choose Instance Type** (choosing the compute/memory/storage of your virtual machine)
- **Configure Instance**
- **Add Storage**
- **Add Tags**
- **Configure Security Group**
- **Review**

You might be starting to understand what I was talking about earlier when I mentioned flexibility versus speed! Luckily, we only really need to start with a few of these, starting with choosing our AMI from a list of options. When we click the **Launch instance** button, we will see options including, but not limited to, the following:

- Amazon Linux 2 AMI

  This option is Amazon's own option, is free tier-eligible, and is designed to work well with EC2.

- Red Hat Enterprise Linux

  This option is an enterprise version of Linux created by the Red Hat foundation, which creates open source enterprise solutions (`https://www.redhat.com/en`). There are a variety of options depending on versions and volume type.

- Ubuntu Server

  Ubuntu is another open source OS built on Linux similar to Red Hat. They also have a variety of free and paid options, the same as Red Hat.

I would recommend selecting the OS that you are most comfortable with already. If you have already used Ubuntu servers, try the newest Ubuntu option, which is, in this case, Ubuntu Server 20.04. The most commonly used AMI options are all based on Linux, which is an open source OS with many flavors, including Red Hat, Debian, and Ubuntu.

To follow along with this chapter, select the default Amazon option, **Amazon Linux 2**. When you check this option and are taken to the **Choose Instance Type** page, select any type that is free tier-eligible, as shown in the following screenshot. Of course, if you would like to pay for more memory or vCPUs you absolutely can, but they are not necessary at this time:

	Family	Type	vCPUs ⓘ	Memory (GiB)	Instance Storage (GB) ⓘ	EBS-Optimized Available ⓘ	Network Performance ⓘ	IPv6 Support ⓘ
☐	t2	t2.nano	1	0.5	EBS only	-	Low to Moderate	Yes
☐	t2	t2.micro Free tier eligible	1	1	EBS only	-	Low to Moderate	Yes
☐	t2	t2.small	1	2	EBS only	-	Low to Moderate	Yes

Figure 8.5 – AWS AMI options

Next, we can skip past the next few options until you get to the sixth tab entitled **Configure Security Group**. There are a few edits that we need to make here:

- TCP Rule

  We need to set our **Security** settings in a way to allow other users online to interact with our web app by adding a new **Transmission Control Protocol (TCP)** rule by clicking **Add Rule** and setting the **Port Range** column to `8501`, the custom Streamlit port.

- Access Source

  We also need to allow anyone to access our app, so we will also set the source to **Anywhere**, as shown in the following screenshot:

Step 6: Configure Security Group

A security group is a set of firewall rules that control the traffic for your instance. On this page, you can add rules to allow specific traffic to reach your instance. For example, if you want to set up a web server and allow Internet traffic to reach your instance, add rules that allow unrestricted access to the HTTP and HTTPS ports. You can create a new security group or select from an existing one below. Learn more about Amazon EC2 security groups.

Assign a security group: ◉ Create a **new** security group
                          ○ Select an **existing** security group

Security group name: launch-wizard-11

Description: launch-wizard-11 created 2021-07-01T20:21:50.897-04:00

Type	Protocol	Port Range	Source	Description
SSH	TCP	22	Custom 0.0.0.0/0	e.g. SSH for Admin Desktop
Custom TCP F	TCP	8501	Anywhere 0.0.0.0/0, ::/0	Streamlit Port

Add Rule

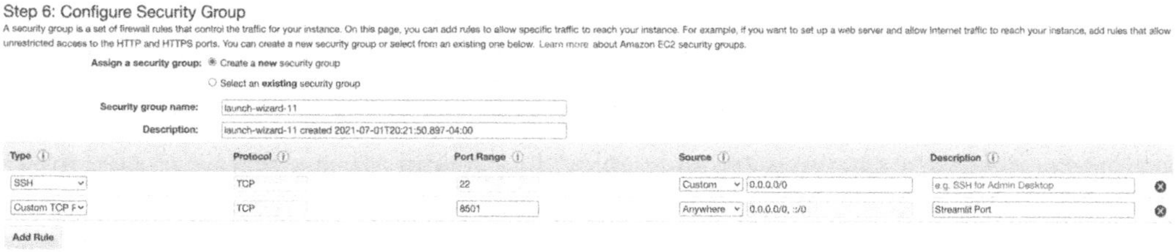

Figure 8.6 – Security settings

Now, we are ready to launch! Head over to the seventh tab, **Review**, and click the **Launch** button if everything looks correct. What will pop up next is a way to create a public and private key, one held by AWS and the other held by you, to allow you to access this new virtual computer from your command line, as shown in the following screenshot:

Select an existing key pair or create a new key pair   ✕

A key pair consists of a **public key** that AWS stores, and a **private key file** that you store. Together, they allow you to connect to your instance securely. For Windows AMIs, the private key file is required to obtain the password used to log into your instance. For Linux AMIs, the private key file allows you to securely SSH into your instance. Amazon EC2 supports ED25519 and RSA key pair types. ED25519 keys are smaller and faster while offering the same level of security as RSA keys. Use ED25519 keys to improve the speed of authentication or if you have regulatory requirements that mandate the use of ED25519 keys.

Note: The selected key pair will be added to the set of keys authorized for this instance. Learn more about removing existing key pairs from a public AMI.

Create a new key pair

Key pair name

Download Key Pair

💬 You have to download the **private key file** (*.pem file) before you can continue. **Store it in a secure and accessible location.** You will not be able to download the file again after it's created.

Cancel   Launch Instances

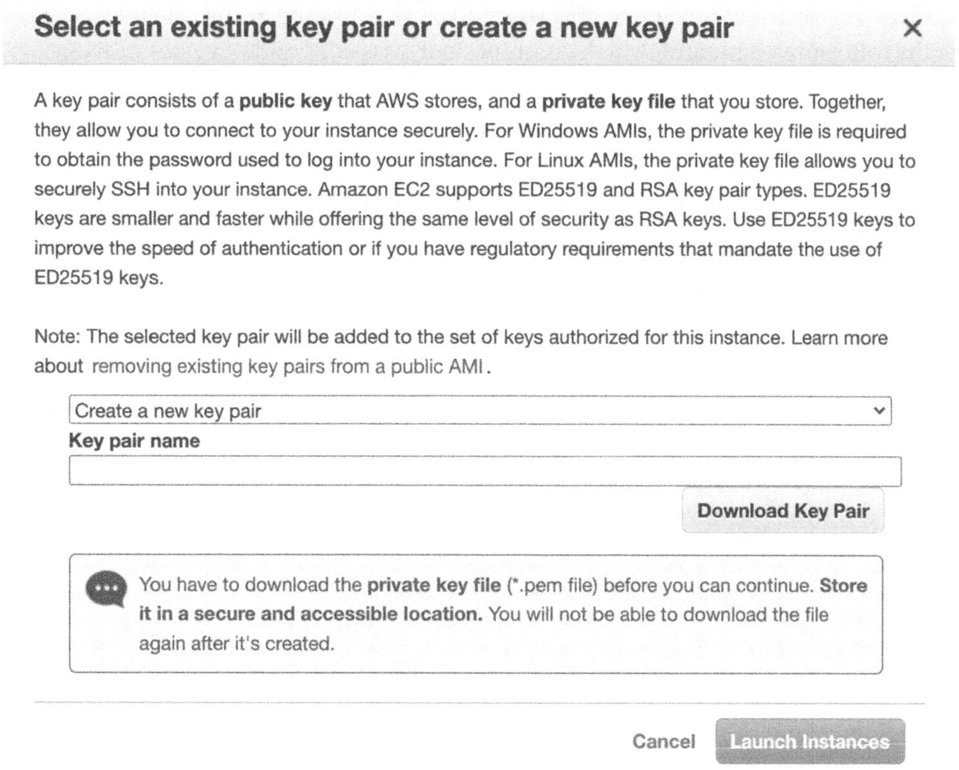

Figure 8.7 – Key-value pairs

Think of it like a unique password that is downloaded as its own file. You can keep this file wherever is easiest and most secure for you, but make sure to never upload this file to a public location, such as a GitHub repository, otherwise, others could come and access your virtual machine! Now that we have launched our EC2 instance, we can access it from our command line and download our app.

Installing the necessary software

For this example, we are going to try and deploy the penguin ML app that we created in *Chapter 4*, *Using Machine Learning with Streamlit*, and deployed in *Chapter 5*, *Deploying Streamlit with Streamlit Sharing*, on Streamlit Sharing. Now that we have our virtual machine and our objective, we need to access our virtual machine from our command line. To begin, we need to first find out the AWS instance's public DNS. Locate your AWS instance using this link, `https://console.aws.amazon.com/ec2/v2/home#Instances`, and look for **Public DNS**, which will be in the format `ec2-10-857-84-485.compute-1.amazonaws.com`. I made up those numbers, but yours should be close to this.

Now, we can access our virtual machine using SSH, which is the Secure Shell Protocol, using the following command, which combines our password and our public DNS:

```
ssh -i "path_to_private_key.pem" ec2-user@<insert_Public_DNS>
```

Often, AWS commands feel like magic incantations, especially when you are first getting started. After some experience, you will certainly get more comfortable with this. At this point, AWS may ask you some questions on the command line about allowing certain types of access depending on how your security settings are set up on your local machine, and after you confirm that you would like to connect, you will know that you are connected if you see something similar to the following screenshot:

```
[→  Downloads ssh -i "streamlit_demo_app.pem" ec2-user@ec2-50-19-244-235.compute-1.amazonaws.com
[Last login: Sat Apr 17 18:07:56 2021 from c-73-189-60-197.hsd1.ca.comcast.net

      __|  __|_  )
      _|  (     /    Amazon Linux 2 AMI
      ___|\___|___|

https://aws.amazon.com/amazon-linux-2/
36 package(s) needed for security, out of 54 available
Run "sudo yum update" to apply all updates.
[ec2-user@ip-172-31-52-196 ~]$
```

Figure 8.8 – AWS login

This is your own new virtual computer! There are no programs, folders, or really almost anything else on this computer; it is brand new right out of the Amazon box. Each computer that we rent out using ec2 starts out with next to nothing, so we have to download all that we need for this project. There are a good number of ways in which to do this. We can do the following:

- Install everything manually.

- Install a prepackaged installer such as Anaconda or Miniconda.

- Use Docker to create a set of installation instructions.

I would advise going with the second option for most use cases, as Anaconda or Miniconda are designed to handle all the difficulties that come with installing Python, dealing with our path, and also with installing various Python and R packages. Anaconda, and its bootstrapped (that is, smaller) version, Miniconda, are notorious for making installation difficult outside of their environment on your computer. If you require other installations of Python on your virtual or local machine, I would advocate either *option 1* or *option 3*.

For installing and setting up Miniconda on our virtual machine, we can run the following commands, which use wget to download Miniconda to the file location, ~/ miniconda.sh, then run the installation file using bash, and then change our path so that we can use conda more easily to download packages:

```
wget https://repo.continuum.io/miniconda/Miniconda3-latest-
Linux-x86_64.sh -O ~/miniconda.sh
bash ~/miniconda.sh -b -p ~/miniconda
export PATH="$HOME/miniconda/bin":$PATH
```

Great! Now we have the latest versions of python, pip, and a whole host of Python packages. Miniconda does not come with Streamlit, however, so we will use the next command to download, install, and test the installation of Streamlit by launching the Streamlit demo app:

```
pip install Streamlit
streamlit hello
```

When we run this command, we should see the following in our terminal (albeit with different network and external URLs):

```
[ec2-user@ip-172-31-52-196 ~]$ streamlit hello

Welcome to Streamlit. Check out our demo in your browser.

Network URL: http://172.31.52.196:8501
External URL: http://50.19.244.235:8501

Ready to create your own Python apps super quickly?
Head over to https://docs.streamlit.io

May you create awesome apps!
```

Figure 8.9 – First Streamlit command

When you head over to the external URL from any browser, you will see the Streamlit demo app, as shown in the following screenshot:

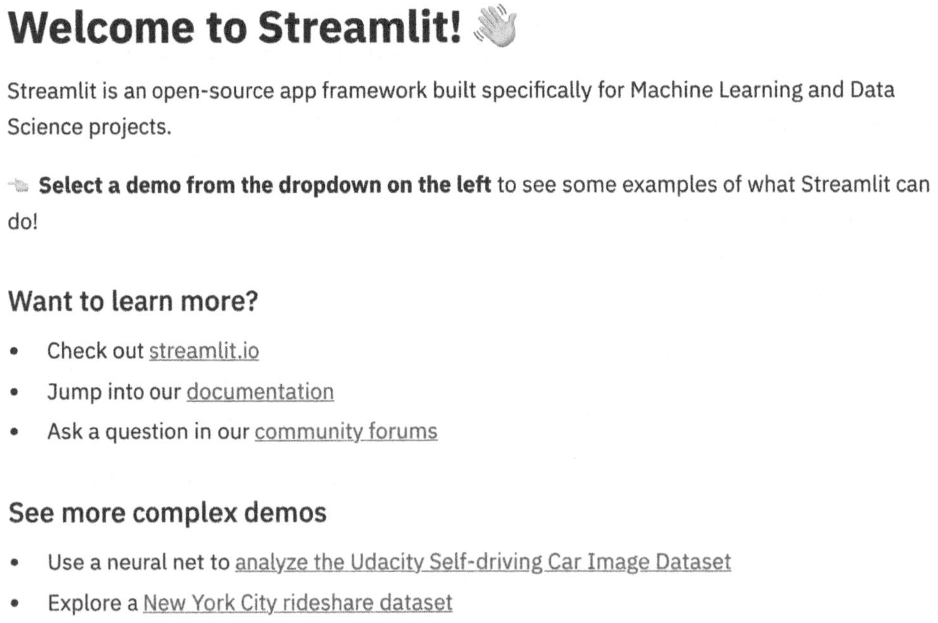

Welcome to Streamlit! 👋

Streamlit is an open-source app framework built specifically for Machine Learning and Data Science projects.

👈 **Select a demo from the dropdown on the left** to see some examples of what Streamlit can do!

Want to learn more?

- Check out streamlit.io
- Jump into our documentation
- Ask a question in our community forums

See more complex demos

- Use a neural net to analyze the Udacity Self-driving Car Image Dataset
- Explore a New York City rideshare dataset

Figure 8.10 – Streamlit demo

We have now deployed our very first Streamlit app from AWS. Now, to deploy a Streamlit app that we have built.

Cloning and running your app

We now have a virtual machine that can run Streamlit, and our next step is to download our own app onto our machine. The most straightforward method for doing this is by using Git and cloning the repository where your penguin machine learning app is held. If you have not already done this in *Chapter 5, Deploying Streamlit with Streamlit Sharing*, feel free to use my GitHub repository at `https://github.com/tylerjrichards/penguin_ml.git`. The following code downloads `git` and then downloads our app from GitHub:

```
conda install git
git clone https://github.com/tylerjrichards/penguin_ml.git
```

This will make a new folder in our current directory called `penguin_ml`, which contains all the files for the Streamlit app. This app requires a few more libraries than come from Miniconda, such as Seaborn and scikit-learn, so we need to download them before we run our app. We have already placed the names of these libraries into a file called `requirements.txt`, so we need to point `pip` to the file using the next set of commands:

```
cd penguin_ml
pip install -r penguin_ml/requirements.txt
```

Now, our final step is to run our Streamlit app:

```
streamlit run penguins_streamlit.py
```

When we go to the external URL in our AWS terminal, we will see our Streamlit app fully functioning there, as shown in the following screenshot:

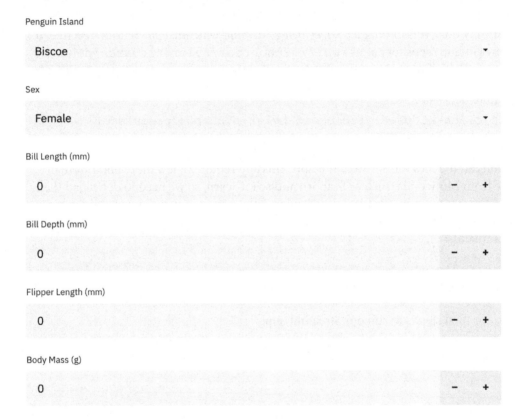

Penguin Classifier: A Machine Learning App

This app uses 6 inputs to predict the species of penguin using a model built on the Palmer's Penguin's dataset. Use the form below to get started!

Penguin Island

Biscoe

Sex

Female

Bill Length (mm)

0

Bill Depth (mm)

0

Flipper Length (mm)

0

Body Mass (g)

0

Predicting Your Penguin's Species:

We predict your penguin is of the Adelie species

We used a machine learning (Random Forest) model to predict the species, the features used in this prediction are ranked by relative importance below.

Figure 8.11 – AWS Penguin app

And there we go! We now have our app running on AWS, visible to the entire world. From this point, we can link to our app from a personal website you may already have or send it to others who may be interested in classifying their own set of penguins.

Long-term AWS deployment

Our final problem is that the SSH session we have running to connect our local machine to AWS needs to be running in order for the Streamlit app to stay up. For most use cases, this will not work as you will ideally want the user to interact with your Streamlit app if your local computer disconnects from AWS. Enter tmux, or the terminal mutiplexer, which can keep a terminal session going regardless of our local connection to it. To download tmux, we can run the following command while connected to our AWS virtual machine:

```
sudo yum install tmux
```

And now, we can begin a new tmux session and kick off our Streamlit app by running these next commands:

```
tmux
```
```
streamlit run penguins_streamlit.py
```

If our connection to AWS gets disconnected, tmux will keep our app running. We can leave the tmux session at any time by pressing *Ctrl + D* and can re-enter the session by running tmux attach.

And that covers deploying Streamlit with AWS! As you can see, Streamlit Sharing handles the majority of these difficulties out of the box, so I would make an effort to make Streamlit Sharing work whenever possible. However, this session should have given you an appreciation for the true breadth of options and configuration controls in front of us when we use AWS, which may come in handy in the future.

Summary

This has been by far the most technical of our chapters so far, so congratulations on making it through! Deploying applications is notoriously difficult and time-consuming, and requires skills from software engineering and DevOps, along with often requiring experience with version control software (such as Git) and Unix-style commands and systems. This is part of the reason why Streamlit Sharing is such a crucial innovation, but in this chapter, we have learned how to push the edge of Streamlit deployment through renting our own virtual machines and deploying these on AWS and Heroku. We have also learned how to figure out what the right deployment strategy is before starting out, which will save hours or days of work (nothing is worse than finishing the deployment of an app and finding out you need to use another platform!).

Next, we'll be moving on to the third and final section of this book, which will focus on the various applications of Streamlit, starting with improving job applications with Streamlit. This next chapter will focus on impressing hiring managers and recruiters with Streamlit applications, on using Streamlit apps within actual job application sections, such as the infamous take-home portion of many interviews, and also on proof-of-skill data projects for improving on the data science résumé.

Section 3: Streamlit Use Cases

Now that we understand how to create and deploy Streamlit apps, this section will focus on the various use cases of Streamlit. We'll go through practical examples of complicated projects and interview power users to find out everything that they can do using Streamlit.

The following chapters are covered in this section:

- *Chapter 9, Improving Job Applications with Streamlit*
- *Chapter 10, The Data Project – Prototyping Projects in Streamlit*
- *Chapter 11, Using Streamlit for Teams*
- *Chapter 12, Interviews with Power Users*

9
Improving Job Applications with Streamlit

At this point in this book, you should already be an experienced Streamlit user. You have a good grasp of everything – from Streamlit design to deployment, to data visualization, and everything in between. This chapter is designed to be application-focused; it will show you some great use cases for Streamlit applications so that you can be inspired to create your own! We will start by demonstrating how to use Streamlit for *Proof Of Skill Data Projects*. Then, we will then move on to discuss how to use Streamlit in the *Take Home* sections of job applications.

In this chapter, we will cover the following topics:

- Using Streamlit for proof of skill data projects
- Improving job applications in Streamlit

Technical requirements

The following is a list of software and hardware installations that are required for this chapter:

- `streamlit-lottie`: To download this library, run the following code in your Terminal:

```
pip install streamlit-lottie
```

  Interestingly, `streamlit-lottie` uses the `lottie` open source library, which allows us to add web-native animations (such as a GIF) to our Streamlit apps. Frankly, it is a wonderful library that you can use to beautify Streamlit apps and was created by Andy Fanilo, a prolific Streamlit app creator.

- The job application example folder: The central repository for this book can be found at https://github.com/tylerjrichards/Getting-Started-with-Streamlit-for-Data-Science. Within this repository, the `job_application_example` folder will contain some of the files that you will need for the second section of the chapter, covering job applications. If you do not have this main repository downloaded already, use the following code in your Terminal to clone it:

```
git clone https://github.com/tylerjrichards/Getting-Started-with-Streamlit-for-Data-Science
```

Now that we have everything set up, let's begin!

Using Streamlit for proof of skill data projects

Proving to others that you are a skilled data scientist is notoriously difficult. Anyone can put Python or machine learning on their résumé or even work in a research group at a university that might do some machine learning. But often, recruiters, professors you want to work with, and data science managers rely on things on your résumé that are proxies for competence, such as having attended the "right" university or already having a fancy data science internship or job.

Prior to Streamlit, there were not many effective solutions to this problem. If you put a Python file or Jupyter Notebook on your GitHub profile, the time it would take for someone to understand whether the work was impressive or not was too much of a risk to take. If the recruiter has to click on the right repository in your GitHub profile and then click through numerous files until they find the Jupyter notebook with unreadable code (without comments), you've already lost them. If the recruiter sees "machine learning" on your résumé, but it takes five clicks to see any machine learning product or code that you've written, you've already lost them. Most interested parties will spend a very small amount of time on your résumé; on average, visitors to my personal portfolio site (`www.tylerjrichards.com`) spend around 2 minutes on the site before moving elsewhere.

One solution to this issue is to try creating and sharing Streamlit apps that are specific to the skills that you would like to showcase the most broadly. For instance, if you have a lot of experience in fundamental statistics, you might create a Streamlit app that proves, or illustrates, a fundamental statistical theorem such as the central limit theorem – just as we did earlier in this book. If instead, you have experience in natural language processing, you could create an app that shows off a new text-generating neural network that you have created. The point here is to minimize the number of clicks someone would need to make until they get proof of your competence within a desired area.

Many of the Streamlit apps that we have created already do serve this purpose. Let's run through a few examples.

Machine learning – the Penguins app

In *Chapter 4, Using Machine Learning with Streamlit*, we created a random forest model that was trained on our Palmer's Penguin dataset to predict the species of penguin according to features such as weight, island of habitation, and bill length. Then, we saved that model so that we could use it in our Streamlit app.

To produce our Streamlit app, we need (in the first iteration) to run the following code. This will create the model to be deployed:

```python
import pandas as pd
from sklearn.metrics import accuracy_score
from sklearn.ensemble import RandomForestClassifier
from sklearn.model_selection import train_test_split
import pickle


penguin_df = pd.read_csv('penguins.csv')
penguin_df.dropna(inplace=True)
output = penguin_df['species']
features = penguin_df[['island', 'bill_length_mm', 'bill_depth_
mm',
                       'flipper_length_mm', 'body_mass_g',
'sex']]
features = pd.get_dummies(features)
output, uniques = pd.factorize(output)


x_train, x_test, y_train, y_test = train_test_split(
    features, output, test_size=.8)
rfc = RandomForestClassifier(random_state=15)
rfc.fit(x_train, y_train)
y_pred = rfc.predict(x_test)
score = accuracy_score(y_pred, y_test)
print('Our accuracy score for this model is {}'.format(score))
```

In this first section, we import our libraries, load our data, and train/evaluate our model while printing out the evaluation results. Then, we save the model results to the `pickle` files using the following code:

```python
rf_pickle = open('random_forest_penguin.pickle', 'wb')
pickle.dump(rfc, rf_pickle)
rf_pickle.close()
output_pickle = open('output_penguin.pickle', 'wb')
pickle.dump(uniques, output_pickle)
output_pickle.close()
```

Recall that at the end of the chapter, we added a new feature so that if a user uploaded their own dataset, they could use our model training script to train a model entirely on their data (provided it was in the same format; it came with some preconditions).

This app, in its final form, shows that we have, at least, some knowledge about data cleaning, how to do one-hot encoding on our variables, how we think about evaluating our models on test data, and finally, how to deploy our pre-trained models in an application. That alone is going to look much better than just putting "machine learning" on our résumé, and it shows evidence of some of the skills that we have. Without this proof of skill, the recruiter or hiring manager who is looking at our application will have to either trust that we are being entirely honest on our résumé (and from reading hundreds of résumés over the years, that is a bad assumption to make) or use a proxy for confidence such as a university degree (this is also a bad proxy for assessing competence).

In addition to this, when we deployed this app to Streamlit Sharing in *Chapter 5, Deploying Streamlit with Streamlit Sharing*, we discussed an automatic feature that comes free with Streamlit Sharing: the **View app source** button. As you can see in the following screenshot, when we deploy our apps, Streamlit adds a button to the user's **Settings** drop-down menu that allows them to view the source code behind the app:

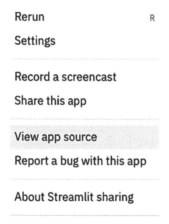

Figure 9.1 – The View app source option

In this way, users can always check to make sure malicious code (for example, whether a researcher's Penguin data is not being stored by the app) is not being deployed by Streamlit Sharing. As a secondary feature, the user can also view the code that you wrote to built the app, which improves the ability for us to use Streamlit as a *Proof of Skill* tool.

Visualization – the Pretty Trees app

In *Chapter 6, Beautifying Streamlit Apps*, we worked on a Streamlit application that could create beautiful and dynamic visualizations of trees in San Francisco, which resulted in the following app:

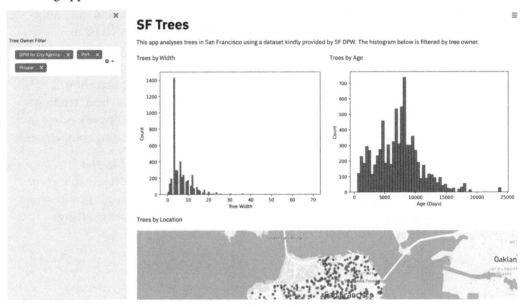

Figure 9.2 – Mapping a web app

Within this app, we had to create multiple different visualizations (that is, two histograms and one map) that dynamically updated based on the user inputs on the right-hand side. With an app like this, we were able to show off our data manipulation skills, our familiarity with the pandas, Matplotlib, and Seaborn libraries, and even that we understood how to deal with datetimes in Python. Let's take a look at the section of the app's code that focuses on visualization:

```
#define multiple columns, add two graphs
col1, col2 = st.beta_columns(2)
with col1:
    st.write('Trees by Width')
    fig_1, ax_1 = plt.subplots()
    ax_1 = sns.histplot(trees_df['dbh'],
        color=graph_color)
    plt.xlabel('Tree Width')
    st.pyplot(fig_1)
with col2:
```

```
      st.write('Trees by Age')
      fig_2, ax_2 = plt.subplots()
      ax_2 = sns.histplot(trees_df['age'],
            color=graph_color)
      plt.xlabel('Age (Days)')
      st.pyplot(fig_2)


st.write('Trees by Location')
trees_df = trees_df.dropna(subset=['longitude', 'latitude'])
trees_df = trees_df.sample(n = 1000, replace=True)
st.map(trees_df)
```

This code is fairly easy to read for anyone who is familiar with Python or other scripting languages, and it is a heck of a lot better than simply putting "data visualization" or "pandas" on a résumé.

At this point, I hope you are convinced. Streamlit apps are an excellent way to showcase your work to recruiters, potential hiring managers, or anyone to whom you need to prove your set of skills. In the next section, we will cover this process in a little more detail and demonstrate how to use Streamlit to bolster your applications to companies that you might want to work for.

Improving job applications in Streamlit

Often, data science and machine learning job applications rely on take-home data science challenges to judge candidates. Frankly, this is a brutal and annoying experience that companies can demand because of the dynamic between the applicant and the employer. For instance, it could take a candidate 5–10 hours to fully complete a data science challenge, but it might only take the employer 10 minutes to evaluate it. Additionally, an individual virtual or telephone interview might take 30–45 minutes for the employer, plus an extra 15 minutes to write up feedback, compared to the same 30–45 minutes for the applicant. Because getting 5–10 hours of work gives them a very high signal per minute of employee time, employers have trended toward including these challenges within their job applications.

You can use the opportunity here to use Streamlit to stand out from the crowd by creating a fully functioning application instead of sending the company a Jupyter Notebook, Word document, or PowerPoint deck.

Questions

Let's walk through a fictional example about a job applicant who is in the middle of applying to a major US airline. They are given two main questions to solve – one has a dataset included:

- **Question 1: Airport distance**

  The first exercise asks, "Given the included dataset of airports and locations (in latitude and longitude), write a function that takes an airport code as input and returns the airports listed from nearest to furthest from the input airport."

- **Question 2: Representation**

  The second question asks, "How would you transform a collection of searches into a numeric vector representing a trip? Assume that we have hundreds of thousands of users and we want to represent all of their trips this way. Ideally, we want this to be a general representation that we could use in multiple different modeling projects, but we definitely care about finding similar trips. How, precisely, would you compare two trips to see how similar they are? What information do you feel might be missing from the preceding data that would help improve your representation?"

> **Note**
> Don't worry about writing code in this section; you can simply describe any transformations of data that you would perform. Your description should be clear enough so that a data scientist reading it would know how to implement your solution if necessary.

Now that we have the required questions, we can get a new Streamlit app started. To do this, I went through the same process that we have used in each chapter thus far. We create a new folder for our app within our central folder (`streamlit_apps`), called `job_application_example`. Within this folder, we can create a Python file, called `job_streamlit.py`, in our Terminal, using the following command:

```
touch job_streamlit.py
```

Answering Question 1

It is not hugely important for you to understand exactly how to answer the problem at hand, but the overall framework is quite important. The Streamlit app we create should read like an incredibly dynamic document that answers the question in a unique way, depending on the ability of Streamlit to make an application that could not easily be replicated by an applicant with a Word document.

To begin, we can create a title that introduces us and kicks off the format for the whole application. One improvement here is to add an optional animation at the top of the application using the streamlit-lottie library that we learned about in *Chapter 7, Exploring Streamlit Components*, as shown in the following code:

```python
import streamlit as st
from streamlit_lottie import st_lottie
import pandas as pd
import requests

def load_lottieurl(url: str):
    r = requests.get(url)
    if r.status_code != 200:
        return None
    return r.json()

lottie_airplane = load_lottieurl('https://assets4.lottiefiles.com/packages/lf20_jhu1lqdz.json')
st_lottie(lottie_airplane, speed=1, height=200, key="initial")

st.title('Major US Airline Job Application')
st.write('by Tyler Richards')
st.subheader('Question 1: Airport Distance')
```

The preceding code will create an application with a beautiful airplane animation at the top, as presented in the following screenshot:

Major US Airline Job Application

by Tyler Richards

Question 1: Airport Distance

Figure 9.3 – An airplane GIF

Next, we need to copy and paste the question below our subheader. Streamlit has many options for putting text into applications. One option that we have not used yet is to wrap our text inside three apostrophe signs, which tells Streamlit to write this text using the markdown language. This is useful for large blocks of text, such as the following one, which begins to answer the first question:

```
'''
The first exercise asks us 'Given the table of airports and
locations (in latitude and longitude) below,
write a function that takes an airport code as input and
returns the airports listed from nearest to furthest from
the input airport.' There are three steps here:

1. Load Data
2. Implement Distance Algorithm
3. Apply distance formula across all airports other than the
input
4. Return sorted list of airports Distance
'''
```

As mentioned in the *Technical requirements* section of this chapter, two files are needed to complete this application. The first is the dataset of the airport locations (called `airport_location.csv`), and the second is a picture that shows the Haversine distance (that is, the distance between two points on a sphere; the file is appropriately named `haversine.png`). Please copy those files into the same folder as the Streamlit application Python file.

Now, we need to complete the first step: loading the data. We need to both complete this step in Streamlit and also show the code to the user. This is different from other Streamlit applications, where the code is hidden in the background. However, because the user definitely wants to see our code, as they will be assessing us on it, we need to do both. We can use the `st.echo()` function, which we used previously, to print out the code block to our app. We can do this with the following code:

```
airport_distance_df = pd.read_csv('airport_location.csv')

with st.echo():
    #load necessary data
    airport_distance_df = pd.read_csv('airport_location.csv')
```

I would like to note here that we have placed a comment at the top of this code. This is not for the purpose of annotating code for you, the reader, but for the application reader. It is good practice to occasionally comment on the purpose of the code that you are writing both within the code and in the blocks of text before and after; this is so that the reader understands the approach you are trying to take. This is especially important in a job application but is good practice for collaborative Streamlit apps, too.

Our next step is to explain the Haversine formula and show the image in our Streamlit application, which we have done in the following code block. It is totally acceptable to take a narrative format in your blocks of text. Simply imagine what you would like to read as a hiring manager and try to replicate that as well as you can:

```
'''
From some quick googling, I found that the haversine distance
is
a good approximation for distance. At least good enough to get
the
distance between airports! Haversine distances can be off by up
to .5%,
because the earth is not actually a sphere. It looks like the
latitudes
and longitudes are in degrees, so I'll make sure to have a way
to account
for that as well. The haversine distance formula is labeled
below,
followed by an implementation in python
'''
st.image('haversine.png')
```

Now, our application should look similar to the following screenshot:

Question 1: Airport Distance

The first exercise asks us 'Given the table of airports and locations (in latitude and longitude) below, write a function that takes an airport code as input and returns the airports listed from nearest to furthest from the input airport.' There are three steps here:

1. Load Data

2. Implement Distance Algorithm

3. Apply distance formula across all airports other than the input

4. Return sorted list of airports Distance

```
#load necessary data
airport_distance_df = pd.read_csv('airport_location.csv')
```

From some quick googling, I found that the haversine distance is a good approximation for distance. At least good enough to get the distance between airports! Haversine distances can be off by up to .5%, because the earth is not actually a sphere. It looks like the latitudes and longitudes are in degrees, so I'll make sure to have a way to account for that as well. The haversine distance formula is labeled below, followed by an implementation in python

$$a = \sin^2(\frac{\Delta\varphi}{2}) + \cos\varphi1 \cdot \cos\varphi2 \cdot \sin^2(\frac{\Delta\lambda}{2})$$

$$c = 2 \cdot atan2(\sqrt{a}, \sqrt{(1-a)})$$

$$d = R \cdot c$$

Figure 9.4 – Loading the data for Question 1

We have our list of items to address, the animation, the Haversine distance formula, and the basic code to read in the data. At this point, we need to implement the Haversine distance formula in Python and also show our implementation:

```
with st.echo():
        from math import radians, sin, cos, atan2, sqrt
        def haversine_distance(long1, lat1, long2, lat2,
degrees=False):
            #degrees vs radians
            if degrees == True:
                long1 = radians(long1)
```

```
        lat1 = radians(lat1)
        long2 = radians(long2)
        lat2 = radians(lat2)


    #implementing haversine
        a = sin((lat2-lat1) / 2)**2 + cos(lat1) * cos(lat2) *
sin((long2-long1) / 2)**2
        c = 2*atan2(sqrt(a), sqrt(1-a))
        distance = 6371 * c #radius of earth in kilometers
    return(distance)
```

The first section of our code does not create our function but instead, prints out the function that we will create to the Streamlit app. This is so that the reader of the application can view both pieces of important code that we have written and interact with the code itself. If we just created a function to implement the Haversine distance, the reader of our application would not really know how we solved the problem at hand! The following code block creates this function:

```
#execute haversine function definition
from math import radians, sin, cos, atan2, sqrt
def haversine_distance(long1, lat1, long2, lat2,
degrees=False):
    #degrees vs radians
    if degrees == True:
        long1 = radians(long1)
        lat1 = radians(lat1)
        long2 = radians(long2)
        lat2 = radians(lat2)


    #implementing haversine
    a = sin((lat2-lat1) / 2)**2 + cos(lat1) * cos(lat2) *
sin((long2-long1) / 2)**2
    c = 2*atan2(sqrt(a), sqrt(1-a))
    distance = 6371 * c #radius of earth in kilometers
    return(distance)
```

We have completed our Haversine implementation! Whenever we want to find the distance between two locations, we can call our formula, input the longitude and latitude, and get the distance in kilometers. This app is useful; however, at the moment, it is not much better than a Word document. Our next step is to allow the user to input their own points to check and see whether the Haversine distance is working. Almost no one knows how many kilometers apart two points on the globe are, so I have included default points and checked the real distance between them:

```
'''
Now, we need to test out our function! The
distance between the default points is
18,986 kilometers, but feel free to try out
your own points of interest.
'''
long1 = st.number_input('Longitude 1', value = 2.55)
long2 = st.number_input('Longitude 2', value = 172.00)
lat1 = st.number_input('Latitude 1', value = 49.01)
lat2 = st.number_input('Latitude 2', value = -43.48)

test_distance = haversine_distance(long1 = long1, long2 =
long2,
          lat1 = lat1, lat2 = lat2, degrees=True)
st.write('Your distance is: {} kilometers'.format(int(test_
distance)))
```

When we put in our default values, the app returns a distance that is approximately 2 kilometers off, as shown in the following screenshot:

Now, we need to test out our function! The distance between the default points is 18,986 kilometers, but feel free to try out your own points of interest.

Longitude 1

2.55   −   +

Longitude 2

172.00   −   +

Latitude 1

49.01   −   +

Latitude 2

−43.48   −   +

Your distance is: 18998 kilometers

Figure 9.5 – Implementing the Haversine distance

At this point, our next step is to combine all of the pieces by using the implemented Haversine distance calculator on our given dataset. This is briefly shown in the following screenshot:

	Airport Code	Lat	Long
0	CDG	49.0128	2.5500
1	CHC	-43.4894	172.5320
2	DYR	64.7349	177.7410
3	EWR	40.6925	-74.1687
4	HNL	21.3187	-157.9220
5	OME	64.5122	-165.4450
6	ONU	-20.6500	-178.7000
7	PEK	40.0801	116.5850

Figure 9.6 – The airport distances that have been given

This dataset has airport codes and their corresponding `lat` and `long` values. The following code block introduces a solution that combines the two distances and leaves out the full `get_distance_list` function, as it is simply a copy of the function that we have implemented twice already:

```
'''
We have the Haversine distance implemented, and we also have
proven to ourselves that it works reasonably well.
Our next step is to implement this in a function!
'''


def get_distance_list(airport_dataframe, airport_code):
    df = airport_dataframe.copy()
    row = df[df.loc[:,'Airport Code'] == airport_code]
    lat = row['Lat']
    long = row['Long']
    df = df[df['Airport Code'] != airport_code]
    df['Distance'] = df.apply(lambda x: haversine_
distance(lat1=lat, long1=long,
        lat2 = x.Lat, long2 = x.Long, degrees=True), axis=1)
    return(df.sort_values(by='Distance').reset_index()['Airport
Code'])


with st.echo():
    def get_distance_list(airport_dataframe, airport_code):
        *copy of function above with comments*
```

Finally, we can implement this distance formula on the dataframe we have been given. We can allow the user to input their own airport code from the options that we have data on and return the correct values:

```
'''
To use this function, select an airport from the airports
provided in the dataframe
and this application will find the distance between each one,
and
return a list of the airports closest to furthest.
```

```
'''
```

```
selected_airport = st.selectbox('Airport Code', airport_
distance_df['Airport Code'])
distance_airports = get_distance_list(
    airport_dataframe=airport_distance_df, airport_
code=selected_airport)
st.write('Your closest airports in order are {}'.
format(list(distance_airports)))
```

This is the end of our first question. We can add an optional section at the end about how we would change our implementation if we had more time to work on this problem. This is always a good idea if you know you only want to spend a few hours on the total application, but you also want to demonstrate that you know how to improve it if you had more time. An example of this is shown in the following code block, to be placed directly after the preceding code block:

```
'''
This all seems to work just fine! There are a few ways I would
improve this if I was working on

this for a longer period of time.

1. I would implement the [Vincenty Distance](https://
en.wikipedia.org/wiki/Vincenty%27s_formulae)

instead of the Haversine distance, which is much more accurate
but cumbersome to implement.

2. I would vectorize this function and make it more efficient
overall.

Because this dataset is only 7 rows long, it wasn't
particularly important,

but if this was a crucial function that was run in production
we would want to vectorize it for speed.
'''
```

Alternatively, you could always just end with a statement about the preceding code and move on to the second question. At this point, our answer to *Question 1* is complete and should look similar to the following screenshot:

To use this function, select an airport from the airports provided in the dataframe and this application will find the distance between each one, and return a list of the airports closest to furthest.

Airport Code

DYR

Your closest airports in order are ['OME', 'PEK', 'HNL', 'EWR', 'CDG', 'ONU', 'CHC']

This all seems to work just fine! There are a few ways I would improve this if I was working on this for a longer period of time.
1. I would implement the Vincenty Distance instead of the Haversine distance, which is much more accurate but cumbersome to implement.
2. I would vectorize this function and make it more efficient overall. Because this dataset is only 7 rows long, it wasn't particularly important, but if this was a crucial function that was run in production we would want to vectorize it for speed.

Figure 9.7 – Taking user input

We have now successfully answered *Question 1*! We can always check the distances between these airports by hand to obtain the same result. But let's move on to the second question in our application.

Answering Question 2

The second question is far more straightforward and only asks for text responses. Here, the trick is to try to add some lists or Python objects in order to break up large paragraphs of text. To begin, we will explain our attempt at answering the question and then demonstrate how it might look inside a dataframe:

```
'''
For this transformation, there are a few things
that I would start with. First, I would have to define
what a unique trip actually was. In order to do this, I would
group by the origin, the destination, and the departure date
(for the departure date, often customers will change around
```

```
this departure date, so we should group by the date plus or
minus at least 1 buffer day to capture all the correct dates).
Additionally, we can see that often users search from an entire
city,
and then shrink that down into a specific airport. So we should
also
consider a group of individual queries from cities and airpots
in the
same city, as the same search, and do the same for destination.
From that point, we should add these important columns to each
unique search.
'''
```

Now, we can think of some columns that would be useful for when we are making a representation of when a user is searching for flights on this major US airline. We can put them into an example dataframe, as follows:

```
example_df = pd.DataFrame(columns=['userid', 'number_
of_queries', 'round_trip', 'distance', 'number_unique_
destinations',
                  'number_unique_origins', 'datetime_first_
searched','average_length_of_stay',
                  'length_of_search'])
example_row = {'userid':98593, 'number_of_queries':5, 'round_
trip':1,
                  'distance':893, 'number_unique_
destinations':5,
                  'number_unique_origins':1, 'datetime_
first_searched':'2015-01-09',
                  'average_length_of_stay':5, 'length_of_
search':4}
st.write(example_df.append(example_row, ignore_index=True))
```

For the remainder of the question, we can add a bit of knowledge regarding how to find the distance between two points using different methods and then call it a day:

```
'''
For answering the second part of the question, we should take
the euclidian distance
on two normalized vectors. There are two solid options for
comparing two
```

```
entirely numeric rows, the euclidian distance (which is just
the straight line
```

```
difference between two values), and the manhattan distance
(think of this as the
```

```
distance traveled if you had to use city blocks to travel
diagonally across manhattan).
```

```
Because we have normalized data, and the data is not high
dimensional or sparse, I
```

```
would recommend using the euclidian distance to start off. This
distance would tell
```

```
us how similar two trips were.
```

```
'''
```

The second question's answer should be similar to the following screenshot:

Question 2: Representation

For this transformation, there are a few things that I would start with. First, I would have to define what a unique trip actually was. In order to do this, I would group by the origin, the destination, and the departure date (for the departure date, often customers will change around this departure date, so we should group by the date plus or minus at least 1 buffer day to capture all the correct dates).

Additionally, we can see that often users search from an entire city, and then shrink that down into a specific airport. So we should also consider a group of individual queries from cities and airpots in the same city, as the same search, and do the same for destination.

From that point, we should add these important columns to each unique search.

	userid	number_of_queries	round_trip	distance	number_unique_destinat…
0	98593	5	1	893	5

For answering the second part of the question, we should take the euclidian distance on two normalized vectors. There are two solid options for comparing two entirely numeric rows, the euclidian distance (which is just the straight line difference between two values), and the manhattan distance (think of this as the distance traveled if you had to use city blocks to travel diagonally across manhattan). Because we have normalized data, and the data is not high dimensional or sparse, I would recommend using the euclidian distance to start off. This distance would tell us how similar two trips were.

Figure 9.8 – Answering Question 2

As you can see, this example demonstrates how to approach take-home data assignments with the help of the Streamlit library to make more impressive applications. The final step of this work is to deploy this Streamlit app and share the link with the recruiter. I would strongly advise you to deploy this on Heroku to guarantee that no one else can view the questions or the data that has been provided by the company. You can also take further precautions, such as putting a textbox at the beginning of the application that functions as a hacky password protector for the application, as shown in the following code block:

```
password_attempt = st.text_input('Please Enter The Password')
if password_attempt != 'example_password':
    st.write('Incorrect Password!')
    st.stop()
```

Now, the entire application will not run unless the user inputs example_password into the textbox. This is certainly not secure, but it is useful for relatively unimportant (at least, in terms of secrecy) applications such as a take-home application:

Please Enter The Password

example_password

Major US Airline Job Application

by Tyler Richards

Figure 9.9 – Entering the password

As you can see, the only way for this application to load is if the correct password has been entered. Otherwise, the user will see a blank page. Alternatively, you can also set the password in Streamlit Sharing using Streamlit secrets, which is currently a feature in Streamlit for Teams and will be covered in *Chapter 11, Using Streamlit for Teams*.

Summary

This chapter is the most application-focused chapter we have created so far. We have focused heavily on job applications and the application cycle for data science and machine learning interviews. Additionally, we have learned how to password protect our applications, how to create applications that prove to recruiters and data science hiring managers that we are the skilled data scientists that we know we are, and how to stand out in take-home data science interviews by creating Streamlit apps. The next chapter will focus on Streamlit as a toy, and you will learn how to create public-facing Streamlit projects for the community.

10

The Data Project – Prototyping Projects in Streamlit

In the previous chapter, we discussed how to create Streamlit applications that are specific to job applications. Another fun application of Streamlit is to try out new and interesting data science ideas and create interactive apps for others. Some examples of this include applying a new machine learning model to an existing dataset, carrying out an analysis on some data uploaded by users, or creating an interactive analysis on a private dataset. There are numerous reasons for making a project like this, such as personal education or community contribution.

In terms of personal education, often, the best way to learn a new topic is to observe how it actually works by applying it to the world around you or a dataset that you know closely. For instance, if you are trying to learn how *Principal Component Analysis* works, you can always learn about it in a textbook or watch someone else apply it to a dataset. However, I have found that my comprehension of a topic goes through the roof when I actually apply it myself in practice. Streamlit is perfect for this. It allows you to give new ideas a shot in a responsive, fun environment that can be easily shared with others. Learning data science can be collaborative, which leads me to the next reason for creating data projects in Streamlit.

In terms of community contribution, one of the best parts of Streamlit – and, frankly, data science – is the growing community around the tools and toys we routinely play with. By learning with others and sharing Streamlit apps on Twitter (`https://twitter.com/tylerjrichards`), LinkedIn, and the Streamlit forums (`https://discuss.streamlit.io/`), we can turn away from the zero-sum experience that is taught in most schools and universities (where if your classmate gets a good grade, that usually comparatively hurts you) and toward a positive-sum experience, where you directly benefit from the lessons learned by others. To use the previous example, if you create an app that helped you understand the statistics behind principal component analysis, sharing that with others will probably teach them something, too.

In this chapter, we will run through one thorough data project from end to end, starting with an idea and ending with the final product. Specifically, we will cover the following topics:

- Data science ideation
- Collecting and cleaning data
- Making a **Minimum Viable Product** (**MVP**)
- Iterative improvement
- Hosting and promotion

Technical requirements

In this section, we will utilize the website *Goodreads.com*, which is a popular website owned by Amazon, that is used to track everything about a user's reading habits, from when they started and finished books to what they would like to read next. It is recommended that you first head over to `https://www.goodreads.com/`, sign up for an account, and explore around a little (perhaps you can even add your own book lists!).

Data science ideation

Often, coming up with a new idea for a data science project is the most daunting part. You might have numerous doubts. What if I start a project that no one likes? What if my data actually doesn't work out well? What if I can't think of anything? The good news is that if you are creating projects that you actually do care about and would use, then the worst-case scenario is that you have an audience of one! And if you send me (*tylerjrichards@gmail.com*) your project, I promise to read it. So that makes it an audience of two at the very least.

Some examples I have either created or observed in the wild include the following:

- Recording ping-pong games for a semester to determine the best player with an Elo model (`http://www.tylerjrichards.com/Ping_pong.html`)

- Using natural language processing to determine the quality of Wi-Fi in hostels (`https://www.racketracer.com/2015/11/18/practical-natural-language-processing-for-determing-wifi-quality-in-hostels/`)

- Analyzing thousands of pizza reviews to find the best NYC pizza near you (`https://towardsdatascience.com/adventures-in-barstools-pizza-data-9b8ae6bb6cd1`)

- Analyzing your reading habits with Goodreads data (`http://www.tylerjrichards.com/books_reco.html`)

Only one of these data projects uses Streamlit, as the rest came out before the library was released. However, all of these could have been improved by deploying them on Streamlit rather than just uploading them to a Jupyter Notebook (*project #1*) or a Word document/HTML file (*projects #2 and #3*).

There are many different methods that you can use to come up with your own idea for a data project, but the most popular methods generally fall into three categories:

- Finding data that only you could gather (for example, your friend's ping-pong games)

- Finding data that you care about (for example, Goodreads' reading data)

- Thinking of an analysis/app you wish existed to solve a problem you have and executing it (for example, hostel Wi-Fi analysis or finding the best pizza near you in NYC).

You can try one of these or start with another idea that you have already. The best method is the one that works best for you! For this chapter, we will walk through and recreate the Goodreads Streamlit app, in depth, as an example of a data project. You can access it again at `http://www.tylerjrichards.com/books_reco.html`.

This app is designed to scrape a user's Goodreads history and create a set of graphs to inform them about their reading habits since they started using Goodreads. The sets of graphs should be similar to the following screenshot:

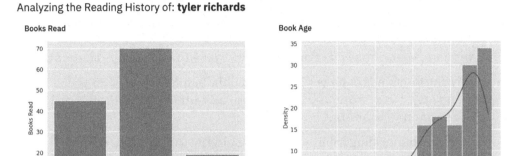

Figure 10.1 – Examples of Goodreads' graphs

I came up with this idea by doing a personal analysis of my book history, and then thinking to myself that others might also be interested in this analysis! There really was no better reason than that, and often, the most fun projects start out that way. To begin, we will work on collecting and cleaning the user data that exists on Goodreads.

Collecting and cleaning data

There are two ways in which to get data from Goodreads: through their **Application Programming Interface** (**API**), which allows developers to programmatically access data about books, and through their manual exporting function. Sadly, Goodreads is deprecating their API in the near future and, as of December 2020, are not giving access to more developers.

The original Goodreads app uses the API, but our version will rely on the manual exporting function that the Goodreads website has instead. To get your data, head over to `https://www.goodreads.com/review/import` and download your own data. If you do not have a Goodreads account, feel free to use my personal data for this, which can be found at `https://github.com/tylerjrichards/goodreads_book_demo`. I have saved my Goodreads data in a file, called `goodreads_history.csv`, in a new folder, called `streamlit_goodreads_book`. To make your own folder with the appropriate setup, run the following in your Terminal:

```
mkdir streamlit_goodreads_book
cd streamlit_goodreads_book
touch goodreads_app.py
```

Now we are ready to get started. We really have no idea what this data looks like or what is in this dataset, so our first steps are to do the following:

- Put titles and an explanation at the top of our app.

- Allow the user to upload their own data with ours as the default if they have no data of their own.

- Write the first few rows of data to the app so that we can take a look at it.

The following code block does all of this. Feel free to change the text so that your app has your name, and also add links to a profile of you that people can view! As of now, around 10 percent of the traffic to my personal website comes from the Streamlit apps I have produced:

```python
import streamlit as st
import pandas as pd


st.title('Analyzing Your Goodreads Reading Habits')
st.subheader('A Web App by [Tyler Richards](http://www.
tylerjrichards.com)')


'''
Hey there! Welcome to Tyler's Goodreads Analysis App. This app
analyzes (and never stores!)
the books you've read using the popular service Goodreads,
including looking at the distribution
of the age and length of books you've read. Give it a go by
uploading your data below!
'''


goodreads_file = st.file_uploader('Please Import Your Goodreads
Data')
if goodreads_file is None:
    books_df = pd.read_csv('goodreads_history.csv')
    st.write("Analyzing Tyler's Goodreads history")
else:
    books_df = pd.read_csv(goodreads_file)
    st.write('Analyzing your Goodreads history')
st.write(books_df.head())
```

Now, when we run this Streamlit app, we should get an app that looks similar to the following screenshot:

Analyzing Your Goodreads Reading Habits

A Web App by Tyler Richards

Hey there! Welcome to Tyler's Goodreads Analysis App. This app analyzes (and never stores!) the books you've read using the popular service Goodreads, including looking at the distribution of the age and length of books you've read. Give it a go by uploading your data below!

Please Import Your Goodreads Data

⬆	Drag and drop file here Limit 200MB per file							Browse files

	Book Id	Title	Author	Author l-f	Additional Authors	ISBN	ISBN13	My Rating	Average Rat
0	18749286	How to Get Rich: One o…	Felix Dennis	Dennis, Felix	nan	=""	=""	0	4.2
1	34376766	Blood, Sweat, and Pixe…	Jason Schreier	Schreier, Jason	nan	=""	=""	0	4.2
2	13530973	Antifragile: Things Th…	Nassim Nicholas Taleb	Taleb, Nassim Nicholas	nan	="1400067820"	="9781400067824"	5	4.0
3	45697427	Dark Matter	Blake Crouch	Crouch, Blake	nan	=""	=""	0	4.1
4	42041926	The Scout Mindset: Why…	Julia Galef	Galef, Julia	nan	="0735217556"	="9780735217553"	0	4.3

Figure 10.2 – The first five rows

As you can see, we get a dataset where each book is a unique row. Additionally, we get a ton of data about each book, including the title and author, the average rating of the book, your rating of the book, the number of pages, and even if you have read the book, are planning to read the book, or are in the middle of reading the book. The data looks mostly clean but with some weirdness; for instance, the data having both a publication year and an original publication year, and the fact that the ISBN (International Standard Book Number) comes in the format of *="1400067820"*, which is just odd. Now that we know more about the data at hand, we can switch over to try to build some interesting graphs for users.

Making an MVP

Looking at our data, we can start by asking a basic question: what are the most interesting questions I can answer with this data? After looking at the data and thinking about what information I would want from my Goodreads reading history, here are a few questions that I have thought of:

- How many books do I read each year?
- How long does it take for me to finish a book that I have started?
- How long are the books that I have read?
- How old are the books that I have read?
- How do I rate books compared to other Goodreads users?

We can take these questions, figure out how to modify our data to visualize them well, and then make the first go at our product by printing out all of the graphs.

How many books do I read each year?

For the first question about books read per year, we have the Date Read column with the data presented in the format of *yyyy/mm/dd*. The following code block will do the following:

- Convert our column into datetime format.

- Extract the year from the Date Read column.

- Group the books by this column and make a count for books per year.

- Graph this using Plotly.

The following code block does this, starting with the datetime conversion. It is important to note here that as with all things, I didn't get this right on the very first try. In fact, it took me some time to figure out exactly how I needed to manage and convert this data. When you are creating projects of your own, do not feel bad if you find that data cleaning and converting are taking a long time! Very often, it is the hardest step:

```python
        goodreads_file = st.file_uploader('Please Import Your
Goodreads Data')
if goodreads_file is None:
        books_df = pd.read_csv('goodreads_history.csv')
        st.write("Analyzing Tyler's Goodreads history")
else:
        books_df = pd.read_csv(goodreads_file)
        st.write('Analyzing your Goodreads history')

books_df['Year Finished'] = pd.to_datetime(books_df['Date
Read']).dt.year
books_per_year = books_df.groupby('Year Finished')['Book Id'].
count().reset_index()
books_per_year.columns = ['Year Finished', 'Count']

fig_year_finished = px.bar(books_per_year, x='Year Finished',
y='Count', title='Books Finished per Year')
st.plotly_chart(fig_year_finished)
```

The preceding code block will create the following graph:

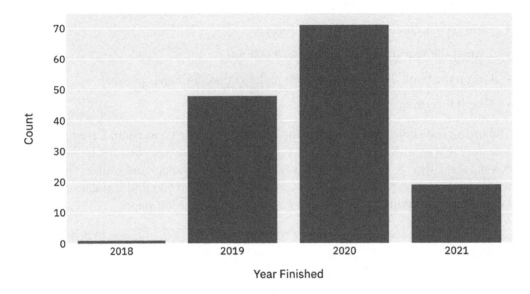

Figure 10.3 – Year Finished bar plot

We actually made an assumption here, that is, we assumed the year in the Date Read column represents when we read the book. But what if we start a book in the middle of December and finish it on January 2? Or, what if we start a book in 2019 but only get a few pages into it, and then pick it back up during 2021? We know this will not be a perfect approximation of the number of books read per year, but it will be better to express this as the number of books finished per year.

How long does it take for me to finish a book that I have started?

Our next question is about the time it takes for us to finish a book once we have started it. To answer this, we need to find the difference between two columns: the Date Read column and the Date Added column. Again, this is going to be an approximation, as we do not have the date of when the user started reading the book but only when they added the book to Goodreads. Given this, our next steps include the following:

- Convert the two columns into datetime format.

- Find the difference between the two columns in days.

- Plot this difference in a histogram.

The following code block starts with the conversion, as we have done previously, and then moves through our list of tasks:

```
books_df['days_to_finish'] = (pd.to_datetime(
         books_df['Date Read']) - pd.to_datetime(books_
df['Date Added'])).dt.days
fig_days_finished = px.histogram(books_df, x='days_to_finish')
st.plotly_chart(fig_days_finished)
```

The previous code block can be added to the bottom of your current Streamlit app, which, when run, should show a new graph:

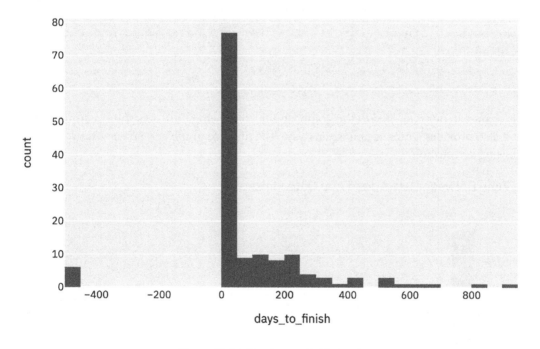

Figure 10.4 – The days to finish graph

This is not the most helpful graph for my data. It looks as though, at some point, I added books that I had read in the past to Goodreads, which show up in this chart. We also have a set of books that have not been finished yet or are on the to-read bookshelf, which exist as null values in this dataset. We can do a few things here, such as filtering the dataset to just include books where the number of days is positive and filtering the data to only finished books, which the following code block does:

```
books_df['days_to_finish'] = (pd.to_datetime(
        books_df['Date Read']) - pd.to_datetime(books_
df['Date Added'])).dt.days
books_finished_filtered = books_df[(books_df['Exclusive Shelf']
== 'read') & (books_df['days_to_finish'] >= 0)]
fig_days_finished = px.histogram(books_finished_filtered,
 x='days_to_finish', title='Time Between Date Added And Date
Finished',
      labels={'days_to_finish':'days'})
st.plotly_chart(fig_days_finished)
```

This change in our code makes the graph significantly better. It makes some assumptions, but it also provides a more accurate analysis. The finished graph can be viewed in the following screenshot:

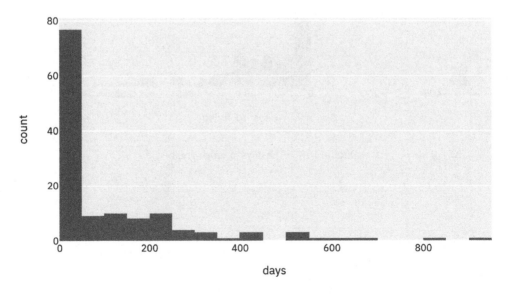

Figure 10.5 – The improved days to finish graph

This looks much better! Now, let's move on to the next question.

How long are the books that I have read?

The data for this question is already in a fairly good state. We have a single column called `Number of Pages`, which, you guessed it, has the number of pages in each book. We just need to pass that column to another histogram, and we will be good to go:

```
fig_num_pages = px.histogram(books_df, x='Number of Pages',
title='Book Length Histogram')
st.plotly_chart(fig_num_pages)
```

This code will produce something similar to the following screenshot, showing a histogram of book length as measured in pages:

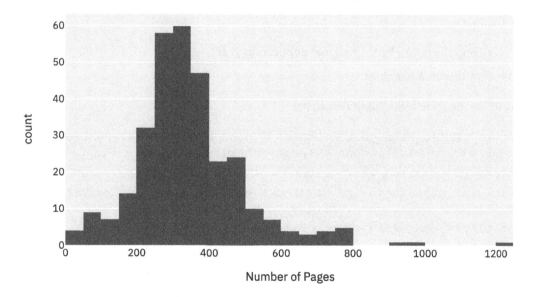

Figure 10.6 – The Number of Pages histogram

This makes sense to me; a ton of books are in the 300–400 page range, with a few giant books that have 1,000+ pages. Now, let's move on to the age of these books!

How old are the books that I have read?

Our next graph should be straightforward. How do we figure out how old the books that we read are? Are our tendencies to go for the newest set of books that are published or to shoot toward reading classics? There are two columns that we can get this information from, the publication year and the original publication year. There is very little documentation on this dataset, but I think we can safely assume that the original publication year is what we are looking for, and the publication year exists for when a publisher republishes a book. The following code block checks this assumption by printing out all the books where the original publication year is later than the publication year:

```
st.write('Assumption check')
st.write(len(books_df[books_df['Original Publication Year'] >
books_df['Year Published']]))
```

When we run this, the app should return zero books with the original publication year as greater than the year published. Now that we have checked this assumption, we can do the following:

1. Group the books by the original publication year.

2. Plot this on a bar chart.

The following code block takes two steps:

```
books_publication_year = books_df.groupby('Original Publication
Year')['Book Id'].count().reset_index()
books_publication_year.columns = ['Year Published', 'Count']
fig_year_published = px.bar(books_publication_year, x='Year
Published', y='Count', title='Book Age Plot')
st.plotly_chart(fig_year_published)
```

When we run this app, we should get the following graph:

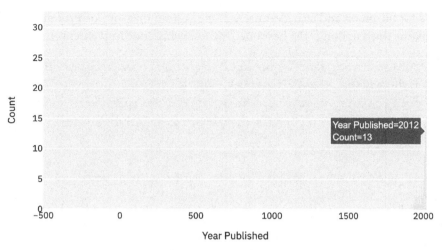

Figure 10.7 – Book Age Plot

At first glance, this graph does not appear to be incredibly useful, as there are quite a few books written so far back in history (for example, Plato's writings in -375 BCE) that the entire graph is hard to read. However, Plotly is interactive by default, and it allows us to zoom into sections of history that we care about more than others. For example, the following screenshot shows us what happens when we zoom into the period of 1850 to the present, where most of the books that I've read happen to be in:

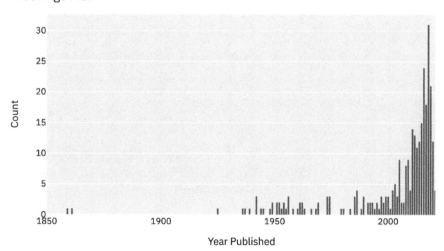

Figure 10.8 – Zooming in on Year Published

This is a much better graph! There are a couple of options going forward. We can start with the graph that is not as useful and tell users to zoom in, we can filter our dataset for only younger books (which would defeat the main purpose of the graph), or we can set a default zoom state for the graph and also alert users at the bottom that they can zoom in as they'd like. I think the third option is the best one. The following code implements this option:

```
Books_publication_year = books_df.groupby('Original Publication
Year')['Book Id'].count().reset_index()
books_publication_year.columns = ['Year Published', 'Count']
st.write(books_df.sort_values(by='Original Publication Year').
head())


fig_year_published = px.bar(books_publication_year, x='Year
Published', y='Count', title='Book Age Plot')
fig_year_published.update_xaxes(range=[1850, 2021])
st.plotly_chart(fig_year_published)
st.write('This chart is zoomed into the period of 1850-
2021, but is interactive so try zooming in/out on interesting
periods!')
```

When we run this code, we should get our final plot:

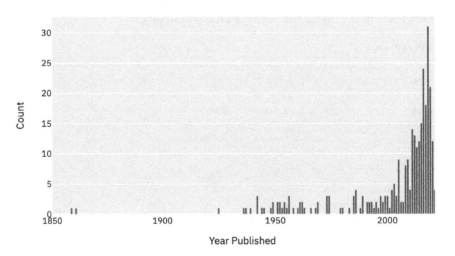

This chart is zoomed into the period of 1850-2021, but is interactive so try zooming in/out on interesting periods!

Figure 10.9 – A default zoom with helpful text

Four questions down, we have one to go!

How do I rate books compared to other Goodreads users?

For this final question, we really need two separate graphs. First, we need to plot how we have rated the books. Then, second, we need to plot how other users have rated the books that we also rated. This isn't a perfect analysis, because Goodreads just shows us the average rating of the books – we have not read the distribution. For example, if we had read *The Snowball*, a biography of Warren Buffett, and rated it 3 stars, and half of Goodreads' readers rated it a 1 star while the other half rated it 5 stars, we would have rated it exactly the same as the average rating, but we would not have rated it the same as any individual rater! However, we do what we can with the data we have. So, we can do the following:

- Filter the books according to the ones we have rated (and, therefore, read).

- Create a histogram of the average rating per book for our first graph.

- Create another histogram for your own ratings.

This next code block does exactly that:

```
books_rated = books_df[books_df['My Rating'] != 0]
fig_my_rating = px.histogram(books_rated, x='My Rating',
title='User Rating')
st.plotly_chart(fig_my_rating)


fig_avg_rating = px.histogram(books_rated, x='Average Rating',
title='Average Goodreads Rating')
st.plotly_chart(fig_avg_rating)
```

As you can see in the following screenshot, the first graph with the user rating distribution looks great. It looks as though I mainly rate books either 4 or 5 stars, which are, overall, pretty lenient ratings:

User Rating

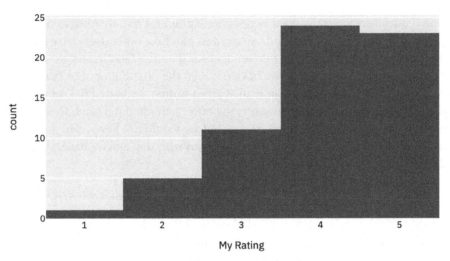

Figure 10.10 – The User Rating distribution

When we also look at the second graph, we see a fairly clean distribution. However, we run into the problem that we have addressed before – all the rating averages are more tightly bundled than the user ratings:

Average Goodreads Rating

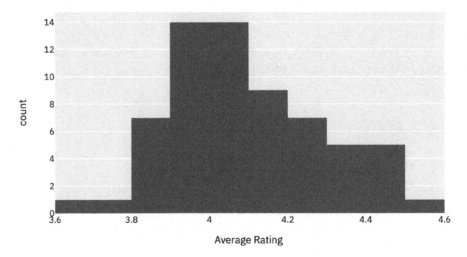

Figure 10.11 – Average Goodreads Ratings

We can always set the *x*-axis range to 1–5 for both graphs, but this will not help our actual problem. Instead, we can leave both of the graphs but also calculate whether, on average, we rate books higher or lower than the Goodreads average. The following code block will calculate this and add it underneath the average Goodreads rating graph:

```
Fig_avg_rating = px.histogram(books_rated, x='Average Rating',
title='Average Goodreads Rating')
st.plotly_chart(fig_avg_rating)
import numpy as np
avg_difference = np.round(np.mean(books_rated['My Rating'] -
books_rated['Average Rating']), 2)
if avg_difference >= 0:
    sign = 'higher'
else:
    sign = 'lower'
st.write(f"You rate books {sign} than the average Goodreads
user by {abs(avg_difference)}!")
```

This code block makes our average and creates a dynamic string that will either say that the Goodreads user rates books higher or lower than the average Goodreads user. The result for my data is as follows:

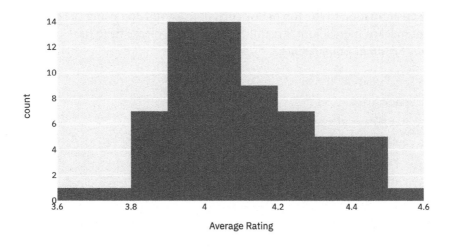

Average Goodreads Rating

You rate books lower than the average Goodreads user by 0.11!

Figure 10.12 – Adding an average difference

This is better and completes our MVP. Our app is in a decent state, and the difficult manipulation and visualization steps are pretty much complete. However, our app certainly doesn't look great and is just a bunch of graphs that appear in a row. This might be good for an MVP, but we need to add some styling to really improve our state. That leads us to our next section: iterating on this idea to make it even better.

Iterative improvement

So far, we have been almost purely in production mode with this app. Iterative improvement is all about editing the work we have already done and organizing it in a way that makes the app more usable and, frankly, nicer to look at. There are a few improvements that we can shoot for here:

- Beautification via animation

- Organization using columns and width

- Narrative building through text and additional statistics

Let's start by using animations to make our apps a bit prettier!

Beautification via animation

In *Chapter 7, Exploring Streamlit Components*, we explored the use of various Streamlit components: one of these was a component called `streamlit-lottie`, which gives us the ability to add animation to our Streamlit applications. We can improve our current app by adding an animation to the top of our current Streamlit app using the following code. If you want to learn more about Streamlit components, please head back over to *Chapter 7, Exploring Streamlit Components*:

```
import streamlit as st
import pandas as pd
import plotly.express as px
import numpy as np
from streamlit_lottie import st_lottie
import requests


def load_lottieurl(url: str):
    r = requests.get(url)
    if r.status_code != 200:
        return None
```

```
    return r.json()
```

```
file_url = 'https://assets4.lottiefiles.com/temp/1f20_aKAfIn.
json'
lottie_book = load_lottieurl(file_url)
st_lottie(lottie_book, speed=1, height=200, key="initial")
```

This Lottie file is an animation of a book flipping its pages, as shown in the following screenshot. These animations are always a nice touch for longer Streamlit apps:

Analyzing Your Goodreads Reading Habits

A Web App by Tyler Richards

Hey there! Welcome to Tyler's Goodreads Analysis App. This app analyzes (and never stores!) the books you've read using the popular service Goodreads, including looking at the distribution of the age and length of books you've read. Give it a go by uploading your data below!

Please Import Your Goodreads Data

 Drag and drop file here
Limit 200MB per file   Browse files

Figure 12.13 – Goodreads animation

Now that we have added our animation, we can move on to how to organize our app a bit better.

Organization using columns and width

As we discussed earlier, our app does not look very good with each graph appearing one after the other. Another improvement we can make is to allow our app to be in wide, rather than narrow, format, and then put our apps side by side in each column.

To begin, at the top of our app, we need the first Streamlit call to be the one that sets the configuration of our Streamlit app to wide rather than narrow, as shown in the following code block:

```
import requests
```

```
st.set_page_config(layout="wide")
def load_lottieurl(url: str):
    r = requests.get(url)
    if r.status_code != 200:
        return None
    return r.json()
```

This will set our Streamlit to our wide format. So far, in our app, we have called each graph a unique name (such as `fig_year_finished`) to make this next step easier. We can now remove all of our `st.plotly_chart()` calls, and create a set of two columns and three rows where we can place our six graphs. The following code creates each of these. We name each space first, and then fill them with one of our graphs:

```
row1_col1, row1_col2 = st.beta_columns(2)
row2_col1, row2_col2 = st.beta_columns(2)
row3_col1, row3_col2 = st.beta_columns(2)

with row1_col1:
    st.plotly_chart(fig_year_finished)
with row1_col2:
    st.plotly_chart(fig_days_finished)
with row2_col1:
    st.plotly_chart(fig_num_pages)
with row2_col2:
    st.plotly_chart(fig_year_published)
    st.write('This chart is zoomed into the period of 1850-
2021, but is interactive so try zooming in/out on interesting
periods!')
with row3_col1:
    st.plotly_chart(fig_my_rating)
with row3_col2:
    st.plotly_chart(fig_avg_rating)
    st.write(f"You rate books {sign} than the average
Goodreads user by {abs(avg_difference)}!")
```

This code will create the app that appears in the following screenshot, which has been cropped to the top two graphs for brevity:

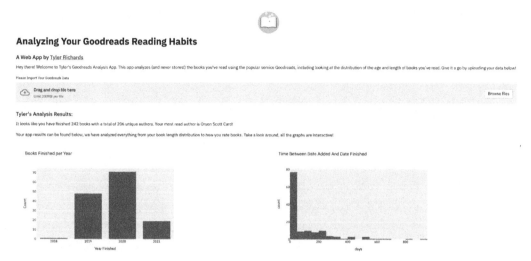

Figure 12.14 – The wide format example

This makes our graphs much easier to read and easily allows us to compare them. We have intentionally paired our two graphs according to ratings, and the rest also appear to fit quite well next to each other. Our final step is to add a bit more text to make the entire app easier to read.

Narrative building through text and additional statistics

These graphs are already quite helpful for understanding how the user reads, but we can bolster the readability of this app by adding some useful statistics and text underneath each graph and at the beginning of the app.

Right above where we start to define our columns, we can add an initial section that shows the unique number of books that we have read, the unique authors, and our favorite author, all in one. We can use these basic statistics to kick off the app and tell the user that each graph is also interactive:

```
if goodreads_file is None:
    st.subheader("Tyler's Analysis Results:")
else:
    st.subheader('Your Analysis Results:')
books_finished = books_df[books_df['Exclusive Shelf'] ==
'read']
u_books = len(books_finished['Book Id'].unique())
u_authors = len(books_finished['Author'].unique())
mode_author = books_finished['Author'].mode()[0]
st.write(f'It looks like you have finished {u_books} books with
a total of {u_authors} unique authors. Your most read author is
{mode_author}!')
st.write(f'Your app results can be found below, we have
analyzed everything from your book length distribution to
how you rate books. Take a look around, all the graphs are
interactive!')

row1_col1, row1_col2 = st.beta_columns(2)
```

Now we need to add four new text sections below the four graphs that do not have any annotated text as of yet. For the first three graphs, the following code will add some statistics and text to each:

```
row1_col1, row1_col2 = st.beta_columns(2)
row2_col1, row2_col2 = st.beta_columns(2)
row3_col1, row3_col2 = st.beta_columns(2)

with row1_col1:
    mode_year_finished = int(books_df['Year Finished'].mode()
[0])
    st.plotly_chart(fig_year_finished)
    st.write(f'You finished the most books in {mode_year_
finished}. Awesome job!')
with row1_col2:
    st.plotly_chart(fig_days_finished)
```

```
        mean_days_to_finish = int(books_finished_filtered['days_
to_finish'].mean())
        st.write(f'It took you an average of {mean_days_to_finish}
days between when the book was added to Goodreads and when you
finished the book. This is not a perfect metric, as you may
have added this book to a to-read list!')
with row2_col1:
        st.plotly_chart(fig_num_pages)
        avg_pages = int(books_df['Number of Pages'].mean())
        st.write(f'Your books are an average of {avg_pages} pages
long, check out the distribution above!')
```

One example graph here is the histogram on book length. The preceding code adds an
average length and some text below the graph, as shown in the following screenshot:

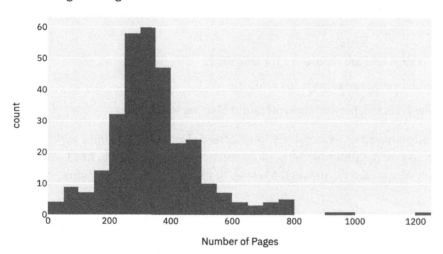

Your books are an average of 346 pages long, check out the distribution above!

Figure 10.15 – The average number of pages text

For the final set of graphs, we can add text to the ones without context:

```
with row2_col2:
        st.plotly_chart(fig_year_published)
        st.write('This chart is zoomed into the period of 1850-
2021, but is interactive so try zooming in/out on interesting
periods!')
```

```
with row3_col1:
    st.plotly_chart(fig_my_rating)
    avg_my_rating = round(books_rated['My Rating'].mean(), 2)
    st.write(f'You rate books an average of {avg_my_rating}
stars on Goodreads.')
with row3_col2:
    st.plotly_chart(fig_avg_rating)
    st.write(f"You rate books {sign} than the average
Goodreads user by {abs(avg_difference)}!")
```

This completes our section on adding text and additional statistics! Now, our final step is to deploy this on Streamlit Sharing.

Hosting and promotion

Our final step is to host this app on Streamlit Sharing. To do this, we need to perform the following steps:

1. Create a GitHub repository for this work.

2. Add a requirements.txt file.

3. Use 1-click deployment on Streamlit Sharing to deploy.

We already covered this extensively in *Chapter 5, Deploying Streamlit with Streamlit Sharing*, so give it a shot now without instruction. If you get stuck, head over to *Chapter 5, Deploying Streamlit with Streamlit Sharing*, to find the exact instructions.

Summary

What a fun chapter! We have learned so much here – from how to come up with data science projects of our own to how to create initial MVPs, to the iterative improvement of our apps. We have done this all through the lens of our Goodreads dataset, and we have taken this app from just an idea to a fully functioning app hosted on Streamlit Sharing. I look forward to seeing all the different types of Streamlit apps that you create. Please create something fun and send it to me on Twitter at *@tylerjrichards*. In the next chapter, we will focus on learning how to use Streamlit at work with the new Streamlit product, *Streamlit for Teams*. See you there!

11
Using Streamlit for Teams

Throughout the past two chapters, we have deeply explored how to use Streamlit for things such as personal data projects, projects for resume building, and even for creating apps for take-home job applications. In this chapter, we will focus on using Streamlit at your place of work, as a data scientist, machine learning engineer, or data analyst. We already know that Streamlit can be used as a convincing tool to influence those around us through thoughtful and interactive analyses, and we will work on applying that to the work data scientists actually do.

Streamlit is both a company and an open source library and makes revenue by being such an excellent tool in a data science toolkit that companies are convinced to pay for special features and customizations that increase the productivity of their own data scientists. The best part about this is that the company is directly incentivized to make the experience of using the tool as useful and valuable as possible; if you're a better data scientist because of Streamlit, your company is more likely to pay more for access.

Additionally, Streamlit is already designed to be collaborative. If another developer has access to a GitHub repository that is being used for a Streamlit app, then any edits they make will pop up on the deployed app automatically. Because of this, Streamlit is a natural collaborative fit for both individual data scientists and groups of data science teams working on similar analyses or applications.

In this chapter, we will discuss the following:

- Analyzing hypothetical survey costs using Streamlit for Teams
- Creating and deploying apps from private repositories
- User authentication with Streamlit

To kick us off for this chapter, we will start with an example of when we would use Streamlit for Teams instead of static analysis at work.

Analyzing hypothetical survey costs using Streamlit for Teams

Imagine you are a data scientist for **Big Internet Company** (**BIC**). BIC sells budgeting software to users, and you are responsible for surveying the users of your app to see where the app could be improved. You work with a fairly typical team made up of a product manager, two software engineers, three project managers, two user experience researchers, and yourself, the lone data scientist. One day, your product manager messages you on Slack and asks you to figure out the right sample of users between the ages of 16 and 24, a crucial segment of the business, to take a 10-question survey about the software. In a brainstorming session, your researchers have found some evidence that giving people a 10% chance at winning a $500 gift card is more effective than giving people $50 for the response rates in your survey, and want you to incorporate that into your analysis.

There are many factors that you need to consider here: how much does the team want to spend? How many samples should we choose? The hardest part here is the trade-off between cost and the representativeness of the sample. We have a few options. We could recommend a sample size without really informing the team why we are recommending a sample size. We could also give the team a few options on costs, describing some of the pros and cons in a list. A better option than any of these is to create a short Streamlit app that will help us make this decision as a team to understand all the trade-offs.

Let's say that we want to do the latter! Our general steps here are going to be to do the following:

1. Setting up a new Streamlit app folder

2. Illustrating the representativeness of the sample

3. Calculating the cost of the sample

4. Using interaction to show trade-offs

Now we need to start with the first option, setting up our folder.

Setting up a new Streamlit app folder

We have taken this step quite a few times in this book before. Go ahead and set up a folder called `random_survey_app` and place within it a file called `app.py`, where we will put our new Streamlit app. Now on to the central problem at hand!

Illustrating the representativeness of the sample

If we are the data scientist for BIC, we know a lot of data about the user population in question. We want to make sure that the sample we grab is representative of the population as a whole, especially in reference to one or more key variables of the business. For this example, we can assume that the most important metric to the business is user time spent on our app. We already know the distribution of user time spent and can represent that within our app using the following code:

```
import streamlit as st
import numpy as np


st.title('Deciding Survey Sample Size')
np.random.seed(1)
user_time_spent = np.random.normal(50.5, 10, 1000)
```

We are using the np.random.seed(1) line so that you will see the same sample as the figures in this book, but when developing a user-facing app, I would recommend leaving this out, otherwise clever users will be more suspicious about your random selection methods! Setting a seed in numpy allows reproducible results with randomly selected data.

Now that we know the distribution of the user time spent on the app, we can show the user how representative different-sized sub-samples will be by drawing the two distributions of user time spent next to each other. While this is not the best method for determining representativeness, it is going to be useful to prove the general point to your audience. The next code block sub-samples 100 from the set of 1,000 samples, and plots each in a histogram:

```python
import streamlit as st
import numpy as np
import plotly.express as px


st.title('Deciding Survey Sample Size')
np.random.seed(1)
user_time_spent = np.random.normal(50.5, 10, 1000)
my_sample = np.random.choice(user_time_spent, 100)


fig = px.histogram(user_time_spent, title='Total Time Spent')
fig.update_traces(xbins=dict(start=0,end=100, size=5))
st.plotly_chart(fig)


fig = px.histogram(my_sample, title='Sample Time Spent')
fig.update_traces(xbins=dict(start=0,end=100, size=5))
st.plotly_chart(fig)
```

This code block will produce the following app, showing that at 100 users, it looks fairly representative of the total time spent:

Deciding Survey Sample Size

Total Time Spent

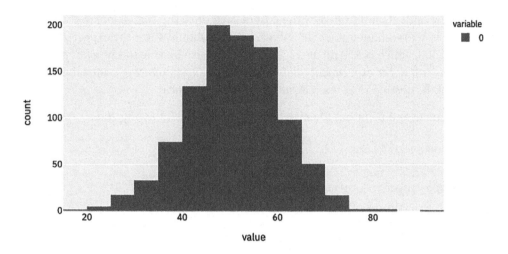

Sample Time Spent

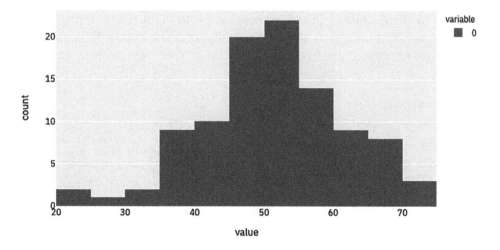

Figure 11.1 – Survey sample size

Now we need to figure out the trade-off – how to determine the cost of a set sample of users.

Calculating the cost of the sample

As we discussed before, we can calculate the cost of the sample by looking at the number of survey respondents multiplied by the cost of each one. The cost of any individual survey respondent is a 10% chance at a $500 gift card, so we should show the expected value as 10% times $500, which is $50 on average. We should also be able to say, *what percent of the time does the cost of the experiment fall below some dollar amount?* dynamically, to assure the group of the costing risks associated with the randomness.

We can calculate and print out the expected cost using the following code:

```
np.random.seed(1)
num_surveys = 100
user_time_spent = np.random.normal(50.5, 10, 1000)
my_sample = np.random.choice(user_time_spent, num_surveys)


expected_cost = 50 * num_surveys
st.write(f'The expected cost of this sample is {expected_
cost}')
```

Once we have this, we can simulate this survey running 10,000 times and count how often the cost of the experiment goes over a certain value, which we call max_cost in the next code block. We use the numpy library again to sample from the binomial distribution, which is the number of successes given a set of independent events with the same probability (for example, if you flipped a coin 10 times, how many times it would land on heads):

```
np.random.seed(1)
num_surveys = 100
user_time_spent = np.random.normal(50.5, 10, 1000)
my_sample = np.random.choice(user_time_spent, num_surveys)

#costing section
expected_cost = 50 * num_surveys
max_amount = 5000
percent_change_over = 100 * sum(np.random.binomial(num_surveys,
```

```
0.1, 10000) > max_amount/500)/10000
st.write(f'The expected cost of this sample is {expected_
cost}')
st.write(f'The percent chance the cost goes over {max_amount}
is {percent_change_over}')
```

For our survey size of 100 and a max cost of $5,000, the expected cost is $5,000 and the
cost goes over our limit ~41% of the time:

Deciding Survey Sample Size

The expected cost of this sample is 5000

The percent chance the cost goes over 5000 is **41.11**

Total Time Spent

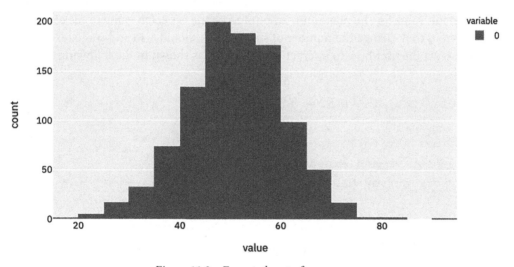

Figure 11.2 – Expected cost of survey

Now that we have all the set pieces, we need to actually make this interactive with
Streamlit features.

Using interaction to show trade-offs

In order to make this app better than a static analysis, we need to let the user interact with our app. We can do this in two ways, first by allowing the user to change the number of people surveyed, and second by changing the max cost variable we assigned. We can do both of those things using the following code block:

```
st.title('Deciding Survey Sample Size')
np.random.seed(1)
num_surveys = 100
num_surveys = st.slider(label='Number of Surveys Sent',
     min_value=5, max_value=150, value=50)
max_amount = st.number_input(label='What is the max you want to
spend?',
     value=num_surveys*50, step=500)
user_time_spent = np.random.normal(50.5, 10, 1000)
my_sample = np.random.choice(user_time_spent, num_surveys)
```

In this block, we set a minimum and maximum value for the Streamlit slider, and also set the default value for the maximum amount to be the expected value to make it easier for the user as they change the number of surveys. We should also add some text above this to instruct the user how to interact with our app, as shown in the following addition to the app:

```
st.title('Deciding Survey Sample Size')
'''
Please use the following app to see how
representative and expensive a set sample
is for our survey design.
'''
np.random.seed(1)
num_surveys = 100
```

These two additions to our app produce the following screenshot:

Deciding Survey Sample Size

Please use the following app to see how representative and expensive a set sample is for our survey design.

Number of Surveys Sent

The expected cost of this sample is 2500

The percent chance the cost goes over 2500 is 37.9

Figure 11.3 – Streamlit sliders with costing

So far, this works perfectly fine. However, because you are working for a company, you want to make sure that none of this information in the app is released to the public or any competitors. Because of this, deploying this app publicly is not an option, and we need to figure out how to privately deploy the application. In *Chapter 9, Improving Job Applications with Streamlit*, we discussed how to make our applications private with password protection, but Streamlit for Teams also allows us to deploy from private GitHub repositories, which is the topic of our next section.

Creating and deploying apps from private repositories

One great feature of the Streamlit for Teams product is the ability to use Streamlit Sharing from private GitHub repositories. This works exactly the same as how we learned in *Chapter 5, Deploying Streamlit with Streamlit Sharing*, but from a private rather than a public repository. To make this change, you will need to have access to Streamlit Teams or get access from the Streamlit team (they might just let you try it out if you ask nicely!).

To create a private GitHub repo, head over to `https://github.com/new` and make sure to click the **Private** rather than **Public** option, as shown in the next screenshot:

Create a new repository

A repository contains all project files, including the revision history. Already have a project repository elsewhere? Import a repository.

Owner *

  🐱 tylerjrichards ▾

Repository name *

  random_survey_app_test ✓

Great repository names are short and memorable. Need inspiration? How about fluffy-computing-machine?

Description (optional)

○ 🖥️ **Public**
    Anyone on the internet can see this repository. You choose who can commit.

◉ 🔒 **Private**
    You choose who can see and commit to this repository.

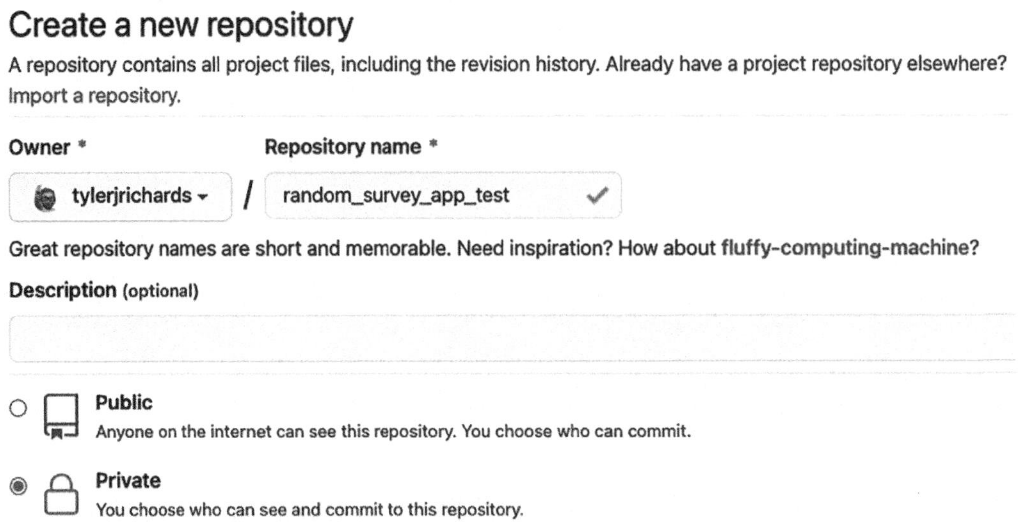

Figure 11.4 – Private repository on GitHub

And after we add our current code to our GitHub repository, we can deploy on Streamlit Sharing just as we normally would, by going over to `https://share.streamlit.io` and following the directions for one-click deployment. I have deployed this Streamlit app using my own private repo, and the Streamlit app can be found at `https://share.streamlit.io/tylerjrichards/random_survey_app/main/app.py`. Our next problem to work on is finding alternatives to the password method that we have already explored, with user-specific authentication with Streamlit.

User authentication with Streamlit

One feature currently in beta on Streamlit for Teams but with an expected release date of late 2021 is Google-based **single sign-on** (**SSO**) authentication for our applications. This will allow us to make our app totally private, only viewable by users that we put on an allow list. The first step we need to take is to link our own Google account, by heading over to `https://share.streamlit.io` and clicking on **Settings** in the top-right corner. Once we are there, we will see the screen shown in the next screenshot:

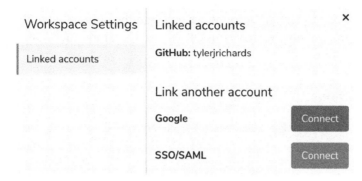

Figure 11.5 – Linking Google accounts

We can now click the blue **Connect** button and then sign in to our Google account. Once that is finished, we need to head over to our main page at `https://share.streamlit.io` and figure out which app we want to restrict traffic to:

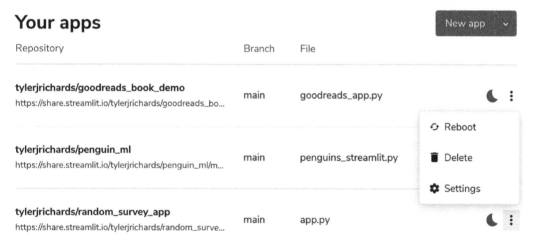

Figure 11.6 – Streamlit sharing options

In this case, I want to limit the reach of the second app, so I will go to the settings of this app by clicking the icon on the far-right side of the page and selecting **Settings**, as we have done before.

Before we connected our Google account, we only had the option to edit the **Secrets** sections of our apps, but now we have this entirely new section called **Viewers**, as shown in the next screenshot:

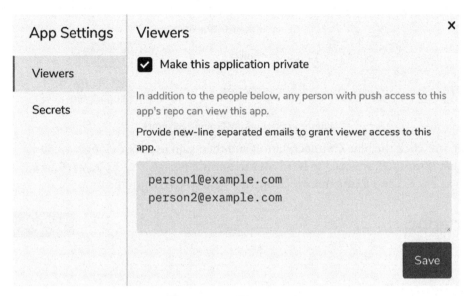

Figure 11.7 – Viewers auth

We can set our app to private with the checkbox and add people with their email to this list. If they are not on the list, they will get a 404 error when trying to reach the app! This works extraordinarily well for a smaller number of users but does not work as well if you are trying to reach hundreds or thousands of users, especially those who do not have Google-related email accounts.

Summary

In this chapter, we explored an example costing analysis, which showed us a job-specific use case for Streamlit. In this example, we discussed how to use interactive Streamlit applications to help improve and inform the data-based decision making of teams. After that, we also learned how to deploy Streamlit applications from private GitHub repositories, and we learned about multiple methods to make our Streamlit applications only available to a private audience with password protection and Google SSO. This concludes the chapter.

In the next chapter, we will focus on interviews with power Streamlit users and creators to learn tips and tricks, why they use Streamlit so extensively, and also where they think the library will go from here. See you there!

12
Streamlit Power Users

Welcome to the final chapter of this book! In this chapter, we will learn from the best, from Streamlit creators with experience creating dozens of apps and components, Streamlit power users turned Streamlit employees, and even the founder of the Streamlit library who now runs the fledgling company supporting the library's development. We sat down and interviewed four different users and learned about their backgrounds, their experience with Streamlit, and what tips they have for users of all experience levels. From these interviews, we will learn how they use Streamlit on a day-to-day basis at work, for teaching, and also about where Streamlit is going from here.

This chapter is grouped into four interviews:

- Fanilo Andrianasolo, Streamlit creator and tech lead at Worldline

- Johannes Rieke, Streamlit creator turned engineer

- Adrien Treuille, Streamlit founder and CEO

- Charly Wargnier, Streamlit creator and SEO consultant

First, let's start with Fanilo!

Interview #1 – Fanilo Andrianasolo

(Tyler) Hey, Fanilo! Before we get started, do you want to introduce yourself to the readers? What's your background? What do you spend your time doing, and who do you work for?

(Fanilo) Hello, everybody! My name is Fanilo Andrianasolo, I'm from Madagascar, and I work at Worldline, which is one of the leading European companies in digital payments and transactional services. I work there as a data science and business intelligence advocate and tech lead, where I help internal product and development teams to prototype new data science use cases, architect those use cases, and then put them into production. So, most of my work is focused on integrating data analytics inside Worldline, which is a huge task because it covers multiple industries from finance, for example, fraud detection, retail, and customer analysis. And I'm also a data science advocate, so I build and present multiple talks internally or to prospective customers where I can show them, "This is data science, don't worry, it's not that hard" or "This is a random forest, don't worry, it's not as complex as what you may think." And on the side, I am a university lecturer in big data and NoSQL in Lyon where I teach about 50 hours a year. It's an amazing opportunity to be able to talk to students and watch them grow into amazing software engineers and data scientists!

(Tyler) That sounds awesome! You basically have, the way that I see it, two very interesting roles where you have to explain data science concepts to others, one at work and then another at university. Do you use Streamlit in both situations?

(Fanilo) Yes, I do! When I discovered Streamlit, it was for internal work. At first, I was working on tracking some metrics from different machines and wanted to showcase them without using Jupyter Notebook, because I didn't want to click and run each cell every time. And I tried Streamlit and I was really hooked by how fast and easy it was to use it to build something.

For my university lectures where I'm doing mostly PySpark, MongoDB, and Elasticsearch lectures, I demo those through their Python plugins. I would show a Streamlit app with the code on the side, I would change the code in front of my students, and all the Python variables would update on the app in real time. When you write this code that builds some MapReduce job, for example, in PySpark, it's easy to show them the code live and even do some coding exercises together. To show how the code works, I just put a function inside the code and the result is directly on the right in the Streamlit app. It's really dynamic and is a really easy way for me to show and tell the code.

(Tyler) Is there a difference in how you develop Streamlit apps for the two groups? I feel like there's a lot of similarities there but what are the differences?

(Fanilo) For students, it's going to be a single script that is going to run from the top to the bottom so it's easy to follow; it's like a live demo for them. Whereas when I'm at my company, I'm going to integrate Streamlit into bigger projects so there is usually already a project structure with a folder dedicated to UI work. For work projects, Streamlit apps are going to use functions from multiple libraries and multiple modules so it's a little bit different. The way we distribute and use the Streamlit app at work is also a little bit different because at university, I can just do anything on my machine. When I'm at work, I have to worry about more, like can I put this into the cache? Can I rewrite a colleague's function because it cannot go into Streamlit hashing? Constraints in my professional work make it a little bit more complex to write Streamlit apps.

(Tyler) I'm curious how you do your deployment at work. Do you do it on Heroku servers to use Streamlit for Teams? Or do you do it all locally?

(Fanilo) We have two servers internally on-prem where I deploy my Streamlit apps. There are not a lot of people using Streamlit inside the company, so I can just host the app on a server temporarily so marketing can play with the app. And the more techy people that don't know Python, I just send them the scripts and tell them how to run it with Anaconda.

(Tyler) So you talked a bit about your first time using Streamlit. Did you find out about it on Twitter, or from a forum somewhere? What got you started? What was your original use case?

(Fanilo) I think I heard about it from Twitter. At first, I dismissed it thinking, "Oh, it's just another Python library, I'll just put it in my to-do list to try one day." And I tried it 2 months later when I was working on a real-time data science demo for a prospective customer. They wanted to track visit metrics from different websites and visualize them. Actually, a good proportion of our customers just ask us for some data analysis. They have not thought of KPIs, analytics business use cases, or business questions to answer through data. Those are always hard to start and I usually build them a small interactive demo to help them understand the data science process. And that's where I thought, "Oh, I should give Streamlit a try."

Before this, I actually did a demonstration for another customer using Jupyter Notebook and the customer was not interested because they saw it as too technical; they didn't like seeing code. And so, I thought for this customer maybe I should try Streamlit to showcase a grid of plots, using sliders just to decide how much of the data you want to visualize. For this problem, we wanted to do windowing over a set of dates to answer what the mean number of visits on those websites is, and wanted to be able to decide on the size of the window. We could just put that in the sidebar in Streamlit, which was a good opportunity to show the customer the results in real time. So we added this slider to the Streamlit app and gave it to the customer, and you can see when there's a spike that you can analyze further. And yeah, that's how I got to know more about Streamlit, just through demoing data science internally and externally.

(Tyler) That's happened to me so often, where the client doesn't exactly know what they'd like when they come with a request. What a great use case! One of the things I wanted to talk to you about is the Streamlit community of which you've become a pretty strong member over the course of the past year. What about Streamlit convinces you to continue investing in the ecosystem?

(Fanilo) For me, the thing that hooked me into Streamlit really was the feedback loop that I missed from when I was doing frontend engineering. I could write some code, and I would see the results on my screen immediately. I could just edit the color in the CSS and see the change. And the fact that this feedback loop is so short in Streamlit, combined with the simplicity of the API, which makes building a basic app really easy, is what really hooked me into the framework. I also had this conversation with Adrian (Streamlit's founder) where I told him the feedback loop really reminded me of the web ecosystem and that for me was Streamlit's secret sauce.

Another thing is the fact that now we can easily integrate web components into Streamlit, which makes it really easy for us to build more diverse web interactive apps for data scientists. I've always got this impression from talking with my students, or other coworkers, or people in meetups that they always struggle to build interactive apps where they can just select something or draw something and use this drawing as an input for their machine learning model. To do this, they needed to pre-draw, and then load the image into a Jupyter notebook, which takes too much time, but there are HTML components to draw on. Streamlit acting as a bridge between Python and the web through components is what gets us as creators hooked into pulling the web ecosystem into Streamlit.

(Tyler) So speaking of web-based platforms, you've spent a lot of time building components like streamlit-lottie (`https://github.com/andfanilo/streamlit-lottie`), which we talked about earlier in the book, streamlit-drawable-canvas (`https://github.com/andfanilo/streamlit-drawable-canvas`), and even streamlit-echarts (`https://github.com/andfanilo/streamlit-echarts`). Can you talk to us a bit about how you come up with ideas for components?

(Fanilo) So for those three components, I've got two different stories. I'm going to start with streamlit-lottie; the idea popped into my head on a Saturday night of boredom and scrolling Twitter. I saw nice animations using Lottie files and I thought to myself, "Oh, that's nice, I'd like to have some cool animations like this in Streamlit," so I just built it. And that's really it, wanting to bring more web components to Streamlit.

For streamlit-echarts and streamlit-drawable-canvas, there was a bigger use case. I was on a tight deadline for a demo using TensorFlow.js years ago. I wanted to do training and inference on drawings and I spent 5 days creating the demo in the JavaScript ecosystem, mixing Fabric.js for drawing on a canvas and Echarts to show the results. It was very tough especially because it was my first real step into the frontend engineering world. And then when Streamlit came out, I wanted to see if other users could build this demo in hours instead of days if the Fabric.js and Echarts components already existed, so I extracted the code of this demo into external libraries and voilà!

The thought process I have is always, what kind of new inputs and outputs can we bring to Streamlit? For example, can we bring real-time music input to Streamlit? Everybody in deep learning today talks about image and sound, so that would be a great component. And as an output, there are so many popular JavaScript libraries to display data in an interactive way that would be helpful for analysis. My goal is always, what kind of input and output that the web enables can I add to Streamlit? Hopefully web developers will want to build more things into Streamlit!

(Tyler) You've probably seen a ton of Streamlit apps that use components of yours. I would imagine that you get really excited by some clever use of streamlit-lottie or streamlit-echarts. Are you just pumped when you see that sort of stuff? Do you have some specific apps that you really enjoy that are built off of some of the components that you have made?

(Fanilo) Those are my first real open source projects, where I've put some effort into building and promoting them. I love that these tools are so flexible and can be used for so many use cases I would have never imagined, especially for streamlit-drawable-canvas. I saw there was a user who would display a side view of a soccer field in Streamlit, then he would draw the limits of the terrain inside the canvas over the field image, and then do some 3D remapping to transform it to a top view and be able to analyze the position of the players. I was like, wow, who does that?

There are people using Streamlit for medical purposes. For example, they want to draw on every slice of a stack of images the position of some molecules so they can draw a kind of 3D version of this molecule. I've even seen an app from Jina AI where they built a Pokémon recognizer (`https://github.com/jina-ai/integration-streamlit-pokemon`)! So you would draw a Pokémon, and it would inject the drawing into a neural network to recognize the Pokémon that you wanted to draw. Never would've predicted that, you know? Yeah, it's amazing.

(Tyler) That sounds amazing. Do you have any tips for beginners getting started in Streamlit? Do you have anything that you wish you would have known, like when you first got started?

(Fanilo) For me, it's consistent experimentation on new libraries. If there is a new Python library, I often just want to understand how it works. What happens if I change this argument, how does each parameter affect the output? So, I just bootstrap a new Streamlit script and import the library. And then for each parameter that you have, you can build a slider, a number input, a date input, and then you begin to build a demo of this unknown library, and Streamlit is only there to help you explore it to the fullest. Then you wonder how you can lay it out better, how to preserve some state for the app, and that's where you begin to dig deep into Streamlit. We talked a lot about the web ecosystem for Streamlit components. But I also think Streamlit is one of the best ways to showcase any Python library, anything from the Python ecosystem.

Other than that, I'd say engage with the community online. The Streamlit community was really my first time interacting with an online community, with people who I didn't know nor meet at all. I don't remember the very first post or topic that I wrote, but I remember putting so much effort into writing it. I know it takes courage to ask questions in public, and I would say: dare to write a new post on the forum. If you're struggling with Streamlit or with Python, it's a good experience to try and post something in the community forums (`https://discuss.streamlit.io/`) because people there are really nice; there are always people willing to help. I would encourage people to play with Streamlit and innovate, and then go on the forums and ask about what they can't figure out. There are a lot of very hidden features that are only available inside the forums, which is why I encourage people to go on the forums.

(Tyler) Yeah, definitely. It's a very interesting case of accumulated knowledge sitting in small places on the internet. It's terrifying to ask because you're always like, "Oh, what if they think I'm really dumb?" That's often the first concern, signaling to others that you know what you're doing. But everyone seems incredibly nice in the Streamlit community, which is, frankly, a big change on the internet.

(Fanilo) Yeah, maybe I'm so used to interacting with students that it helps me understand the fear of asking your very first online question to a "stranger." The worst thing that happened to one of my students is they wanted to clone a Git repo and the log showed that this folder already existed on their machine, so they could not clone over it. The answer is easy, in front of our very eyes written on the log, at least it's easy for us to interpret, right? But when it's your very first time coding, you have no idea what this log means, or that you should even check the log. So, I try to answer questions like I would answer my students coding for the first time and set this as a bar for our community, so everyone realizes we were all beginners at some point and that we should guide them into the gigantic Python/Streamlit world and not respond with "Go read the manual."

One year ago, I was not into online communities at all. I was also scared of doing this. And now here I am, a forum moderator and Streamlit creator. One year ago, I would never have dreamed of doing this. So, ask questions, people!

(Tyler) Thank you so much for your time, Fanilo! For anyone reading who wants to learn more, you can find Fanilo's GitHub at `https://github.com/andfanilo` and his tutorial for building Streamlit components at `https://streamlit-components-tutorial.netlify.app/`.

Interview #2 – Johannes Rieke

(Tyler) Hey, Johannes! Before we get started, do you want to give us a quick intro to yourself? Where have you worked in the past, what do you do, what is your background?

(Johannes) Hello! I'm from Germany, and currently living in Berlin. Well, as you know, I'm currently working at Streamlit and have been for the past 2 months but my background actually is in physics. So I did physics in my undergrad and I somehow got into neuroscience. I took a couple courses, did a few projects, and really loved it, especially the combination with computer science, doing simulations of nerve cells, the brain, all that kind of stuff. I got super interested in that. I decided to do my master's in computational neuroscience, which is kind of a combination of neuroscience on the one hand, but also machine learning on the other. In that program, I did a lot of stuff in all kinds of different areas of machine learning, like medical imaging, natural language processing, graph networks, all kinds of things. After I graduated from my master's program, I got into a couple open source projects. Well actually, I wanted to go traveling for a longer time but Covid came, and I had to get back to Germany earlier than I expected. And then I got into open source projects and started doing a lot with Streamlit, which is where I am today, working as a product engineer at Streamlit.

(Tyler) Very interesting! When did you get started with the Python ecosystem? Was that back in your physics days?

(Johannes) Yeah, that was long ago, basically at the start of my bachelor's or the first year of my bachelor's. I had already done programming since high school. Started out with Java, and then in 2013, during my bachelor's, I got into Python and really fell in love with it. Because for the stuff I was doing, starting with computations and simulations, and later machine learning, Python is just awesome.

(Tyler) Did you do any machine learning in Java? I haven't seen a lot of ML engineers who work in Java or need to write anything in Java.

(Johannes) I definitely worked in Python. Before I studied for my master's, I actually worked at a research lab in a gap year, and I did some computational stuff with C++ in that time but that was just horrible. If I had known about Python back then, I would have probably done everything in Python, and would have finished in a tenth of the time.

(Tyler) I know a lot of people that will do most of their work in Python and then if they have some strong need to make an algorithm much faster, they'll switch to a lower-level language, which is excessive in the best way. So at that point, you were really involved with Python and had been coding in Python for a while, and then you kind of started making these machine learning projects in Streamlit, like your Traingenerator app (`https://traingenerator.jrieke.com/`), which is a multi-purpose app to write machine learning code for you. What was your motivation for creating some of these? To give back to the community, showcase your work, create a personal portfolio, or something totally different?

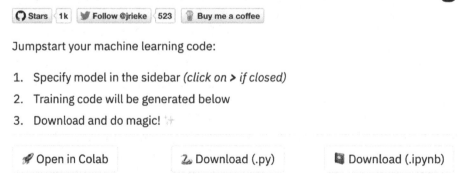

Figure 12.1 – Traingenerator app

(Johannes) Yeah, it's a combination of most of those points. I started using Streamlit in spring last year after I graduated. I had gone traveling after graduation, but with Covid, I had to come back to Germany and had obviously a lot of free time. Some of my friends and former colleagues had started working on an open source project, which was in the area of Covid tracing, and so I joined them. And as part of that, we needed a small dashboard and a friend had told me about Streamlit, and I tried it out and thought it was super cool.

But that's basically how I started using Streamlit for fun. The Traingenerator app that I built actually had more business or start-up intentions. I thought, let's try my own project. And I realized I really liked the idea of training a machine learning model with a single line of code, like FastAI and PyTorch Lightning are doing. PyTorch Lightning is a library in the same area. I have worked a lot in machine learning, and often I've worked with very standard and basic models and just applied them to new datasets or new areas. One thing that has always annoyed me was that you're taking a super standard approach, but you have to write all this code to implement a model, or even if you have an implemented model, you have to test it and tweak it; you have to transform your data to work with that model. And you have to write code to track your metrics and experiments, all that kind of stuff. So my idea was more: could I build something that simplifies this process, maybe also with the prospect of becoming a viable product, a viable business?

I had worked on that for a while, and then the idea for Traingenerator came up when I talked about this project with a friend and how a Python library to simplify this process is great, but it reaches its limits as soon as you want to build something more sophisticated; obviously, because you cannot easily go in and tweak stuff. We thought that it works great for prototypes, but as soon as you want to get a model into production, you have to start all over again.

And then we had this idea of building a web app where you could put in what you want to train and which framework you want to use, and then it generates the code for you. And you can either use that code to train models directly, or you can modify it as you like, which is what Traingenerator does.

The other things I built after that, like the GitHub 2020 app (`http://gh2020.jrieke.com/`), also the best-of-streamlit list, those were more like ideas just for fun, personal projects, certainly also for my portfolio.

(Tyler) All of that is very interesting. I've used Traingenerator a few times and love it. At the time you developed it, which was before Streamlit Sharing was released, you deployed the app with Heroku. I'm curious if you would still do the same thing; what is your decision-making process for where to deploy your apps?

(Johannes) The reason back then was simply that I wanted to have a custom URL that was short; I didn't want it to be a long, non-understandable URL. But I've actually moved it to Streamlit Sharing now! It's just a way better developer experience than Heroku, because the app updates within a second of pushing to GitHub, without rebooting or anything like that. Sharing doesn't support custom URLs by default yet, but there's a hack on the forum, which I'm using for now. And I've already annoyed our product managers quite a bit with this feature request, so I hope it shouldn't take too long!

(Tyler) One other app you created was an app to dynamically create and share a user's GitHub stats called Year on GitHub (`http://gh2020.jrieke.com/`). It became quite popular; I saw it all over the internet fairly consistently. Can you talk us through that story?

Figure 12.2 – GitHub stats app

(Johannes) For sure. So the reason or the idea behind it is actually a super random idea, I have no clue how I got it. There's no big story behind that. I had built Traingenerator already and it was incredibly well received. I did some more stuff with Streamlit, and then a couple days before Christmas, I got the idea to build an app where you just put in your GitHub username and it would show you some stats about what you've done on GitHub in 2020. And then you can tweet it. So it's similar to Spotify Wrapped that they do at the end of every year.

A couple days after I had that idea, literally, a new Python library for GitHub came out actually for the GitHub API, which was super cool. And then I thought, obviously it doesn't make any sense to release something like this in March or April, which means I would need to build it in the next 2 weeks, and release it soon. So I worked on this all throughout my Christmas holidays and it was super, super cool.

I think there were four or five hundred tweets generated with it. The creators of the Julia programming language used it. It was really nice to see and also the Streamlit employees saw all of the tweets, so I think that probably brought me half of my job.

(Tyler) I have this theory that if you really want a job somewhere, you should make a Streamlit app for them that solves a problem of theirs or makes them notice you. And if you do that, you're just way more likely to actually get hired there. I've tried this a couple times and it usually turned into an offer down the line.

(Johannes) It actually wasn't even intended at all. At that time, I hadn't even thought about applying to Streamlit, but it worked pretty well. In retrospect, I think they all loved it internally because it brought a huge spike to the Twitter numbers on the Streamlit account, and was super cool to see all the tweets about this new app.

(Tyler) All of that makes sense to me! So after working on Streamlit for 8 or 9 months, you decided this is where you want to work, applied to a job there, and then got the job. First of all, congratulations. Second of all, what about the library makes you think that it's going to be like a big thing in the data science and machine learning community going forward? I have enough conviction about Streamlit to write a book on it so I clearly agree with you, but can you talk a bit about your conviction for the company in this space?

(Johannes) So in my eyes, what is great about Streamlit is the developer experience and the simplicity of it. In my current job as a product engineer, I also look at lots of other web frameworks and solutions in that space, and I have to play around with them. And there are certainly other tools that have some cool functions that allow you to do more complex things than Streamlit because Streamlit is fairly young, but in terms of developer experience, how simple it is to start something and how fun it is to make apps, none of these tools even comes close to Streamlit. And I think that there are lots of pieces playing into that.

On the simplicity aspect, you can just whip up an app in basically 5 minutes with a few lines of code. And it's just your normal Python script that you're writing anyway; you don't have to learn about other classes or anything about frontend development. It's very intuitive for newcomers.

Then there's the live coding model of Streamlit, which allows you to code your app and Streamlit will rerun your app at the same time. And it's very intelligent about what it reruns, especially if you use the cache. I think that is what makes Streamlit so fun and addictive to work with, because you're getting this super instant feedback by instantly seeing the result.

The other aspect is the community; the Streamlit community is just amazing. I mean, we have so many developers now who really like working with Streamlit. The forums are such a cool place to exchange ideas and to get tips, and there are so many people who are super dedicated, who are just answering questions in their free time for hours each week.

We actually have like three, four, or five people within Streamlit who are working full time on the forum interacting with developers, sending swag to people who build Streamlit apps, which I think for a company that just has about 25 employees is very unique.

(Tyler) I think of that dynamic a lot. When I started out, it felt like Streamlit was just a really good tool. And then I started playing around with it more. And then I realized that it might be closer to a toy, where I just have this constant iteration and feedback loop. And whenever you have something that is both a tool and a toy, it has worked out pretty well in the end.

(Johannes) Yeah, definitely. I think one big aspect of why Streamlit is cool and why I think it's going to become even cooler at some point in the future is that there's a lot of parts to it, too. It's not just the open source library but it's also Streamlit Sharing, which if you want to deploy your model is super nice and easy to use. It's also, as I said, the forums where if you have a problem, you can certainly get help there. I think in the future, there will be lots more parts coming into the equation.

(Tyler) You're about 9 months into your Streamlit developing experience. Do you have any tips for beginners getting started? Things that you wish you would have known?

(Johannes) I actually think that there are not so many tips you can give to beginners, other than just try it out. Because that's the cool thing about Streamlit; if you start with it, you can basically get how it works after around 10 minutes. And it's just super easy to start. I also have a couple friends who I recommended Streamlit to and I didn't have to do a lot of convincing. I just told them about it, and a day later, they came back and knew how to use it. The only tip is to sign up on the forums, and if you have any questions, just ask or reach out to us in any way. There are lots of helpful people on the forums. There are, as I said, lots of people within Streamlit whose job is to interact with developers.

The more complicated stuff, like cache and state, is not easy to get for beginners and needs some explanation, which we are also working a lot on right now.

(Tyler) Thanks, Johannes, for coming and talking to us; I'm sure people got a lot out of this. Johannes's personal site can be found at `https://www.jrieke.com/`.

Interview #3 – Adrien Treuille

(Tyler) Hey, Adrien! Thanks for being willing to be interviewed for this. Before we really get started, do you want to tell me a little bit about yourself? I know you were a professor at Carnegie Mellon, and before that you were working with protein folding. You've also worked on self-driving cars, and now are the founder of Streamlit. So how do you introduce yourself?

(Adrien) First of all, when I was a professor, this whole Python data stack was kind of new. NumPy was certainly pre 1.0, and there was kind of this revelation that there was this amazing library called NumPy, all of a sudden, that made Python as good as MATLAB, and then after a while, way was better than MATLAB. That was the beginning of Python becoming the dominant language of numerical computation, and then ultimately machine learning. Python was a scripting language, a sysadmin language, or maybe a CS 101 language. All of a sudden it had this massive, new, super important industrial application. It started off with a bunch of nerds and professors using it in research, and they found that it was actually very useful, and much easier than writing our own machine learning code or numerical code in C.

The other thing I was doing was creating computer games that allowed people to develop scientific problems, and eventually, millions of people played them. Fast forward a bit, and I went to work at Google. I had a really interesting, cool career at the intersection of tech and machine learning.

Then I started Streamlit. We're building tools that are grounded in that numerical Python stack we were using 15 years ago (before it was cool). The other part of Streamlit is building a community. I think that aspect of Streamlit is very special. These two themes from my research have come full circle: the numerical Python world and the building of online communities.

(Tyler) In the original documentation from October 2019 and the Medium posts thereafter, Streamlit was originally pitched as a tool for machine learning engineers. Now, you see all different types of people using it. I'm not an ML engineer, but I use it all the time. How has the idea of Streamlit changed over time?

(Adrien) At a meta level, I'll say very genuinely that it's very cool for you to observe that. For us inside Streamlit, there are little, subtle shifts in how we talk about our targer user profile. But it doesn't necessarily feel like anyone else is paying attention to these subtle shifts. It's kind of cool to see someone else notice it!

There are a couple of ways to answer this. Streamlit is more fundamental to Python programming than it is to machine learning or data science. It fulfills a need in Python programming that didn't exist in any other tool. You could write command-line scripts. There are also Python GUI frameworks, but those are quite intricate to use because GUI app development is a totally different style of programming than data work. You could go into a Jupyter notebook, but then it was, again, a totally different style of programming.

Streamlit is a mashup of GUI programming and scripting. To me, that's a very useful thing. It actually transcends machine learning, as such. So part of the potential for Streamlit, for example, is to play a role in CS 101. One of the cool things about Streamlit is that there's this idea of the technology, and then there's the idea of how we are applying that to different problems and spaces. How do we prioritize applications for the community's benefit and also to create a sustainable company?

(Tyler) I want to talk a bit more about the community you just mentioned, because you have built a ton of online games before, like FoldIt (`https://fold.it/`), which has a strong crowdsourcing function to it. There are two sides to Streamlit in my mind. One side is very community-focused. It's an open source language on top of which anyone can build, and there are Streamlit components that can be made and added easily. The other side is the company Streamlit, which obviously exists to eventually turn a profit. How do you manage those two sides?

(Adrien) I don't feel like we have to choose. When two things are aligned in their interests, everybody wins. From a business model standpoint, we are trying to put this software out into the world which has lots of use cases in data science. For example, I wrote a computer game for my son's class in Streamlit to help them understand multiplication. It also has a bunch of industrial applications. These two groups are aligned: the more people who are in the community and are contributing to Streamlit, the more our addressable user base grows for those industrial applications.

It's a funnel. Data scientists funnel into Streamlit's open source community, which then flows into our customer base. We try to grow at every stage of the funnel, which is good both for the business model and the community.

(Tyler) What did you learn from your decade building online crowdsource games that you've brought into the Streamlit world? Because the community feels like a meta-game where people are trying to create cool Streamlit apps for other people. How do you nurture that? Is that intentional, or just a function of it being a cool tool?

(Adrien) One interesting similarity between FoldIt and Streamlit is that they're both designed to be toy-like. A "toy" – which is a technical term in game design – is a game without rules that you just want to play with. There's no instruction manual for a GI Joe. It's just something you play by making it do stuff. You can add rules too, but you don't have to.

Here's another game-like aspect of Streamlit: people building Streamlit apps and put them online to communicate ideas, and show off work, and gain praise. That helps others learn about Streamlit who then build more apps and further grow the community. We realized, "Wow, this cycle of publishing and praise is an amazing growth vector for us." We have made some effort to support the people who are putting their work out there, but I don't think we've really explored most of what's possible with this aspect of Streamlit. We just haven't had time to execute on it, because there are so many important things to do.

(Tyler) If we're talking about company prioritization, how do you think about the priority of the company right now? You talked about the funnel, so then there are three main sections, the data scientists, the data scientists who use Streamlit, and then the data scientists who use Streamlit inside their company. Where's the focus of Streamlit at the moment?

(Adrien) There is actually one more stage, which is how many people are viewing the apps created inside those companies, because our present pricing plan is based on viewership, not the number of developers. It's some number of dollars per viewer per month.

So the way we prioritize focuses on another level of that pipeline.

We called the first year after launch "the year of the developer," and it was about growing the open-source community. Going through exponential growth lead to discontinuous changes in operations. We weren't prepared for that. We put the entire engineering team on rotation answering questions in the community forums. They gave super well-informed answers, but the engineering team literally ground to a halt for three months. Then we realized, oh shoot, we can't hire engineers to solve our community problems.

The second year, which we're in now, is "the year of the customer." This is all about building that initial monetization engine and creating a self-serve mechanism so that you can basically be a Streamlit user, click a button, and have Streamlit for Teams. We're not there yet, but all the pieces are coming together!

(Tyler) A lot of people who are going to be reading this are going to be just starting out with their Python development, or they might be in the beginner/intermediate stage of learning Python and data science. They have quite a few other options to choose from, from Django or Flask to no-code tools, to other dashboarding frameworks. They could even switch over to R's Shiny app development. What is your pithy pitch to new users? Why Streamlit?

(Adrien) I'd say you should just try it. There's a lot of sentiment on Twitter around how "cool" Streamlit is. I think it is powerful and cool. Streamlit is grounded in this idea of scripting, which is a very natural and simple paradigm for thinking about dataflow. I don't think anyone else really does that. It should feel kind of magical; coding isn't actually magic, but it's very fun. Super highly educated and incredibly well-paid people make apps just because it's fun, so we enjoy coming at it with that perspective. You should feel like you're getting more back than you spent typing each function call, and if that's the kind of emotional thing you get, then it's exciting to go through this.

(Tyler) In my view, I started because it's easy, and then stayed because it's the best, you know?

(Adrien) I think something that's true (and maybe I'm wrong about this) is that there's a lot in this visualization/dashboarding app/development space, where the more you know how they work and the deeper you get into them, the more disappointed you are. The demos you see look customizable and seem great, but when you actually go through the experience of building or trying to replicate the demo, it's very, very hard to actually achieve this thing that they're promising on their websites.

That's just not true of Streamlit. When you look at all of the demo apps in the gallery (`https://streamlit.io/gallery`), they're really quite accessible. We're not trying to compete in the "Let's build a massive, perfect app" space.

(Tyler) Thanks for coming and talking to us! The main thing that we should point to is obviously the central Streamlit website (`https://streamlit.io/`). You can find Adrien's writing at `https://medium.com/@adrien.g.treuille` and you can find him on Twitter at `https://twitter.com/myelbows`.

Interview #4 – Charly Wargnier

(Tyler) Hey, Charly! Thanks so much for coming and talking to us. To start off, can you introduce yourself to the readers?

(Charly) Hey there! I'm French and have been living in the UK for about 13 years now. And I've been doing mainly digital marketing, business intelligence, and **SEO (Search Engine Optimization)** consulting here in the UK. In the last few years, I have pivoted toward data engineering and data science. Also, I've worked both in-house and on the agency side, and for large companies in retail fashion and at a large range of small businesses as well. But since 2014, it has mainly been enterprises, and the time between 2008 and 2014 was with small businesses.

(Tyler) Let's back up for a half-second; what is it like working in SEO? What does that actually look like?

(Charly) My core skill set is mainly technical SEO. SEO is a vast territory, as you may imagine, and my core skill is with anything regarding the technicalities of a website, the way it has been coded, or the way it is being crawled or being passed by web crawlers. To make sure that Google and Bing can actually crawl these large websites accurately. Obviously, there's a lot of things involved in that, like making sure that paid search is in synergy with SEO.

It's a very versatile kind of job where you have to liaise with not only the SEO people, but also the people developing the website, and even the PR, content, and product people as well. In terms of interactions, that's one of the most versatile jobs around.

(Tyler) Got it, that all makes sense. Another thing we haven't mentioned yet is Streamlit. You use Streamlit quite a bit and are a prolific creator. What is it about Streamlit that makes it so valuable of a tool for you?

(Charly) I used to work a lot providing some Python scripts to people via Google Colab or Jupyter Notebook. And since I've been using Streamlit, I no longer have to send over scripts; I can just literally send those apps! And I can show them some SEO apps or functionality that they wouldn't have been able to use unless they were a developer. It really widens the scope and the user adoption. And in the few companies I've worked with in the last few months, I've been able to bring way more people to start using the SEO apps that I have been designing. There has been a big, big shift.

(Tyler) How interesting! The other option for you in Python is to make Flask for Django applications; did you ever think about doing something like that for SEO apps?

(Charly) Yeah, I did develop some Flask applications back in the day, but it was quite cumbersome for me to develop that because it requires a lot of skills in HTML or JavaScript. But with Streamlit, it has really enabled me to create something very quickly and to share that with people. So no Flask, and I have tried a bit of Django but the learning curve is actually quite steep. It usually takes me ages to design anything in Django. So yeah, there's literally no comparison; I've left Flask and Django aside for now and I'm really prioritizing Streamlit.

(Tyler) Totally agree, I've made a bunch of different data science projects pre-Streamlit and my two options always were to put it in a Jupyter notebook or blog post or make a fully fledged app in Flask. The issue for me used to be that the difference in time and effort to make an entire app, before Streamlit, was way too high. It would double the time on the project! And with Streamlit, it is just a little bit more difficult than making a Jupyter notebook but the output is so much better.

(Charly) I'm trying to learn React at the moment, so I can make something a bit more integrated and polished and use Streamlit as an MVP. So I have used some other web frameworks, but you're right. With regards to quickness, nothing to this day beats Streamlit. I think the closest one is Panel (`https://panel.holoviz.org/`), which is flexible and pretty straightforward, but I think that the big difference between Streamlit and Panel is the community. The Streamlit community has been so welcoming, including yourself and other people too. Even a few years ago, I was barely coding anything in Python and Streamlit is really the application that I've embraced. I think the community is really key.

(Tyler) Speaking of community, you have been really involved with both the SEO and the Streamlit communities. You've created apps like StreamEA (`https://www.charlywargnier.com/post/streamea-entity-analyzer`), which extracts and analyzes entities from web pages; how do you come up with apps like these? Are you solving your own problems and then turning that into an app, or taking older Python scripts from older clients and turning those into apps?

(Charly) So it's really a mix of different things. You've quoted quite a few there. First of all, I'm solving issues I'm having myself, as I've been doing SEO for years so I've regularly bumped into SEO issues and the idea is to solve these by creating an app so others can use the solution as well. I've always been fascinated by web applications; I remember as far back as 2013 where I had a bit of a geeky dream to develop web apps! The other thing that you're right about is that I have a lot of Jupyter notebooks and scripts that I have been using for years, and speaking of user adoption, I wanted to make sure anyone could try them out.

I usually also collect feedback within my companies or from the clients that I've worked for, so I get a lot of user feedback. And sometimes also it is just stumbling upon some new libraries online that I am curious about, just like yourself. The final thing is the paid aspect; there are a lot of SEO options on the market that can be pretty expensive. And I think one of my secret desires, if I may say, is to be able to kind of make those apps available for free. It's my guilty pleasure to take an application that people would pay hundreds or thousands of pounds a month for and recreate it with Python for free. It's a nice satisfaction to have!

(Tyler) I'd love to talk about StreamEA a little bit more, can you talk a bit about any developmental difficulties you had with creating that app? What was that process like?

Entity Analyzer

ℹ - About this app

- StreamEA leverages the power of Google Natural Language API to extract entities from web pages!
- It retrieves entities' salience scores - their overall relevance to the supplied text
- It also highlights missing entities between pages

Figure 12.3 – StreamEA

(Charly) Well, entity analysis is a hot topic in the SEO world. Google has been shifting from pure keywords to different kinds of semantic advancements, like, for example, entities. As Google is putting some ranking value or some weight toward those entities, you want to make sure that your pages or your websites are targeting those entities accurately.

In terms of challenges, there's quite a bit of code, but it wasn't necessarily too challenging. The Google Natural Language API is pretty straightforward. So the way the app is built, you get two main parts, the scraping bits with BeautifulSoup and the entity analysis bits with the API. The difficulty here is that by default, the Natural Language API retrieves some data and you need to create some function that would convert back and forth between dictionaries and data frames, which was a bit of a challenge because when I started last August, my Python knowledge wasn't necessarily great. And I remember struggling with that a lot, to be able to take the API from Google in a way that worked with my data frame. Now, it would be a piece of cake, but I remember it was a bit of a bottleneck and a learning experience for me.

And then you've got a little budget estimator, because the Google NLP API can be pricey if left untamed! A lot of people are scraping Wikipedia, which can have very long pages, so I thought that having this kind of little budget estimator, which estimates the cost for using StreamEA (StreamEA has you upload your own Google API credentials), would be useful.

Recently, I have open sourced another application, which does entity relationship retrieval from Wikipedia URLs. I haven't put any budget estimates on it yet, and people have been a bit grumpy with me, which is why I put a warning on it. It not only scrapes the Wikipedia URLs you input, but it also scrapes any children pages, which can go crazy without limits. The other day, some people were pushing the application to the max with scripting, for example, 100 children from the master page, which was fantastically long. And they were charged hundreds of pounds from Google!

(Tyler) That's the one thing that I've recommended to people at the very beginning when you're setting up your AWS or GCP accounts, that you should absolutely set the budget limit to what you can afford so they turn your services off before you spend anywhere close to that amount of money.

So you kind of got started in Python and Streamlit around the same time, do you have any tips for beginners getting started in Streamlit? Are there things that you kind of wish you would have known when you first started?

(Charly) I started with Python in 2016 or 2017, where I was literally going to GitHub, taking some scripts, and not doing anything to them. Just using Python without necessarily understanding what the stuff was about. And then I started learning online with Jupyter Notebook, and eventually I had this opportunity to start building some web apps.

But to come back to your question, my advice that I would give to new users is to lean on the community. With Streamlit, I think that sets us apart. I would say don't be too shy! People are so helpful there, they will certainly try to help out. And also don't be scared to share anything; embrace Twitter for sharing information with others. Don't be afraid to share your projects and your progress, not just the end product; there is no such thing as an end product anyway. I really have worked in a vacuum, working for myself, and if you don't share your work, then you don't get this good emotional push from the feedback from the community.

It will never be perfect; you will never be ready. So just release it early; release it often! If there are a few issues with the app, don't worry about it. Just caveat it in your tweet or your post, and people will understand that. I mean, besides, your tool is a free tool. So people can't be too demanding.

(Tyler) When I first started developing and doing data science work in school, I would never share anything because I was so nervous that it wouldn't be good enough compared to all the professionals out there. So I would make all this stuff and never show it to anyone because I didn't feel like it was good enough. And then once I figured out that wasn't going to work and I started to share more of my projects, it was just so much better, so much more fun.

(Charly) You've released a lot of projects over the years, it's really great. It's pretty impressive.

(Tyler) Thank you! Do you have any other things you would like to plug that you're working on?

(Charly) Oh, yeah, as you can imagine there are many things on the grill right now. I kind of started some of them around 2 years ago but as a script or a notebook, and I'm slowly converting them to Streamlit apps. I want to turn StreamEA into a paid app that is way more useful for SEO. I also have some machine learning apps in the pipeline, which I'm hopefully planning to release soon.

(Tyler) Thank you so much for coming and talking to us! You can find Charly on Twitter at `https://twitter.com/DataChaz`.

Summary

This concludes *Chapter 12, Streamlit Power Users*, and also the book! We covered so much deep content in this chapter, from talking about the importance of community development with Fanilo to some practical examples of popular applications with Johannes, and even discussing the toy-like features of Streamlit and where Streamlit is heading next with Adrien. We got a brief history lesson of where Streamlit has come from over the past couple of years (2019 and 2020), heard about the SEO ecosystem from Charly, and learned tips and tricks along the way. Some of my favorite tips are to join and post on the forums from Fanilo, to put Streamlit apps online that you think would be interesting from Johannes, and to lean in to the toy-like aspects of Streamlit from Adrien.

I just want to say thank you for reading this book; it has been a labor of love for me and I would like nothing better than for you to reach out to me and let me know how it has affected your Streamlit developer experience. You can find me on Twitter at `https://twitter.com/tylerjrichards`, and I hope you have had as good of a time reading this book as I have writing it. Thank you and go make some awesome Streamlit apps!

Why subscribe?

Other Books You May Enjoy

If you enjoyed this book, you may be interested in these other books by Packt:

Interactive Dashboards and Data Apps with Plotly and Dash

Elias Dabbas

ISBN: 978-1-80056-891-4

- Find out how to run a fully interactive and easy-to-use app

- Convert your charts to various formats including images and HTML files

- Use Plotly Express and the grammar of graphics for easily mapping data to various visual attributes

- Create different chart types, such as bar charts, scatter plots, histograms, maps, and more

- Expand your app by creating dynamic pages that generate content based on URLs Implement new callbacks to manage charts based on URLs and vice versa

Tableau Prep Cookbook

Hendrik Kleine

ISBN: 978-1-80056-376-6

- Perform data cleaning and preparation techniques for advanced data analysis
- Understand how to combine multiple disparate datasets
- Prepare data for different Business Intelligence (BI) tools
- Apply Tableau Prep's calculation language to create powerful calculations
- Use Tableau Prep for ad hoc data analysis and data science flows
- Deploy Tableau Prep flows to Tableau Server and Tableau Online

Packt is searching for authors like you

If you're interested in becoming an author for Packt, please visit `authors.packtpub.com` and apply today. We have worked with thousands of developers and tech professionals, just like you, to help them share their insight with the global tech community. You can make a general application, apply for a specific hot topic that we are recruiting an author for, or submit your own idea.

Share Your Thoughts

Now you've finished *Getting Started with Streamlit for Data Science*, we'd love to hear your thoughts! Scan the QR code below to go straight to the Amazon review page for this book and share your feedback or leave a review on the site that you purchased it from.

`https://packt.link/r/1-800-56550-X`

Your review is important to us and the tech community and will help us make sure we're delivering excellent quality content.

Index

U

W

Made in United States
Orlando, FL
21 November 2021

10597222R00154